Garfield takes his licks

BY JIM DAVIS

Ballantine Books • New York

2012 Ballantine Books Trade Paperback Edition

Copyright © 1993, 2012 by PAWS, Inc. All rights reserved.
"GARFIELD" and the GARFIELD characters are trademarks of PAWS, Inc.

Published in the United States by Ballantine Books, an imprint of The Random House Publishing Group,
a division of Random House, Inc., New York.

Ballantine and colophon are registered trademarks of Random House, Inc.

Originally published in slightly different form in the United States by Ballantine Books, an imprint of
The Random House Publishing Group, a division of Random House, Inc., in 1993.

ISBN 978-0-345-52587-1

Printed in the United States of America

www.ballantinebooks.com

9 8 7 6 5 4 3 2 1

First Colorized Edition

TOP TEN REASONS TO OWN A CAT INSTEAD OF A DOG

SORRY, YOU'RE NOT MY TYPE
Candy

PREMIUM, RIGHT?

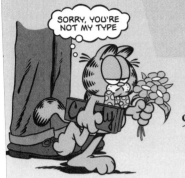

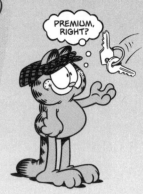

10. No need to drool-proof your home
9. Cat has absolutely no romantic interest in your leg
8. Nothing spooks a burglar like stepping on a cat
7. Dog breath actually killed a guy in Utah
6. Cat always returns your car with a full tank
5. Cat will keep yard free of pesky songbirds
4. Cat won't drag you out into blizzard just to piddle on a tree
3. Ever seen **Cujo**?
2. Dogs... Fetch, roll over, sit up and beg;
Cats... Drive, balance checkbook, give CPR
1. Garfield. Odie. Case closed.

NEED I SAY MORE?

JUST WHEN YOU THINK THEY HAVE TELEVISED EVERY SPORT...
YOW!
THERE'S BLINDFOLDED DARTS
© 1992 PAWS, INC. All Rights Reserved.
JIM DAVIS 2-5

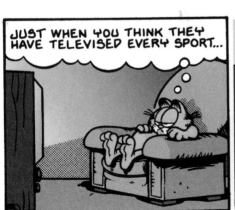

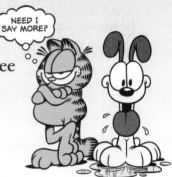

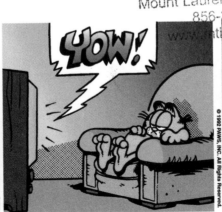

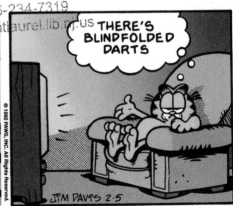

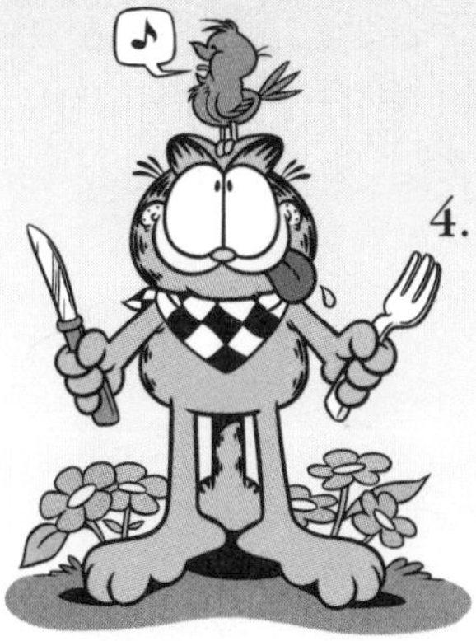

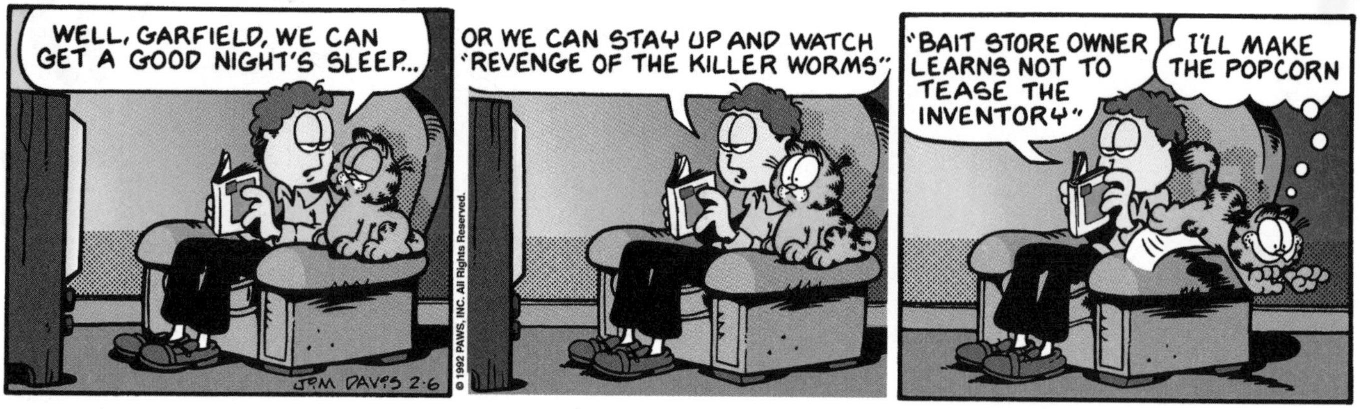
WELL, GARFIELD, WE CAN GET A GOOD NIGHT'S SLEEP...
JIM DAVIS 2-6
© 1992 PAWS, INC. All Rights Reserved.
OR WE CAN STAY UP AND WATCH "REVENGE OF THE KILLER WORMS"
"BAIT STORE OWNER LEARNS NOT TO TEASE THE INVENTORY"
I'LL MAKE THE POPCORN

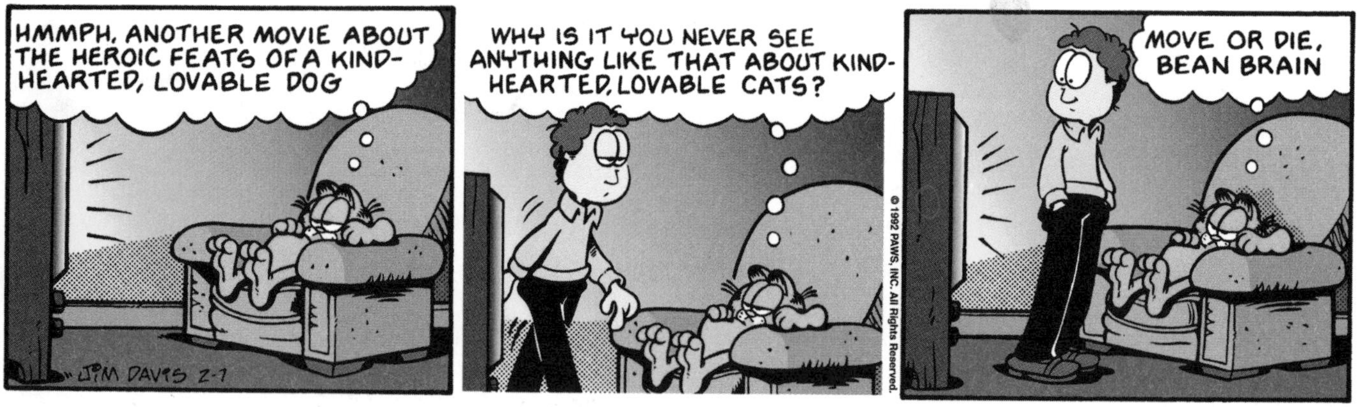
HMMPH, ANOTHER MOVIE ABOUT THE HEROIC FEATS OF A KIND-HEARTED, LOVABLE DOG
JIM DAVIS 2-7
WHY IS IT YOU NEVER SEE ANYTHING LIKE THAT ABOUT KIND-HEARTED, LOVABLE CATS?
© 1992 PAWS, INC. All Rights Reserved.
MOVE OR DIE, BEAN BRAIN

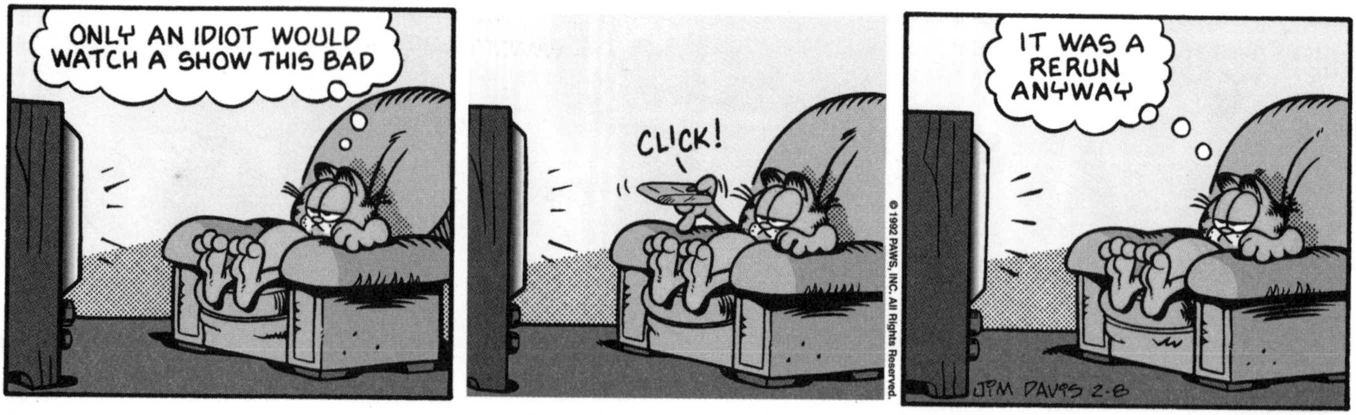
ONLY AN IDIOT WOULD WATCH A SHOW THIS BAD
CLICK!
© 1992 PAWS, INC. All Rights Reserved.
IT WAS A RERUN ANYWAY
JIM DAVIS 2-8

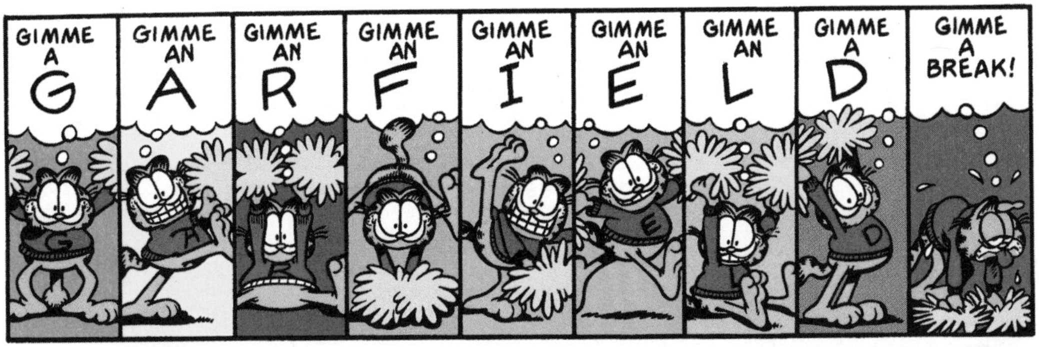
GIMME A G
GIMME AN A
GIMME AN R
GIMME AN F
GIMME AN I
GIMME AN E
GIMME AN L
GIMME A D
GIMME A BREAK!

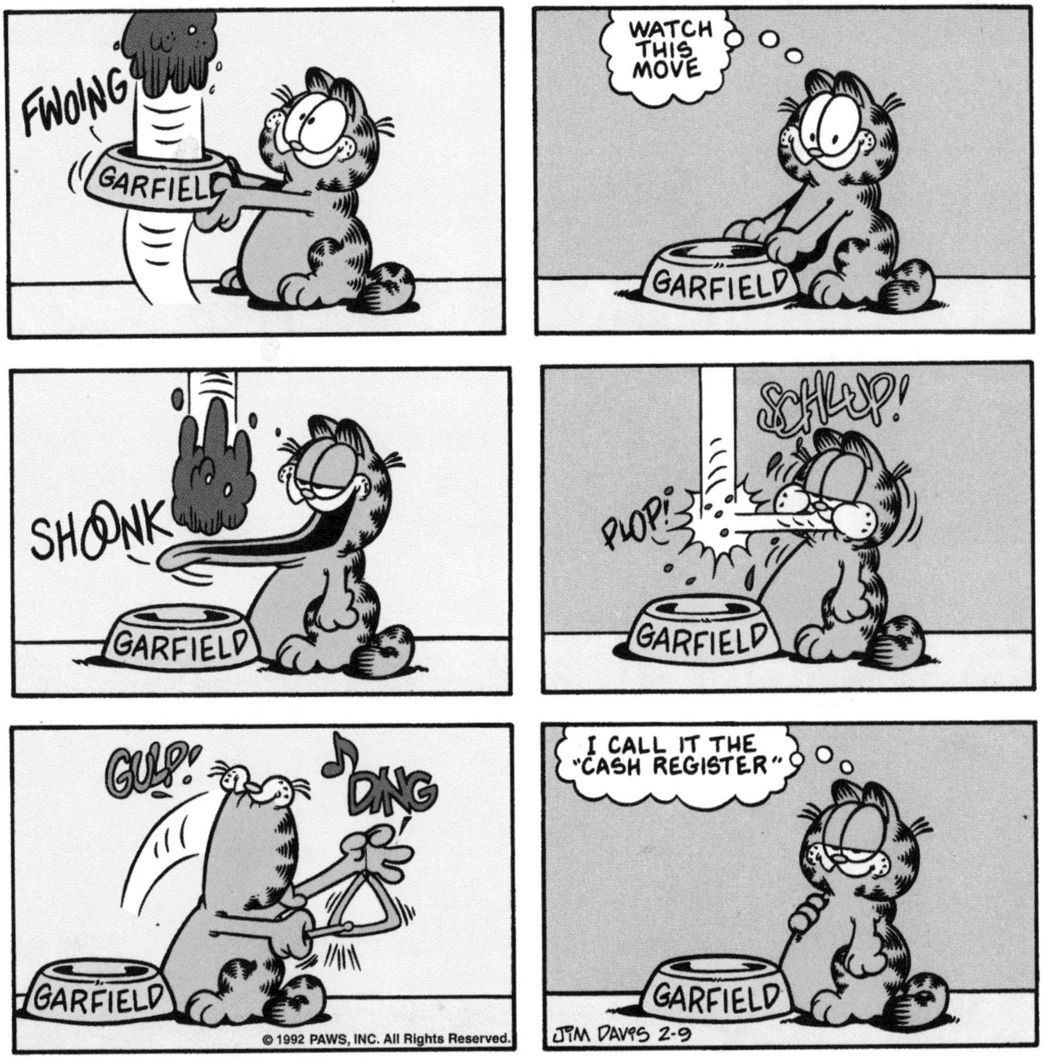
FWOING
GARFIEL
WATCH THIS MOVE
GARFIELD
SHOONK
GARFIELD
SCHLUP!
PLOP!
GARFIELD
GULP!
DING
GARFIELD
© 1992 PAWS, INC. All Rights Reserved.
I CALL IT THE "CASH REGISTER"
GARFIELD
JIM DAVIS 2-9

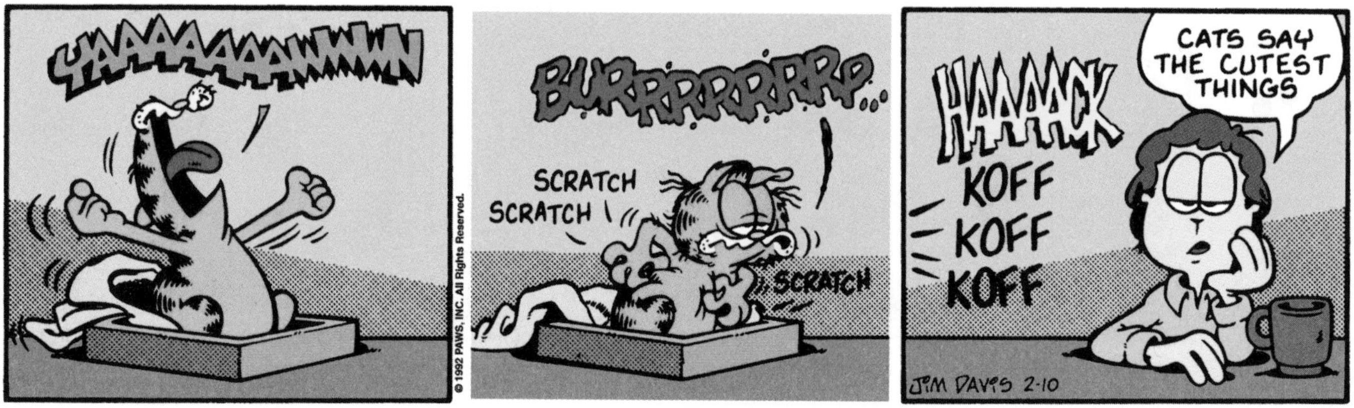
YAAAAAAAWWWN
BURRRRRRRRP...
SCRATCH
SCRATCH
SCRATCH
HAAAACK
KOFF
KOFF
KOFF
CATS SAY THE CUTEST THINGS
JIM DAVIS 2-10

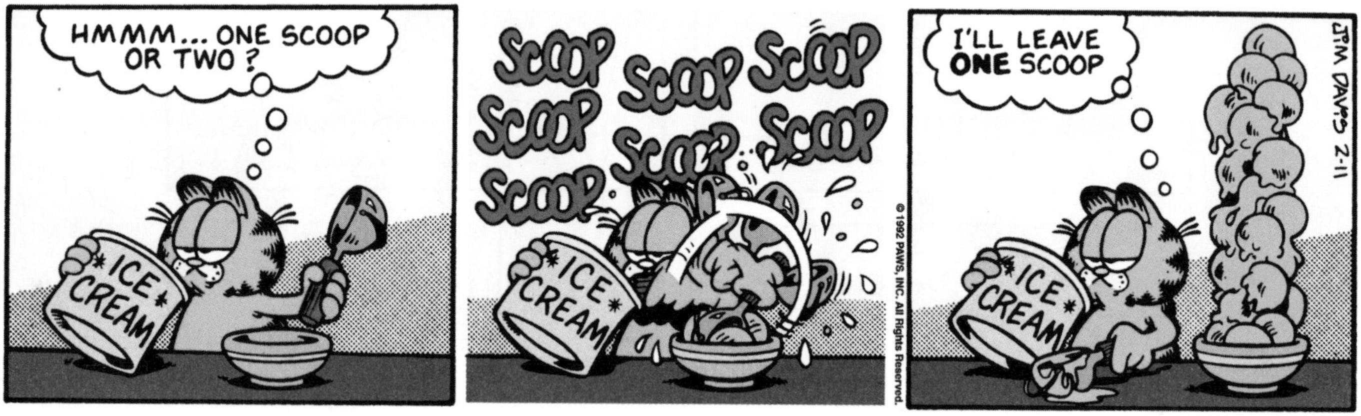
HMMM... ONE SCOOP OR TWO?
ICE CREAM
SCOOP SCOOP SCOOP
SCOOP SCOOP SCOOP
SCOOP
ICE CREAM
I'LL LEAVE **ONE** SCOOP
ICE CREAM
JIM DAVIS 2-11

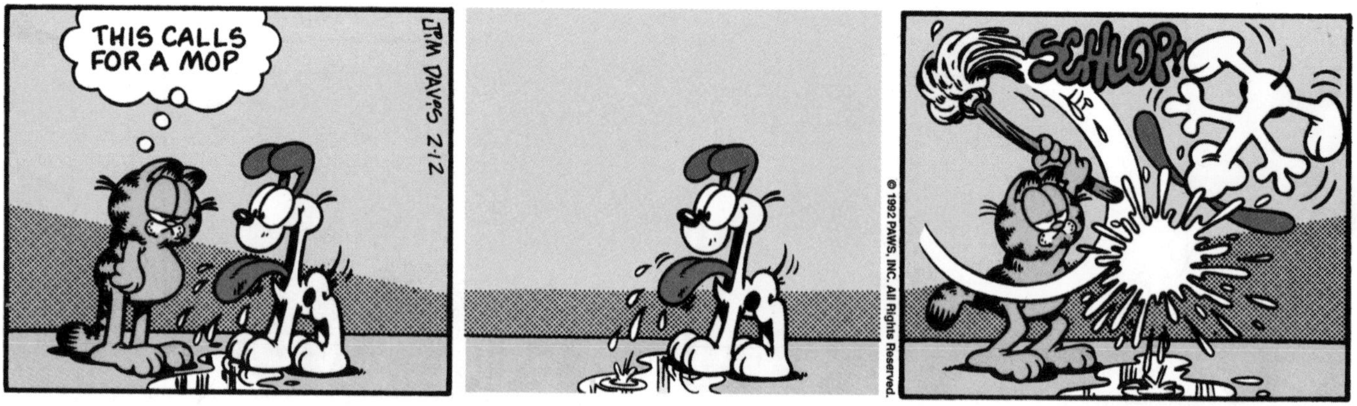
THIS CALLS FOR A MOP
JIM DAVIS 2-12
SCHLOP!

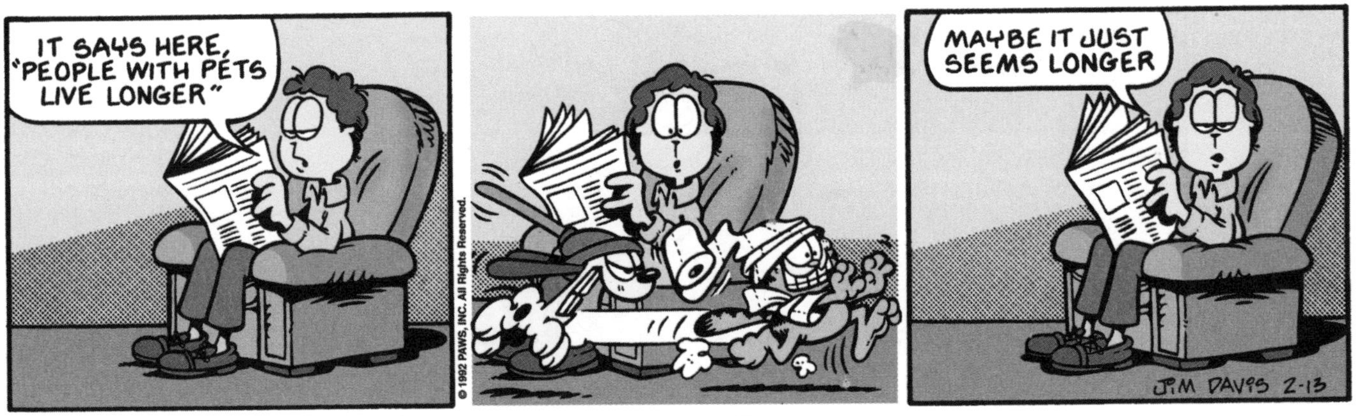
IT SAYS HERE, "PEOPLE WITH PETS LIVE LONGER"
© 1992 PAWS, INC. All Rights Reserved.
MAYBE IT JUST SEEMS LONGER
JIM DAVIS 2-13

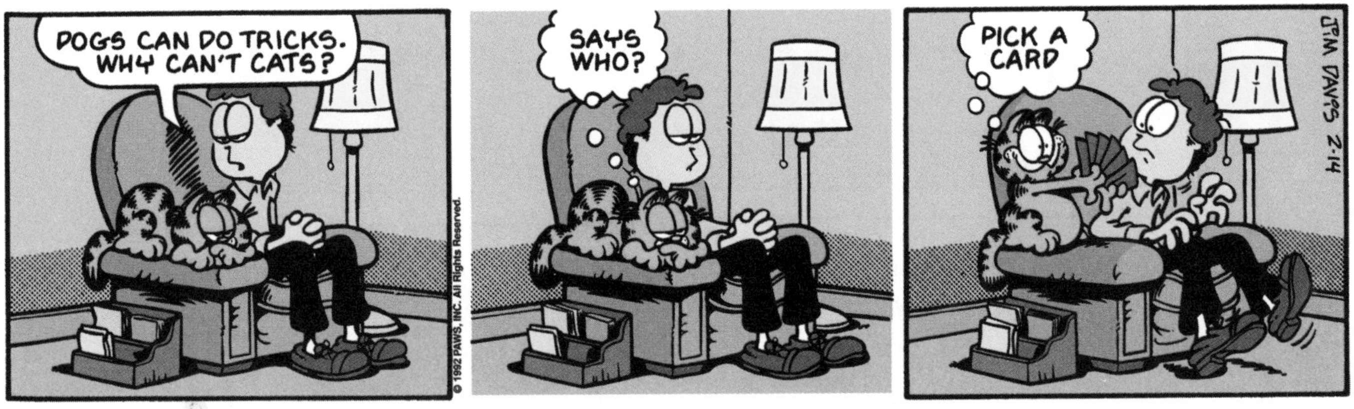
DOGS CAN DO TRICKS. WHY CAN'T CATS?
© 1992 PAWS, INC. All Rights Reserved.
SAYS WHO?
PICK A CARD
JIM DAVIS 2-14

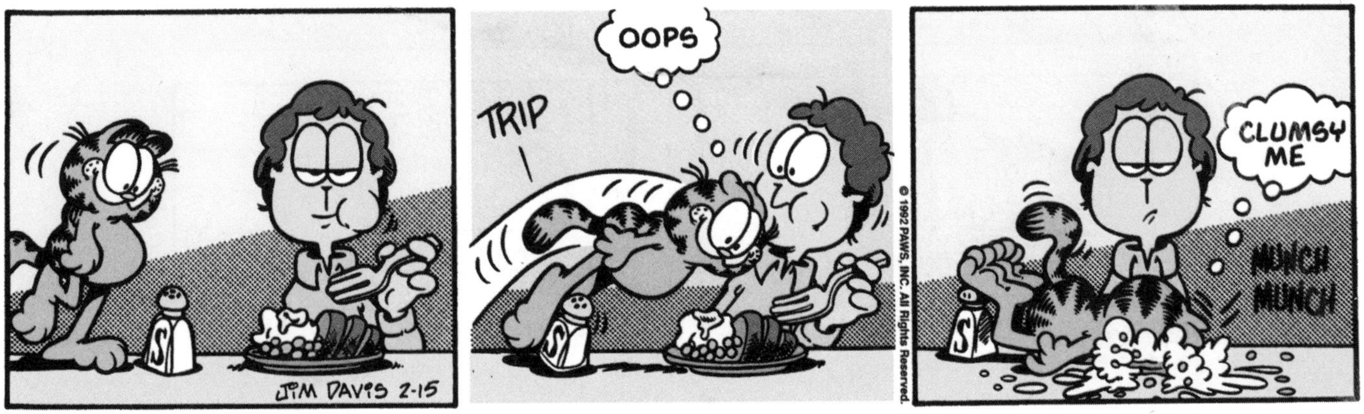
JIM DAVIS 2-15
OOPS
TRIP
© 1992 PAWS, INC. All Rights Reserved.
CLUMSY ME
MUNCH MUNCH

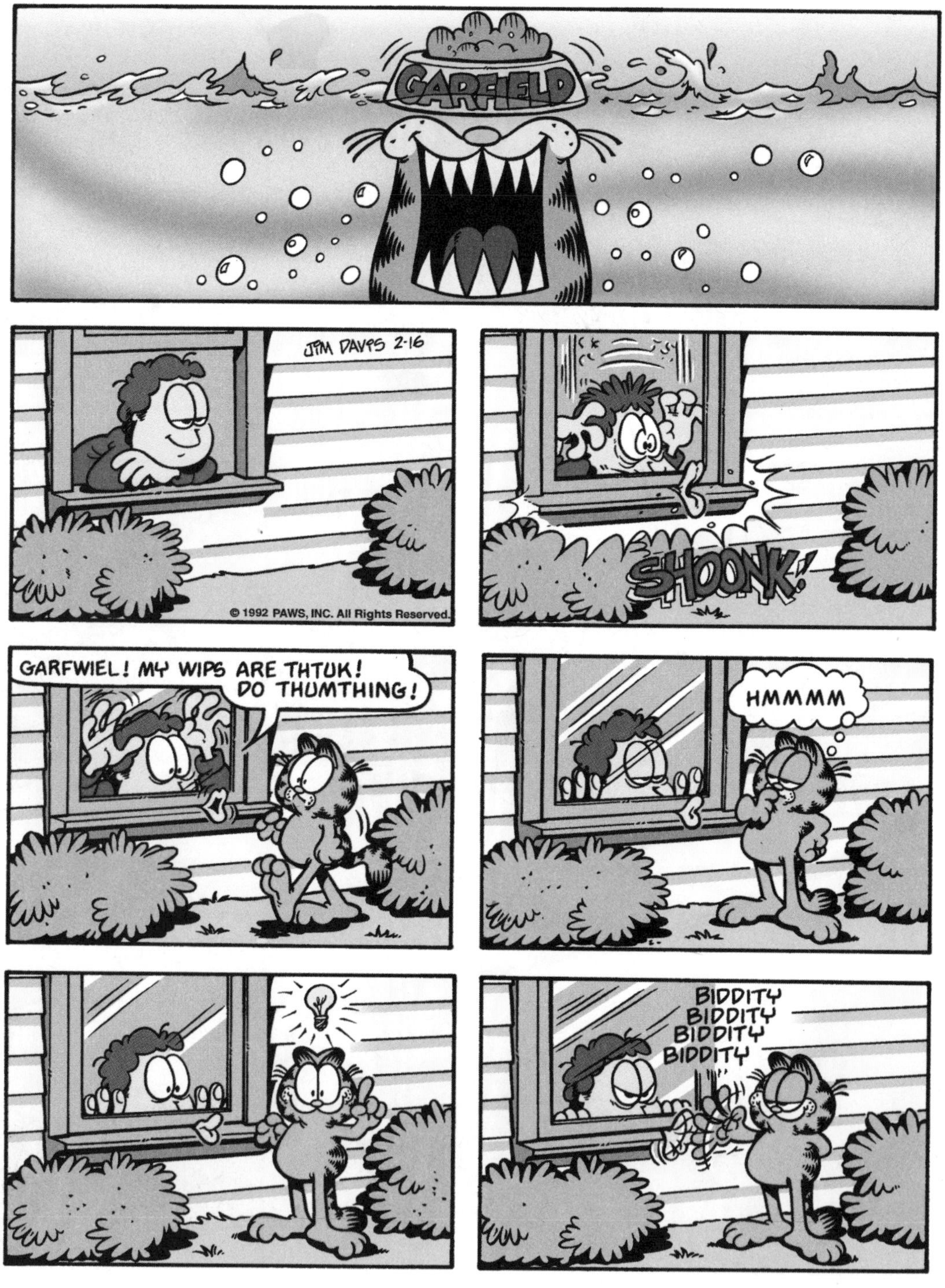
GARFIELD
JIM DAVIS 2-16
© 1992 PAWS, INC. All Rights Reserved.
SHOONK!
GARFWIEL! MY WIPS ARE THTUK! DO THUMTHING!
HMMMM
BIDDITY
BIDDITY
BIDDITY
BIDDITY

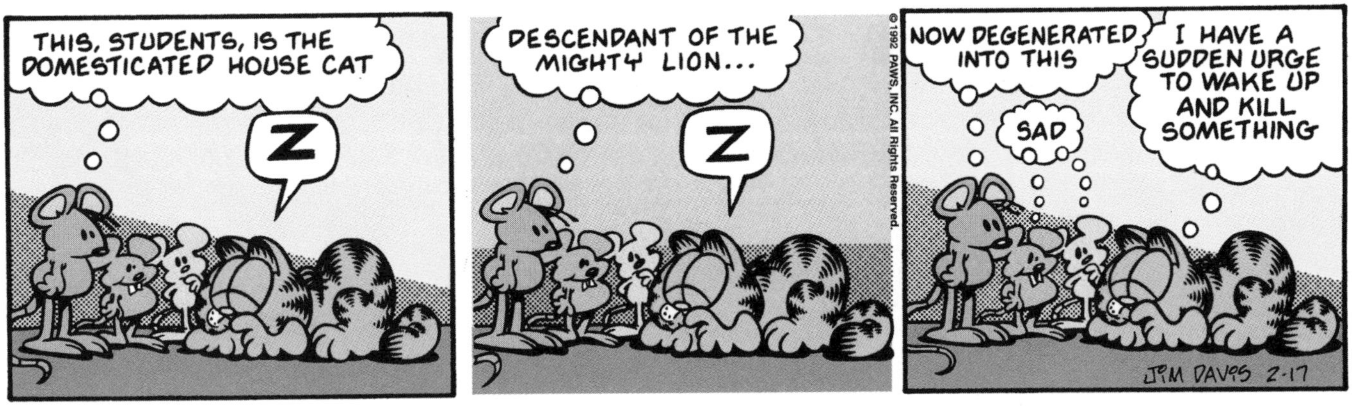
THIS, STUDENTS, IS THE DOMESTICATED HOUSE CAT
Z
DESCENDANT OF THE MIGHTY LION...
Z
© 1992 PAWS, INC. All Rights Reserved.
NOW DEGENERATED INTO THIS
SAD
I HAVE A SUDDEN URGE TO WAKE UP AND KILL SOMETHING
JIM DAVIS 2-17

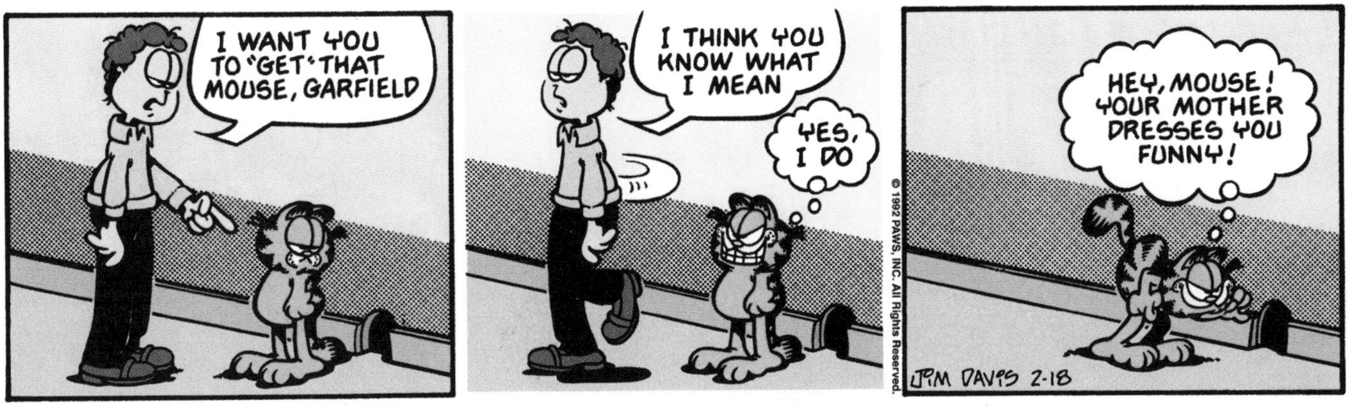
I WANT YOU TO "GET" THAT MOUSE, GARFIELD
I THINK YOU KNOW WHAT I MEAN
YES, I DO
© 1992 PAWS, INC. All Rights Reserved.
HEY, MOUSE! YOUR MOTHER DRESSES YOU FUNNY!
JIM DAVIS 2-18

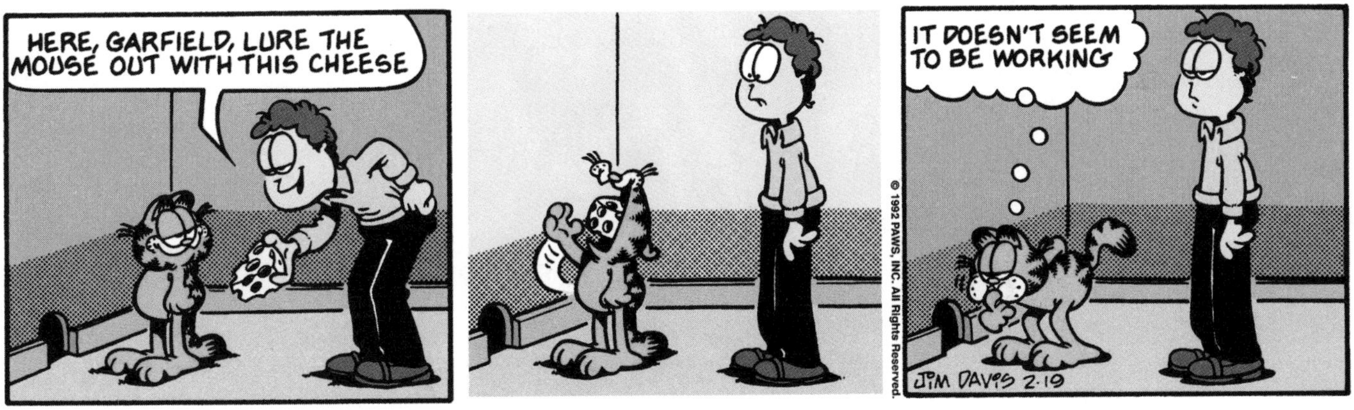
HERE, GARFIELD, LURE THE MOUSE OUT WITH THIS CHEESE
© 1992 PAWS, INC. All Rights Reserved.
IT DOESN'T SEEM TO BE WORKING
JIM DAVIS 2-19

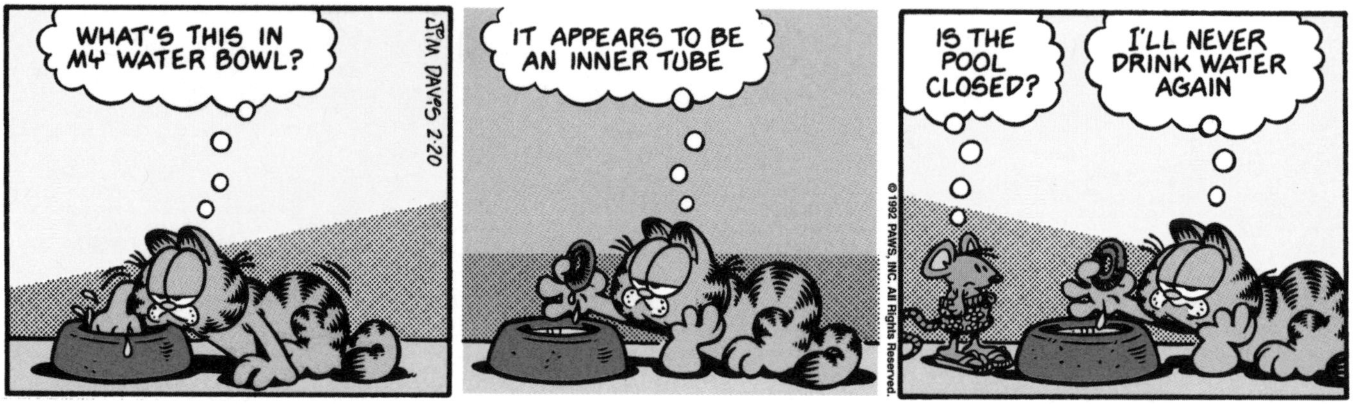
WHAT'S THIS IN MY WATER BOWL?
JIM DAVIS 2-20
IT APPEARS TO BE AN INNER TUBE
© 1992 PAWS, INC. All Rights Reserved.
IS THE POOL CLOSED?
I'LL NEVER DRINK WATER AGAIN

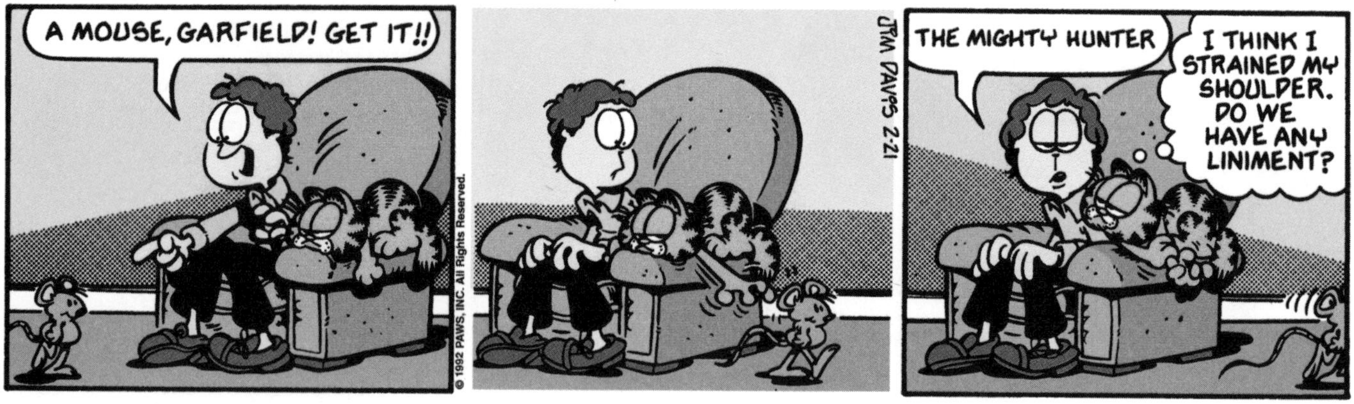
A MOUSE, GARFIELD! GET IT!!
© 1992 PAWS, INC. All Rights Reserved.
JIM DAVIS 2-21
THE MIGHTY HUNTER
I THINK I STRAINED MY SHOULDER. DO WE HAVE ANY LINIMENT?

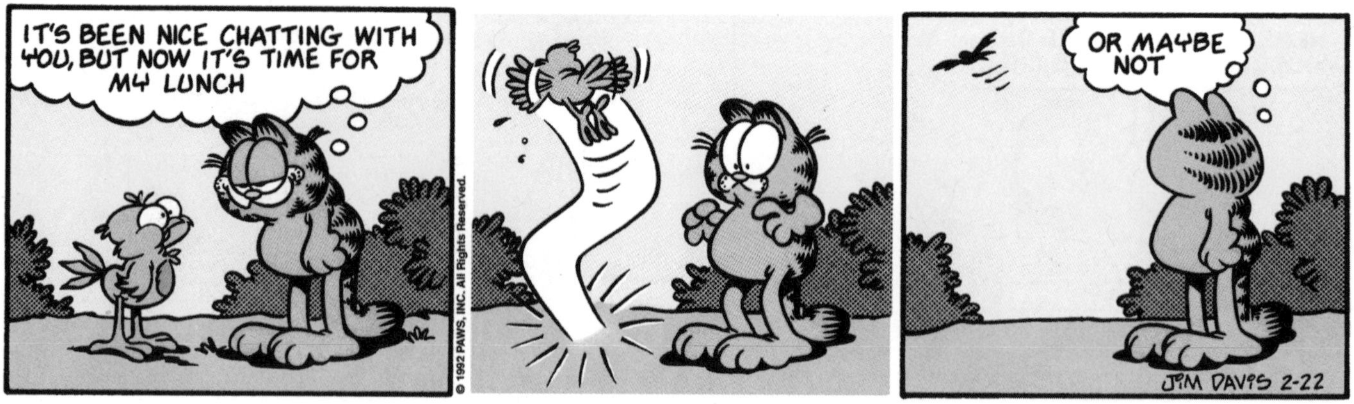
IT'S BEEN NICE CHATTING WITH YOU, BUT NOW IT'S TIME FOR MY LUNCH
© 1992 PAWS, INC. All Rights Reserved.
OR MAYBE NOT
JIM DAVIS 2-22

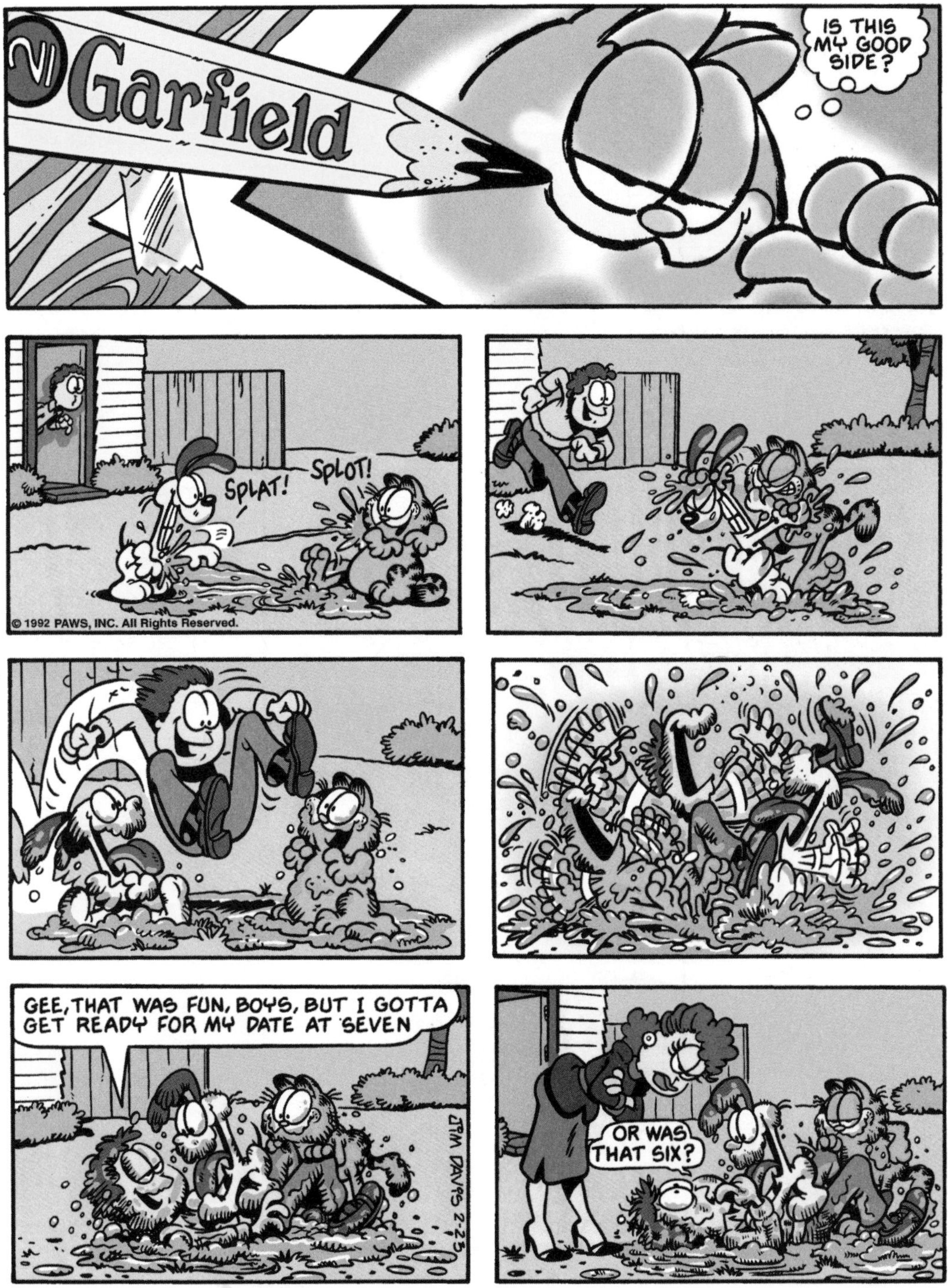
Garfield
IS THIS MY GOOD SIDE?
SPLAT!
SPLOT!
© 1992 PAWS, INC. All Rights Reserved.
GEE, THAT WAS FUN, BOYS, BUT I GOTTA GET READY FOR MY DATE AT SEVEN
JIM DAVIS 2-23
OR WAS THAT SIX?

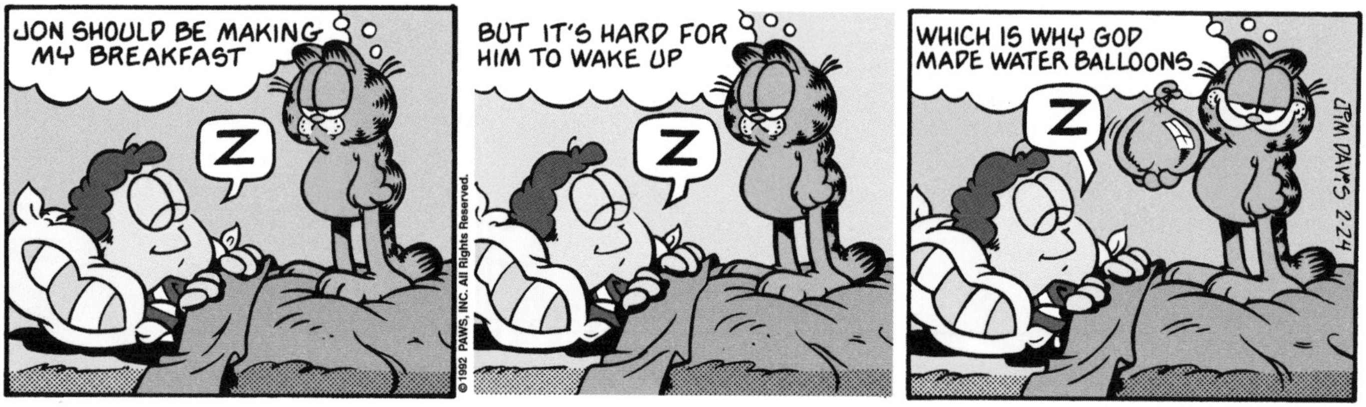
JON SHOULD BE MAKING MY BREAKFAST
Z
© 1992 PAWS, INC. All Rights Reserved.
BUT IT'S HARD FOR HIM TO WAKE UP
Z
WHICH IS WHY GOD MADE WATER BALLOONS
Z
JIM DAVIS 2-24

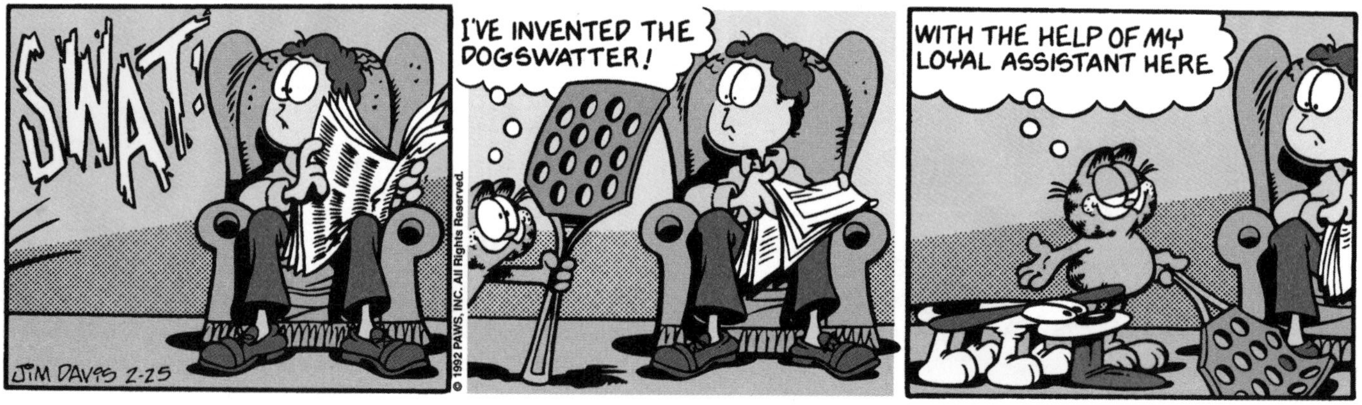
SWAT!
JIM DAVIS 2-25
© 1992 PAWS, INC. All Rights Reserved.
I'VE INVENTED THE DOGSWATTER!
WITH THE HELP OF MY LOYAL ASSISTANT HERE

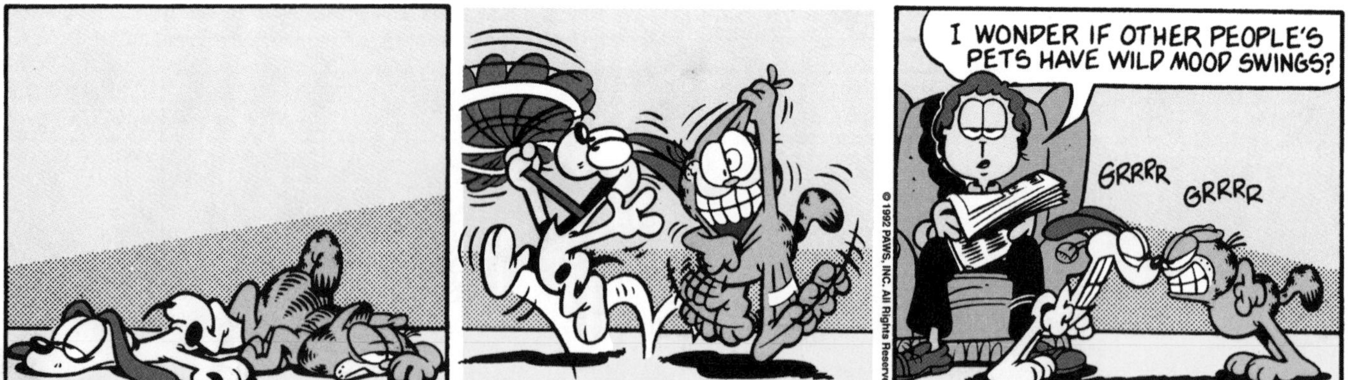
JIM DAVIS 2-26
© 1992 PAWS, INC. All Rights Reserved.
I WONDER IF OTHER PEOPLE'S PETS HAVE WILD MOOD SWINGS?
GRRRR
GRRRR

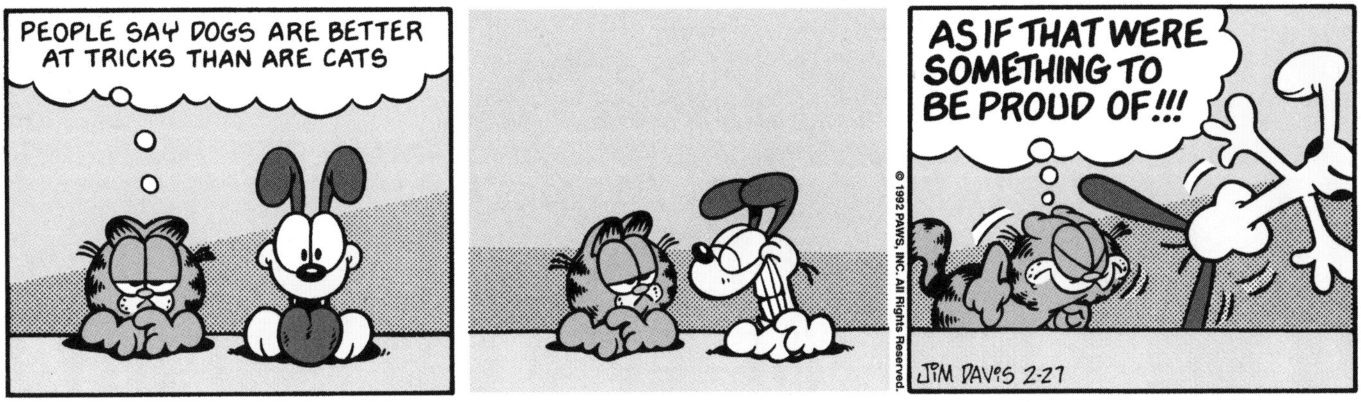
PEOPLE SAY DOGS ARE BETTER AT TRICKS THAN ARE CATS
© 1992 PAWS, INC. All Rights Reserved.
AS IF THAT WERE SOMETHING TO BE PROUD OF!!!
JIM DAVIS 2-27

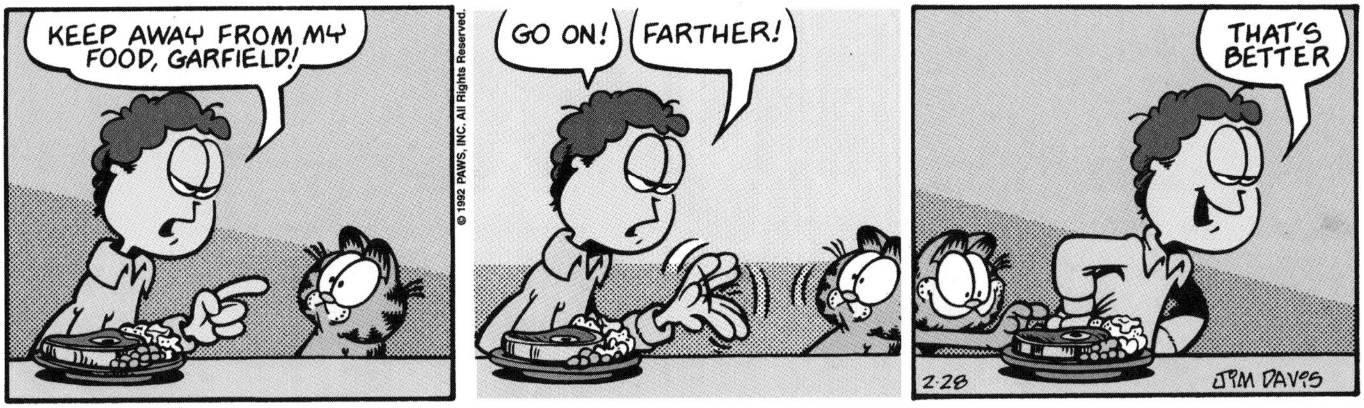
KEEP AWAY FROM MY FOOD, GARFIELD!
© 1992 PAWS, INC. All Rights Reserved.
GO ON!
FARTHER!
THAT'S BETTER
2-28
JIM DAVIS

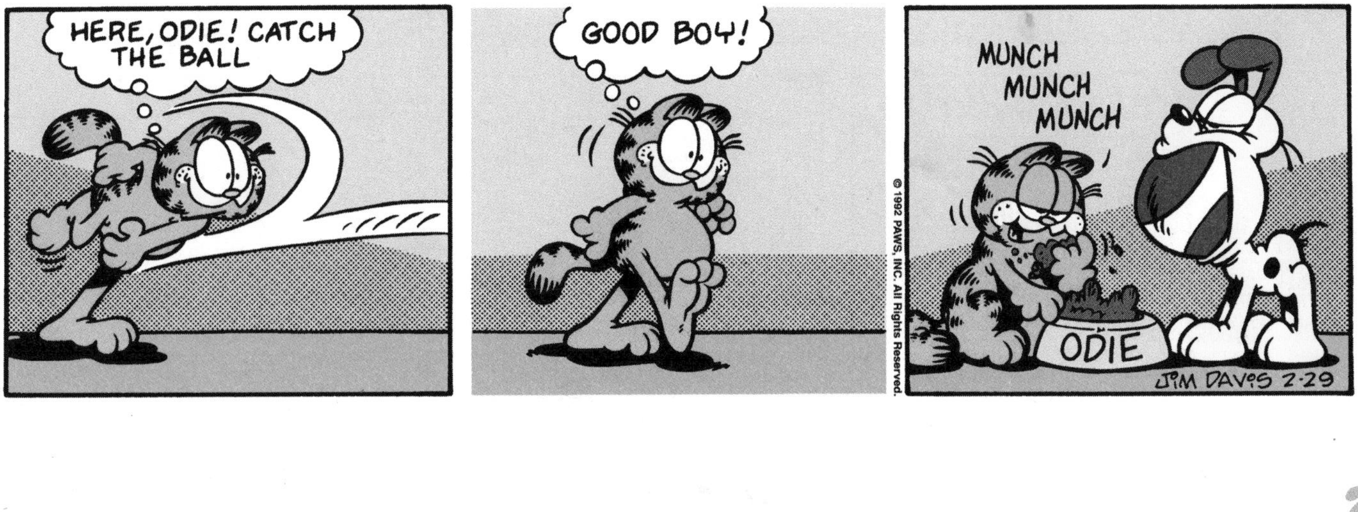
HERE, ODIE! CATCH THE BALL
GOOD BOY!
© 1992 PAWS, INC. All Rights Reserved.
MUNCH
MUNCH
MUNCH
ODIE
JIM DAVIS 2-29

The NEW, IMPROVED Garfield
NOW WITH!
SHARPER CLAWS!
BIGGER APPETITE!
LARGER EGO!
LEMON-FRESH SCENT!!
© 1992 PAWS, INC. All Rights Reserved.
JIM DAVIS 3-1
SIGH... EVERYBODY HAS A TROPHY BUT ME
YAAAAAAHHH!!!
BOOF! THUD! WHOMP! CRAAASH!
MAY I HAVE A WORD WITH YOU, GARFIELD?

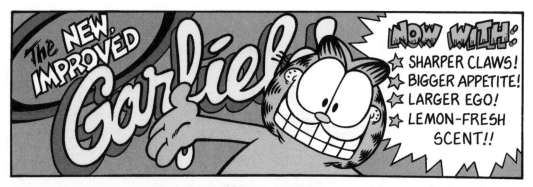

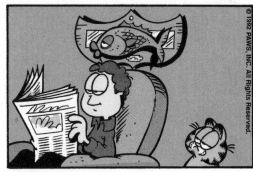

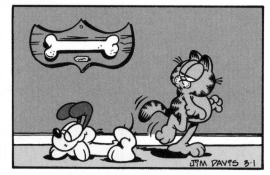

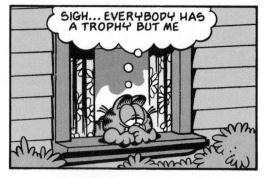

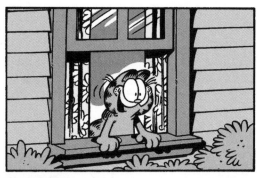

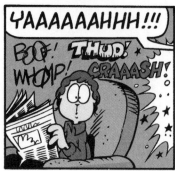

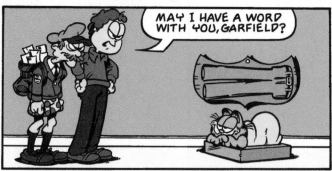

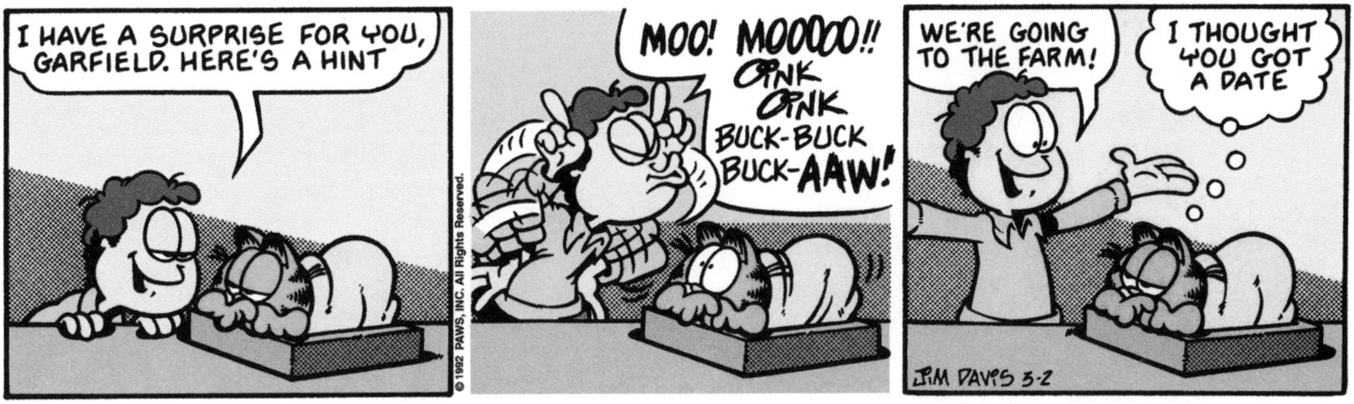
I HAVE A SURPRISE FOR YOU, GARFIELD. HERE'S A HINT
© 1992 PAWS, INC. All Rights Reserved.
MOO! MOOOOO!! OINK OINK BUCK-BUCK BUCK-AAW!
WE'RE GOING TO THE FARM!
I THOUGHT YOU GOT A DATE
JIM DAVIS 3-2

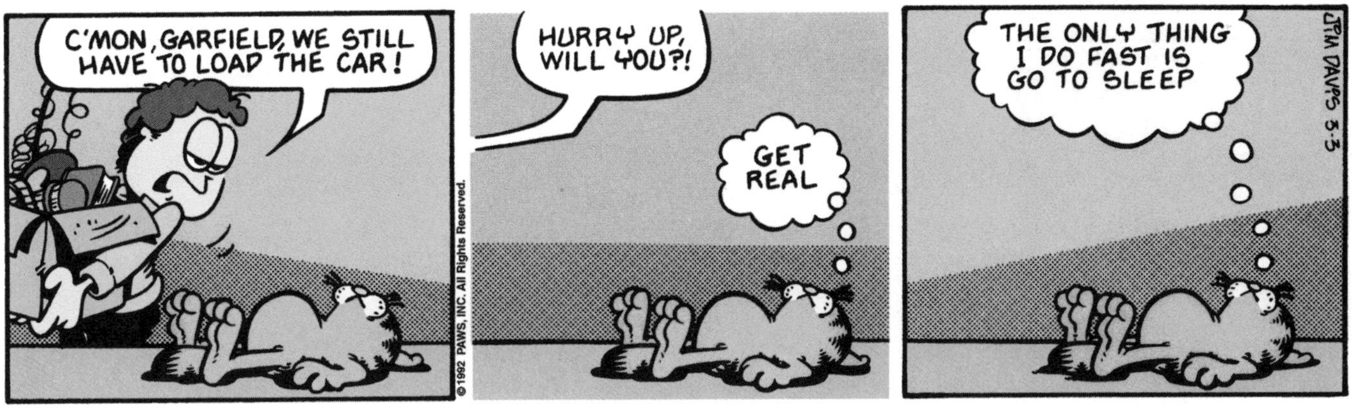
C'MON, GARFIELD, WE STILL HAVE TO LOAD THE CAR!
© 1992 PAWS, INC. All Rights Reserved.
HURRY UP, WILL YOU?!
GET REAL
THE ONLY THING I DO FAST IS GO TO SLEEP
JIM DAVIS 3-3

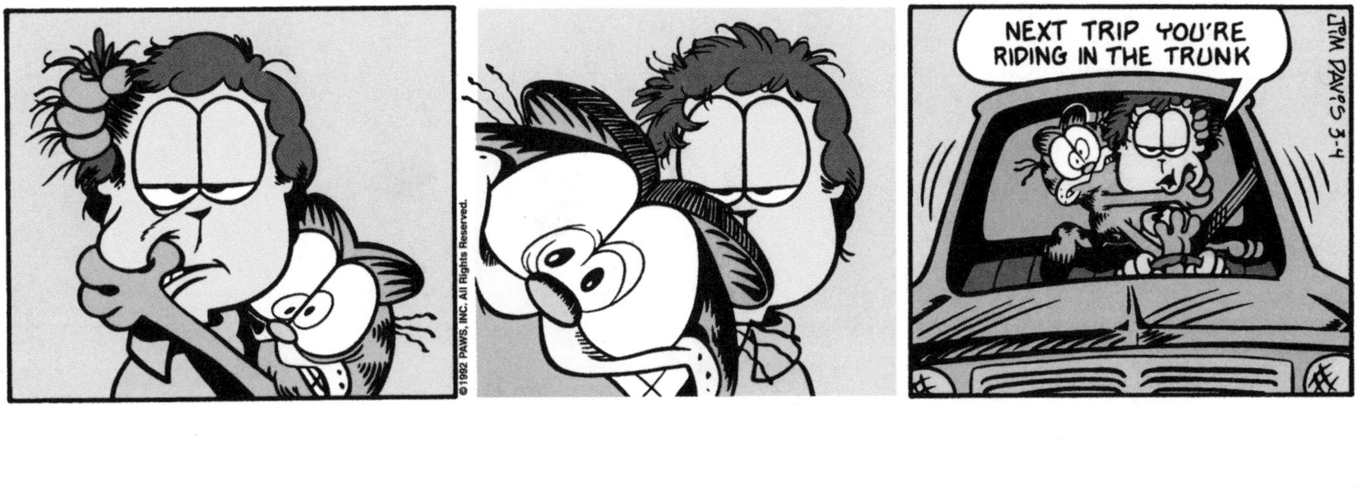
© 1992 PAWS, INC. All Rights Reserved.
NEXT TRIP YOU'RE RIDING IN THE TRUNK
JIM DAVIS 3-4

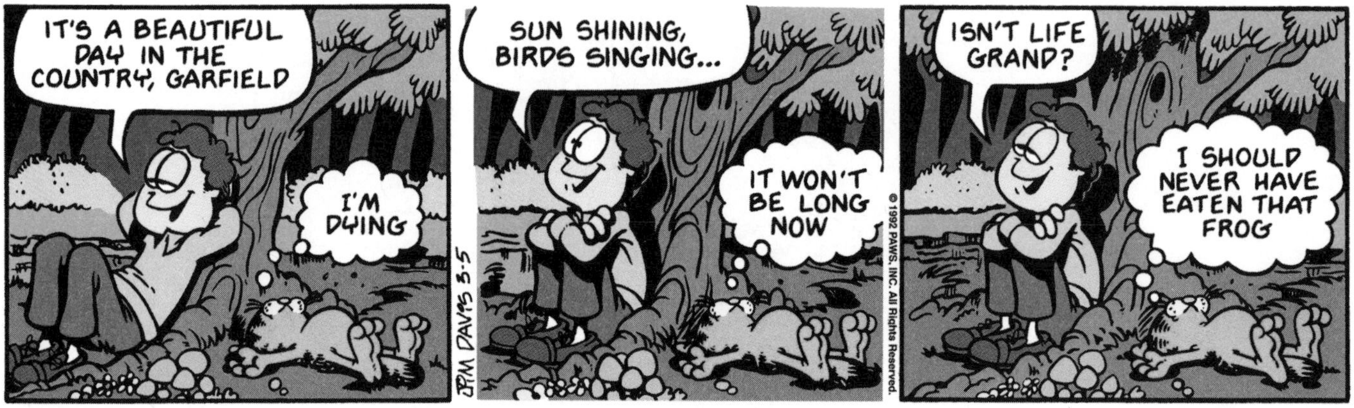
IT'S A BEAUTIFUL DAY IN THE COUNTRY, GARFIELD
I'M DYING
JIM DAVIS 3-5
SUN SHINING, BIRDS SINGING...
IT WON'T BE LONG NOW
© 1992 PAWS, INC. All Rights Reserved.
ISN'T LIFE GRAND?
I SHOULD NEVER HAVE EATEN THAT FROG

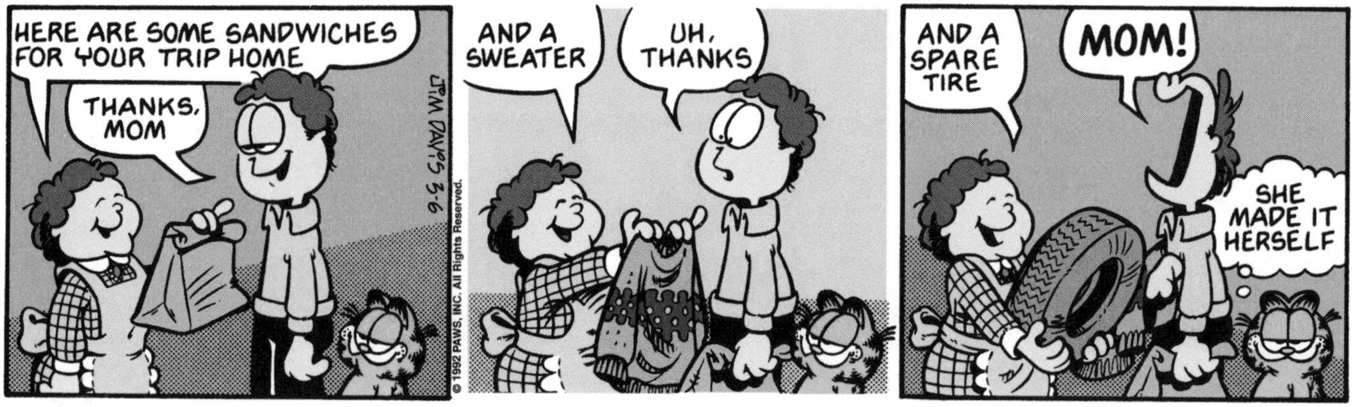
HERE ARE SOME SANDWICHES FOR YOUR TRIP HOME
THANKS, MOM
JIM DAVIS 3-6
© 1992 PAWS, INC. All Rights Reserved.
AND A SWEATER
UH, THANKS
AND A SPARE TIRE
MOM!
SHE MADE IT HERSELF

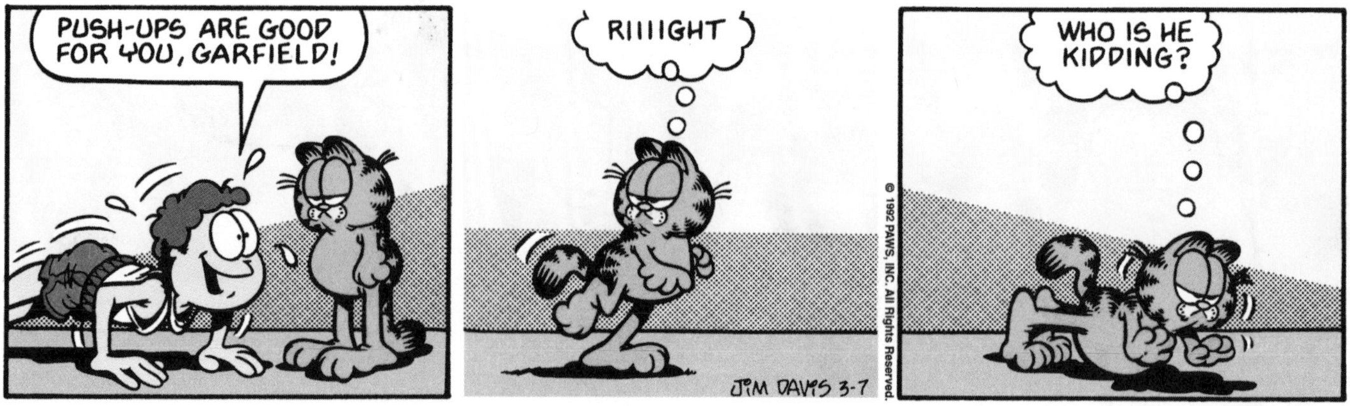
PUSH-UPS ARE GOOD FOR YOU, GARFIELD!
RIIIIGHT
JIM DAVIS 3-7
© 1992 PAWS, INC. All Rights Reserved.
WHO IS HE KIDDING?

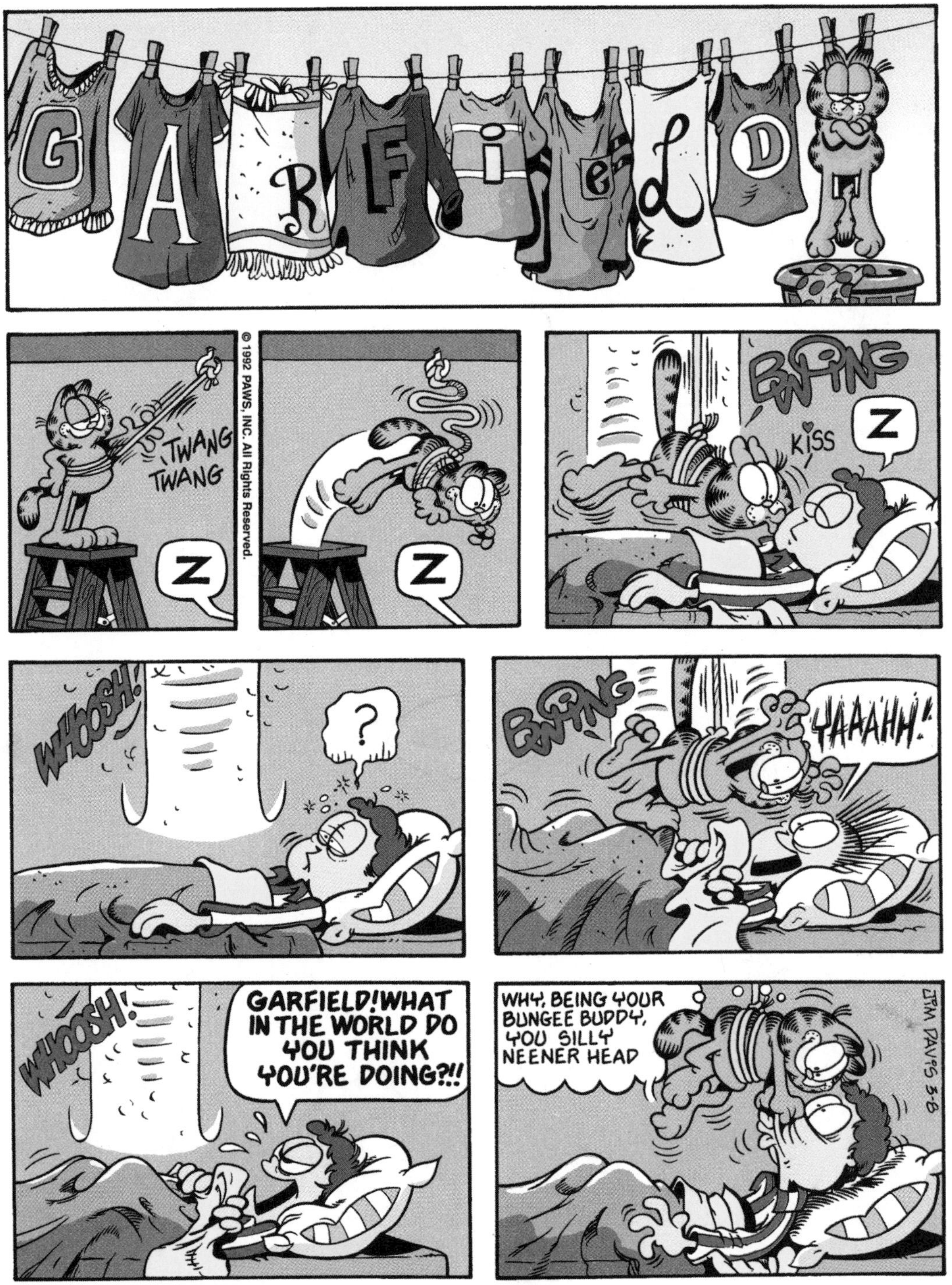
GARFIELD
© 1992 PAWS, INC. All Rights Reserved.
TWANG TWANG
Z
Z
BWING
KISS
Z
WHOOSH!
?
BWING
YAAAHH!
WHOOSH!
GARFIELD! WHAT IN THE WORLD DO YOU THINK YOU'RE DOING?!!
WHY, BEING YOUR BUNGEE BUDDY, YOU SILLY NEENER HEAD
JIM DAVIS 3-8

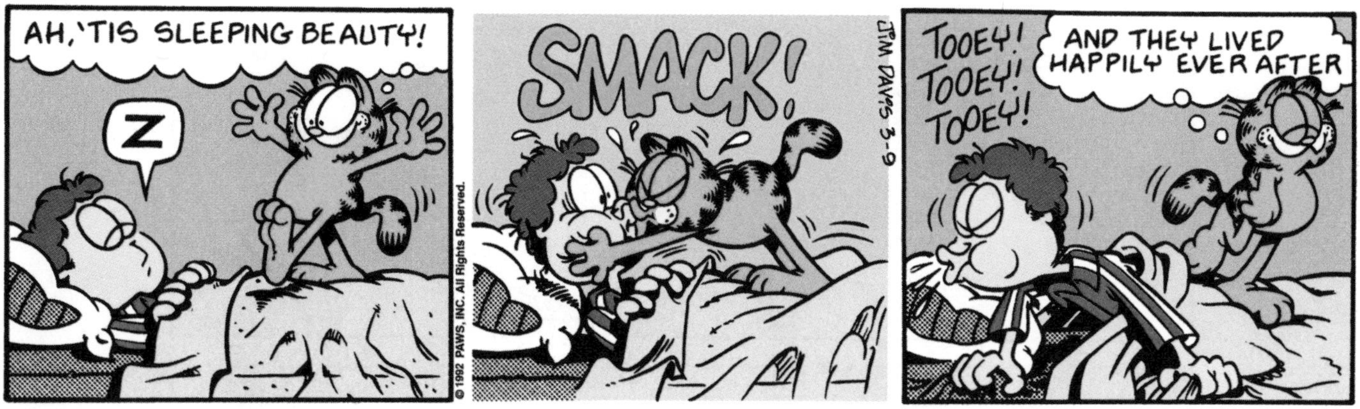
AH, 'TIS SLEEPING BEAUTY!
Z
SMACK!
TOOEY! TOOEY! TOOEY!
AND THEY LIVED HAPPILY EVER AFTER
JIM DAVIS 3-9
© 1992 PAWS, INC. All Rights Reserved.

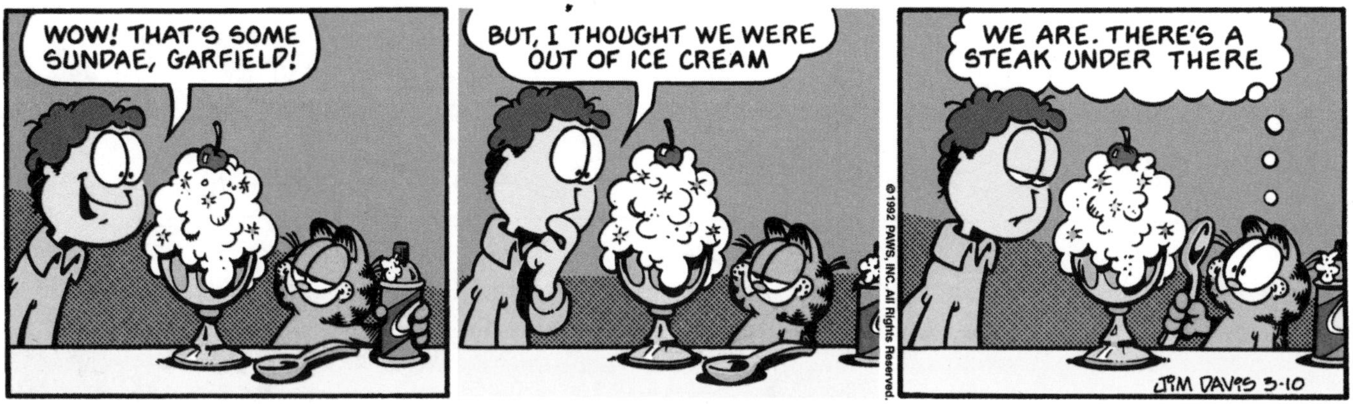
WOW! THAT'S SOME SUNDAE, GARFIELD!
BUT, I THOUGHT WE WERE OUT OF ICE CREAM
WE ARE. THERE'S A STEAK UNDER THERE
JIM DAVIS 3-10
© 1992 PAWS, INC. All Rights Reserved.

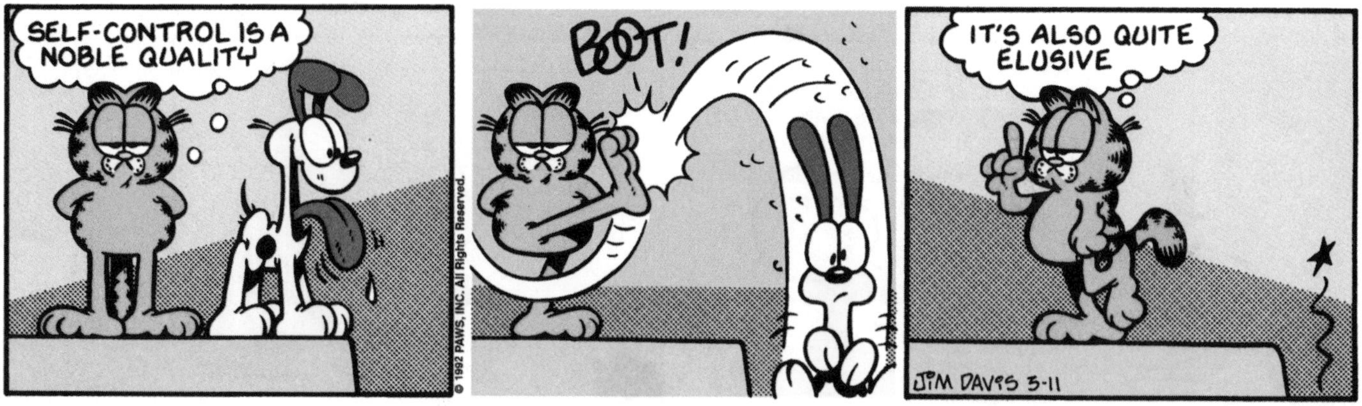
SELF-CONTROL IS A NOBLE QUALITY
BOOT!
IT'S ALSO QUITE ELUSIVE
JIM DAVIS 3-11
© 1992 PAWS, INC. All Rights Reserved.

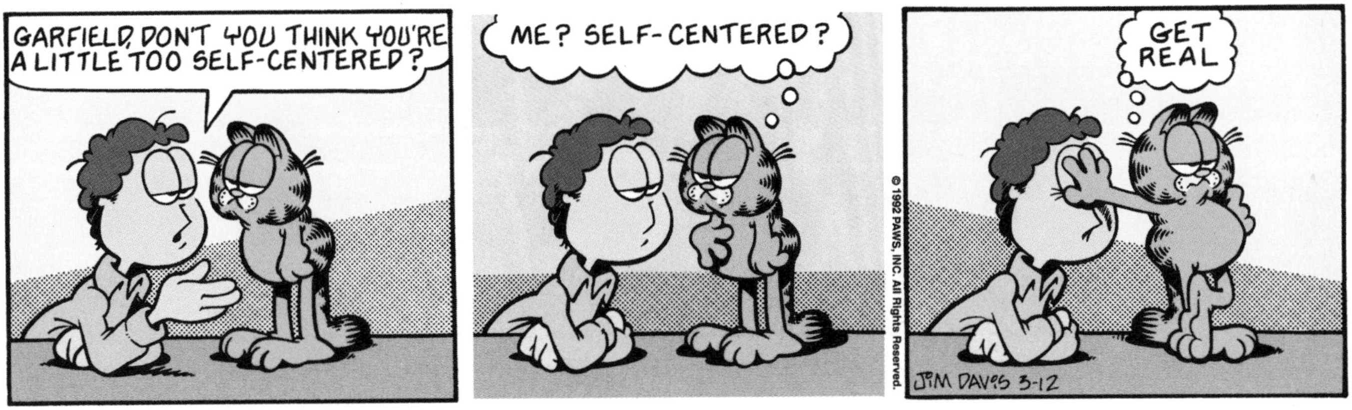
GARFIELD, DON'T YOU THINK YOU'RE A LITTLE TOO SELF-CENTERED?
ME? SELF-CENTERED?
GET REAL
© 1992 PAWS, INC. All Rights Reserved.
JIM DAVIS 3-12

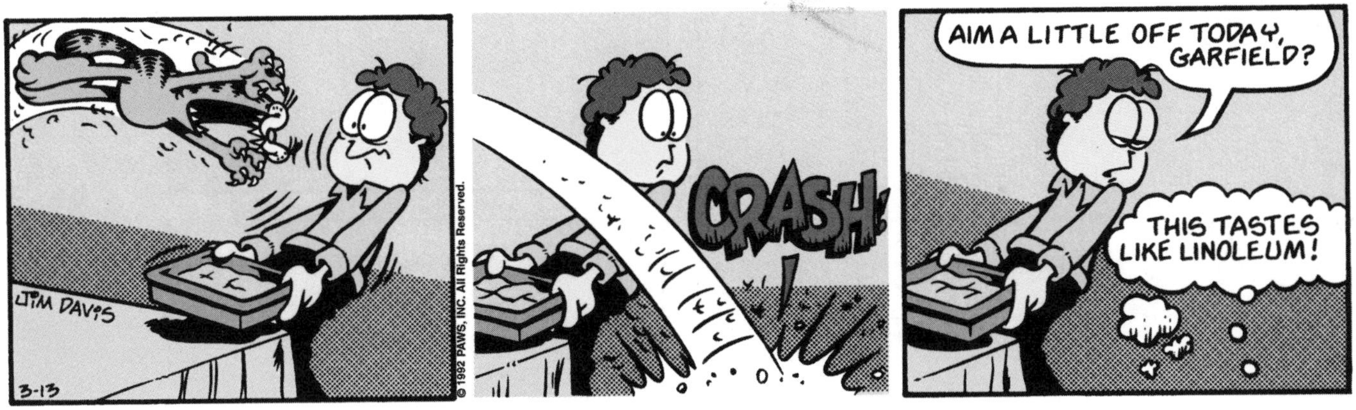
JIM DAVIS
3-13
© 1992 PAWS, INC. All Rights Reserved.
CRASH!
AIM A LITTLE OFF TODAY, GARFIELD?
THIS TASTES LIKE LINOLEUM!

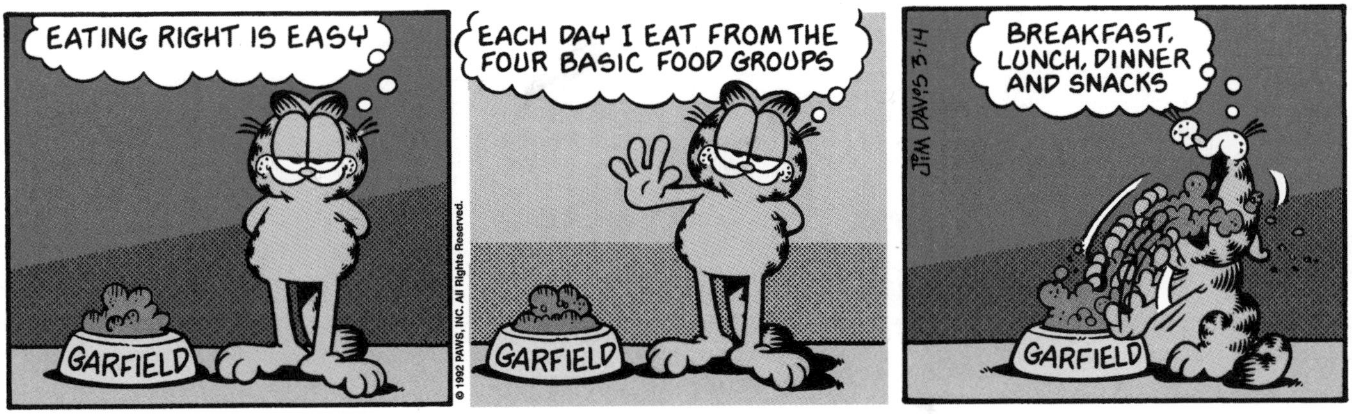
EATING RIGHT IS EASY
GARFIELD
© 1992 PAWS, INC. All Rights Reserved.
EACH DAY I EAT FROM THE FOUR BASIC FOOD GROUPS
GARFIELD
JIM DAVIS 3-14
BREAKFAST, LUNCH, DINNER AND SNACKS
GARFIELD

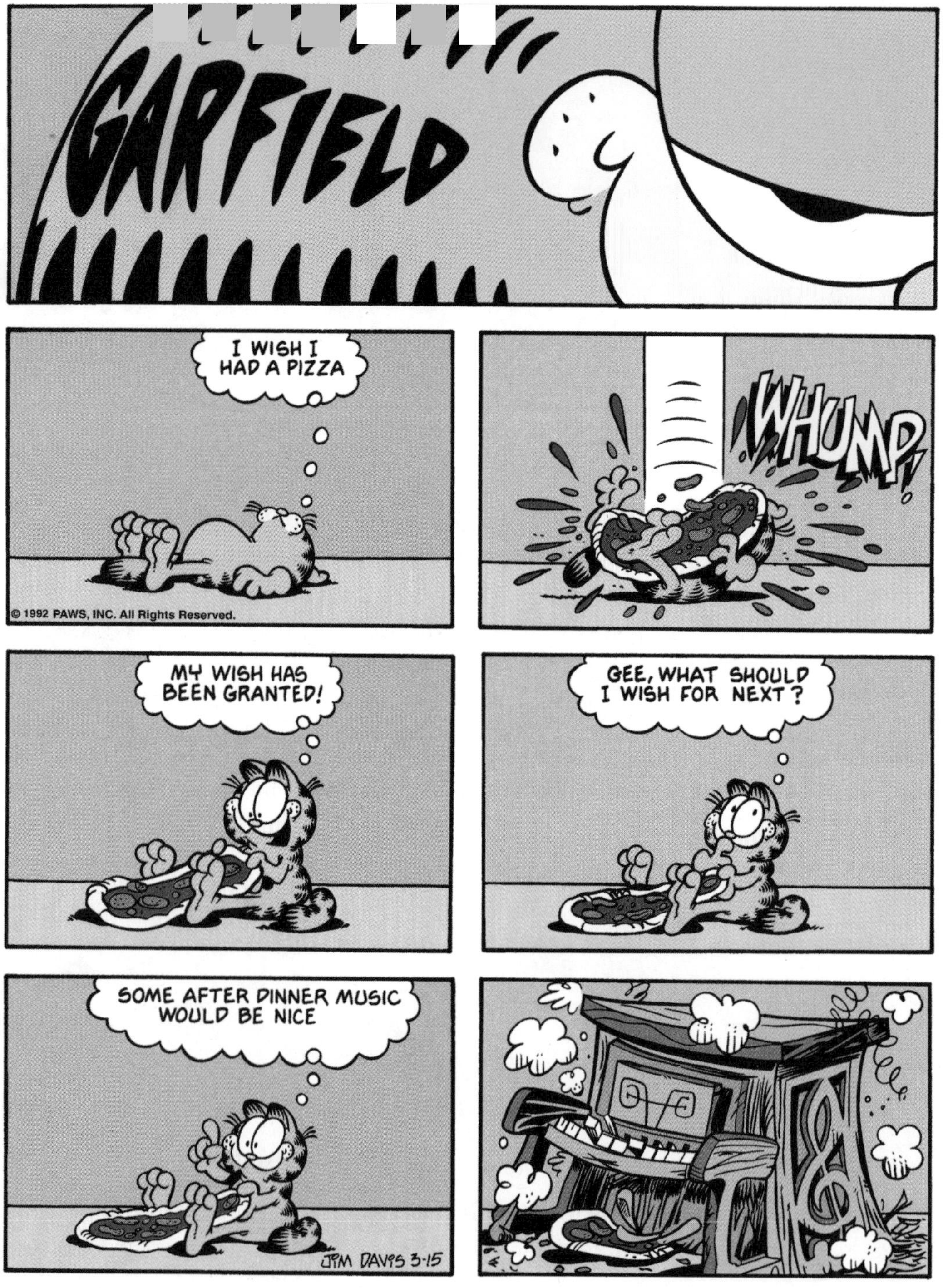
GARFIELD
I WISH I HAD A PIZZA
© 1992 PAWS, INC. All Rights Reserved.
WHUMP
MY WISH HAS BEEN GRANTED!
GEE, WHAT SHOULD I WISH FOR NEXT ?
SOME AFTER DINNER MUSIC WOULD BE NICE
JIM DAVIS 3-15

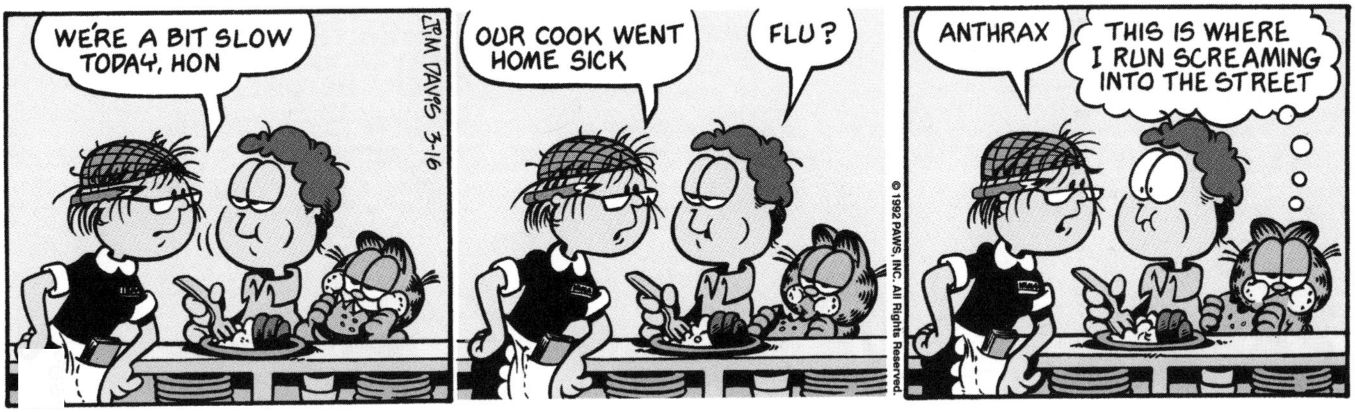
WE'RE A BIT SLOW TODAY, HON
JIM DAVIS 3-16
OUR COOK WENT HOME SICK
FLU?
© 1992 PAWS, INC. All Rights Reserved.
ANTHRAX
THIS IS WHERE I RUN SCREAMING INTO THE STREET

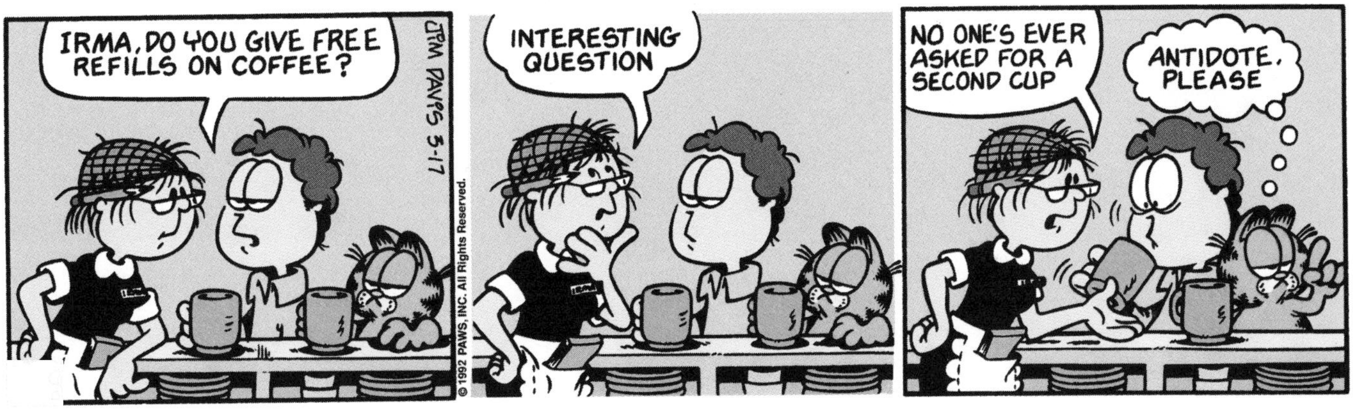
IRMA, DO YOU GIVE FREE REFILLS ON COFFEE?
JIM DAVIS 3-17
© 1992 PAWS, INC. All Rights Reserved.
INTERESTING QUESTION
NO ONE'S EVER ASKED FOR A SECOND CUP
ANTIDOTE, PLEASE

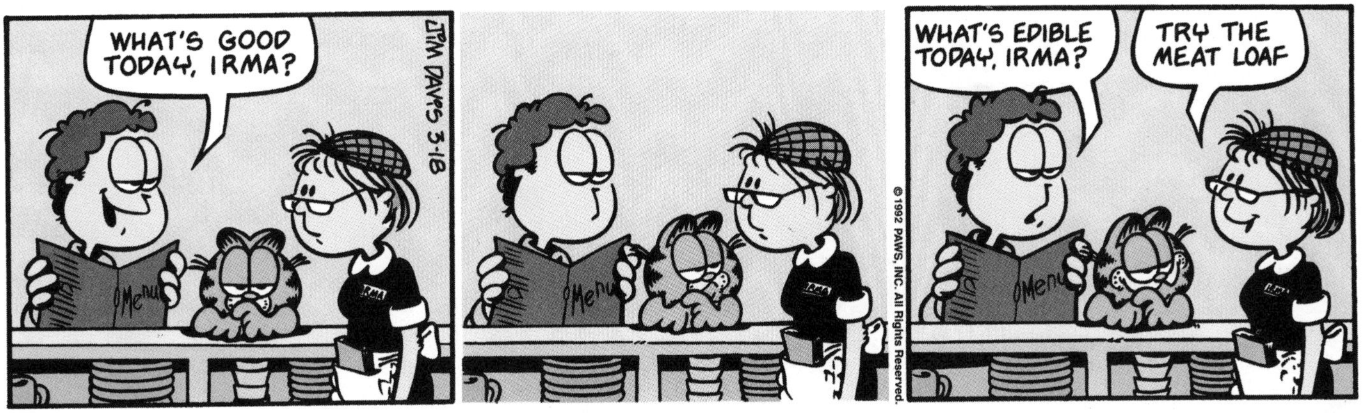
WHAT'S GOOD TODAY, IRMA?
JIM DAVIS 3-18
Menu
© 1992 PAWS, INC. All Rights Reserved.
WHAT'S EDIBLE TODAY, IRMA?
TRY THE MEAT LOAF

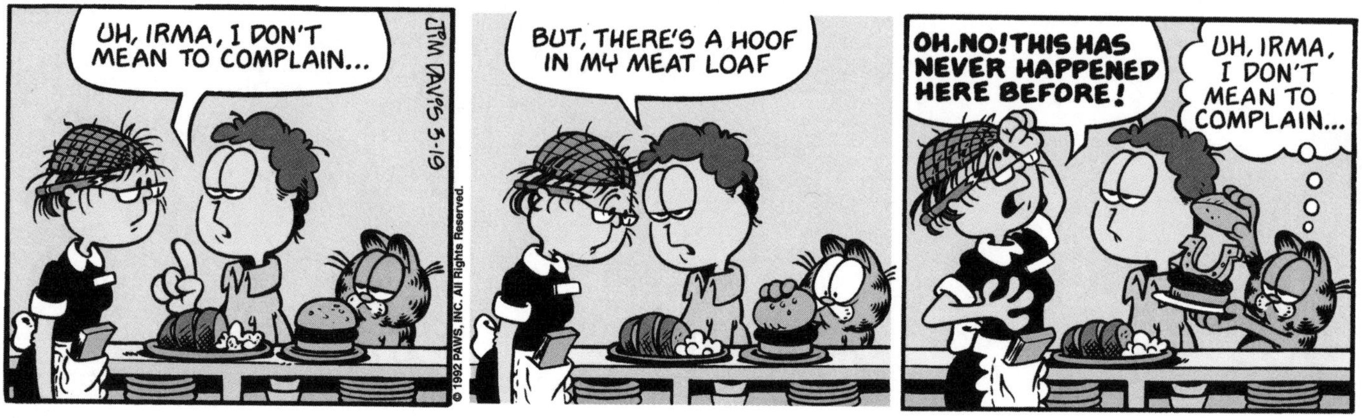
UH, IRMA, I DON'T MEAN TO COMPLAIN...
JIM DAVIS 3-19
BUT, THERE'S A HOOF IN MY MEAT LOAF
© 1992 PAWS, INC. All Rights Reserved.
OH, NO! THIS HAS NEVER HAPPENED HERE BEFORE!
UH, IRMA, I DON'T MEAN TO COMPLAIN...

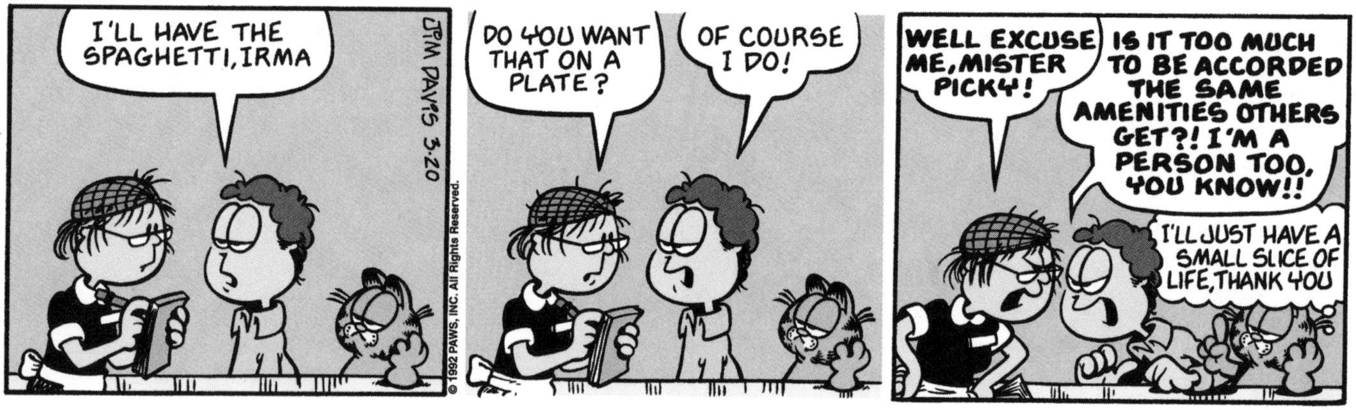
I'LL HAVE THE SPAGHETTI, IRMA
JIM DAVIS 3-20
DO YOU WANT THAT ON A PLATE?
OF COURSE I DO!
© 1992 PAWS, INC. All Rights Reserved.
WELL EXCUSE ME, MISTER PICKY!
IS IT TOO MUCH TO BE ACCORDED THE SAME AMENITIES OTHERS GET?! I'M A PERSON TOO, YOU KNOW!!
I'LL JUST HAVE A SMALL SLICE OF LIFE, THANK YOU

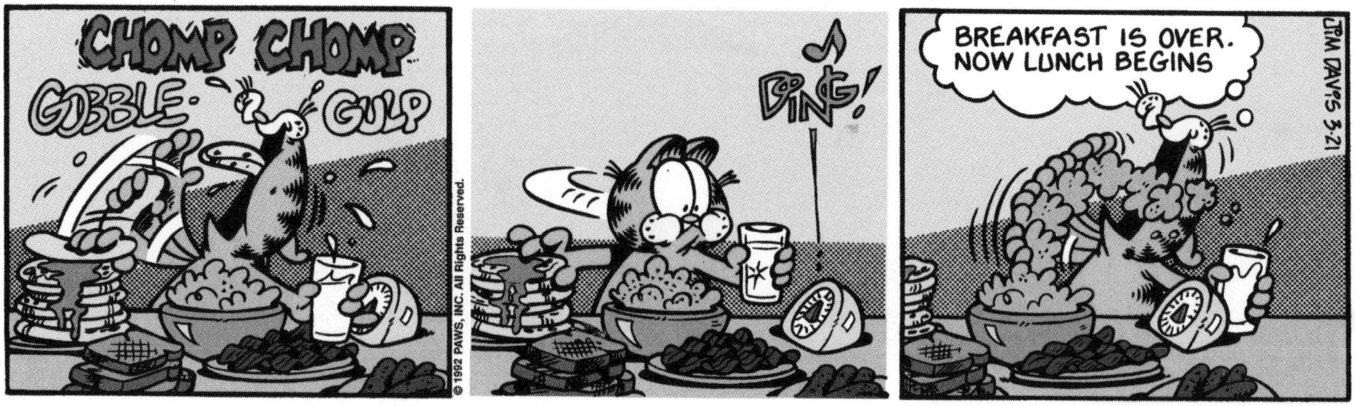
CHOMP CHOMP
GOBBLE
GULP
© 1992 PAWS, INC. All Rights Reserved.
DING!
BREAKFAST IS OVER. NOW LUNCH BEGINS
JIM DAVIS 3-21

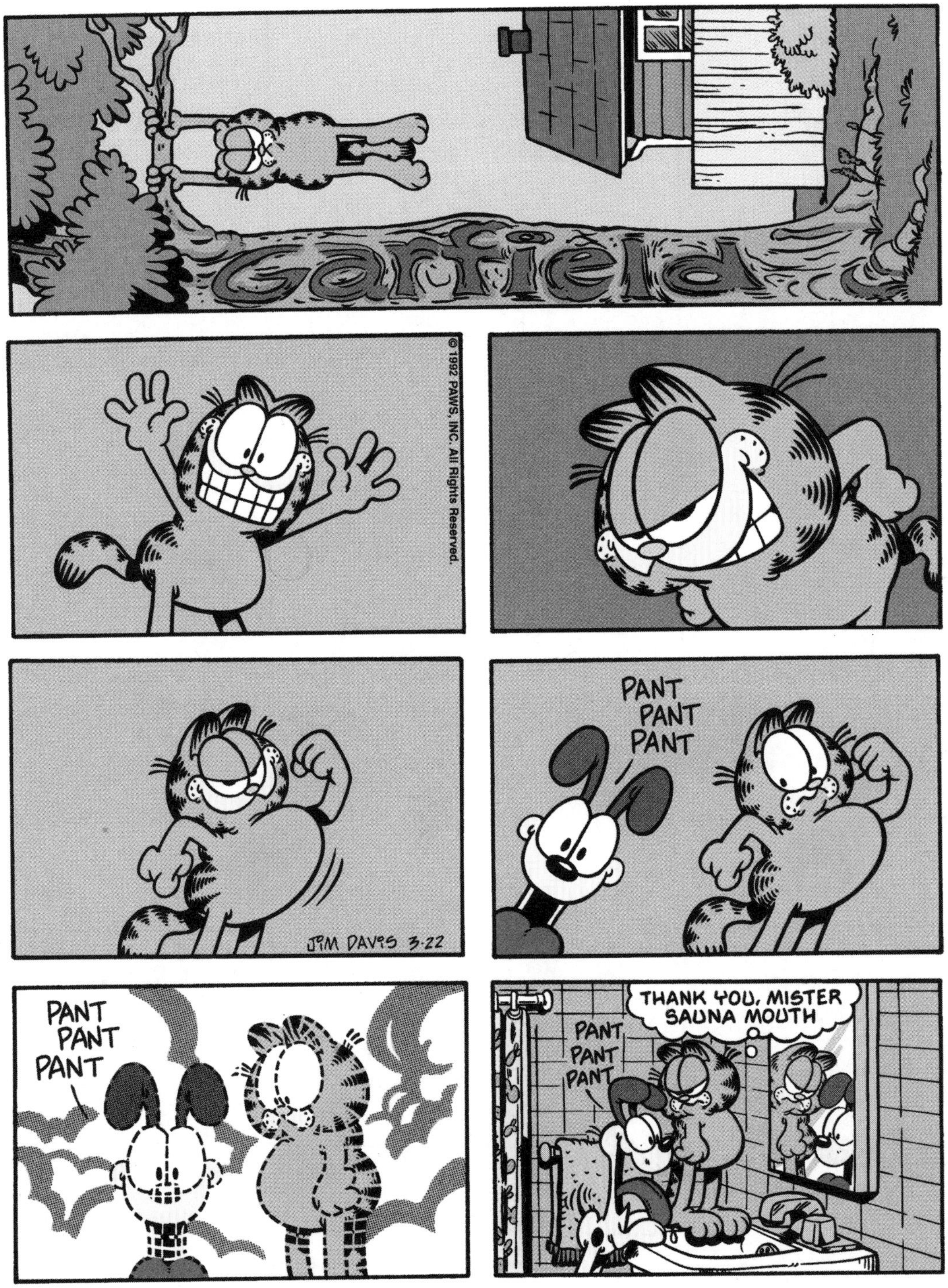
Garfield
© 1992 PAWS, INC. All Rights Reserved.
JIM DAVIS 3-22
PANT
PANT
PANT
PANT
PANT
PANT
PANT
PANT
PANT
THANK YOU, MISTER SAUNA MOUTH

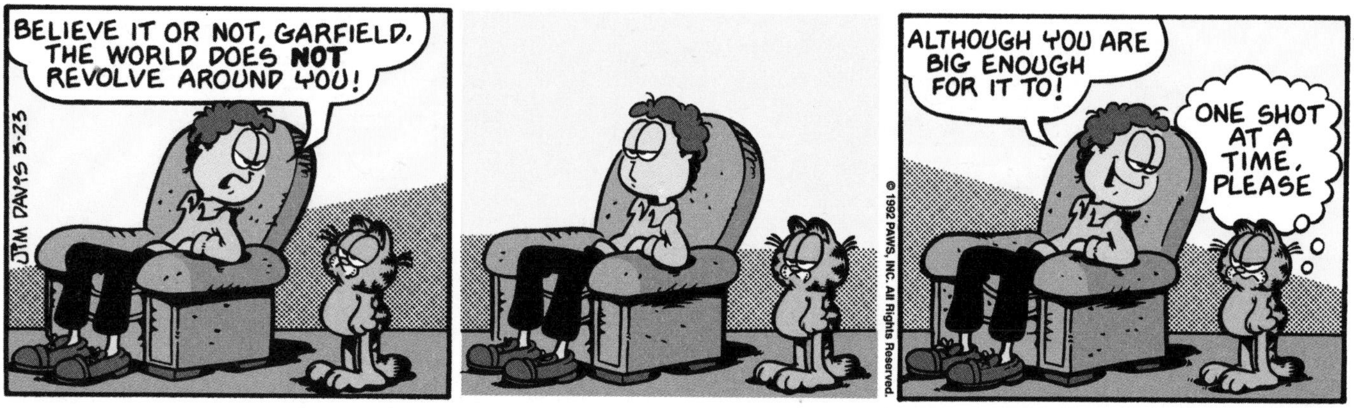
JIM DAVIS 3-23
BELIEVE IT OR NOT, GARFIELD. THE WORLD DOES **NOT** REVOLVE AROUND YOU!
© 1992 PAWS, INC. All Rights Reserved.
ALTHOUGH YOU ARE BIG ENOUGH FOR IT TO!
ONE SHOT AT A TIME, PLEASE

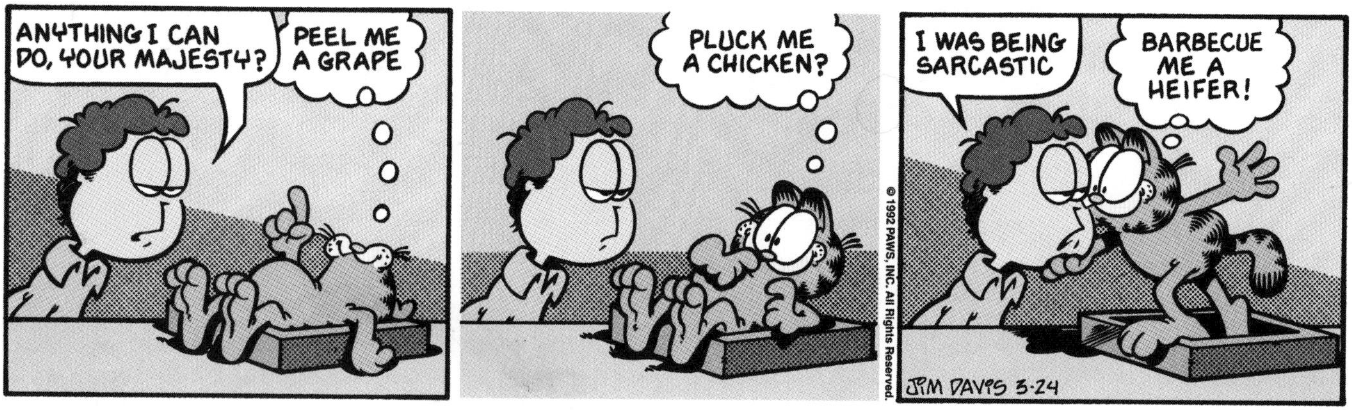
ANYTHING I CAN DO, YOUR MAJESTY?
PEEL ME A GRAPE
PLUCK ME A CHICKEN?
© 1992 PAWS, INC. All Rights Reserved.
I WAS BEING SARCASTIC
BARBECUE ME A HEIFER!
JIM DAVIS 3-24

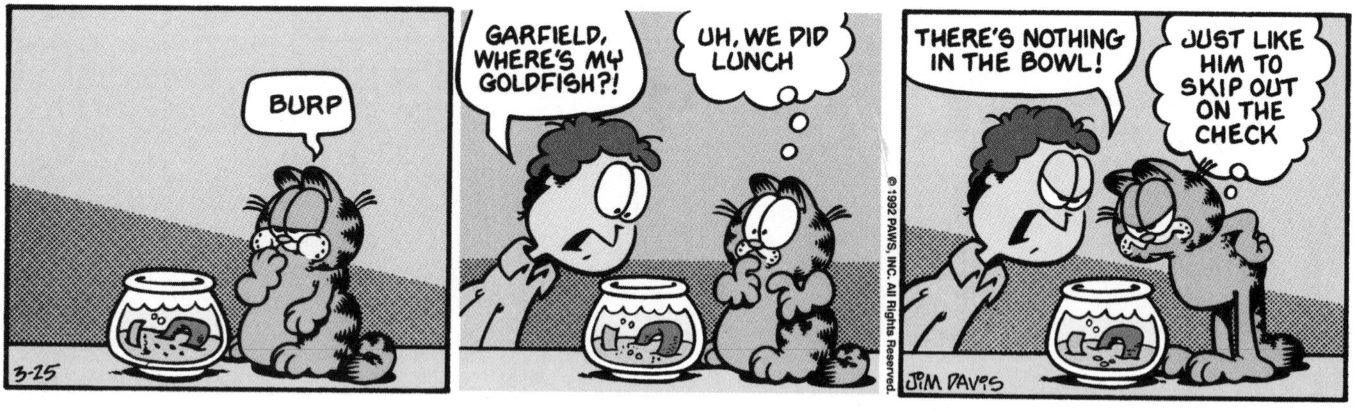
BURP
3-25
GARFIELD, WHERE'S MY GOLDFISH?!
UH, WE DID LUNCH
© 1992 PAWS, INC. All Rights Reserved.
THERE'S NOTHING IN THE BOWL!
JUST LIKE HIM TO SKIP OUT ON THE CHECK
JIM DAVIS

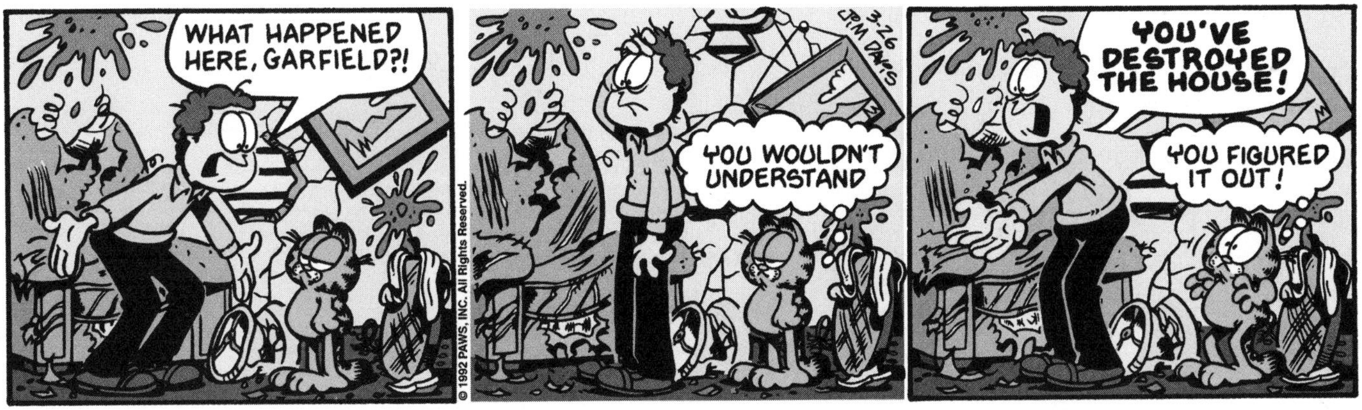
WHAT HAPPENED HERE, GARFIELD?!
© 1992 PAWS, INC. All Rights Reserved.
JIM DAVIS 3-26
YOU WOULDN'T UNDERSTAND
YOU'VE DESTROYED THE HOUSE!
YOU FIGURED IT OUT!

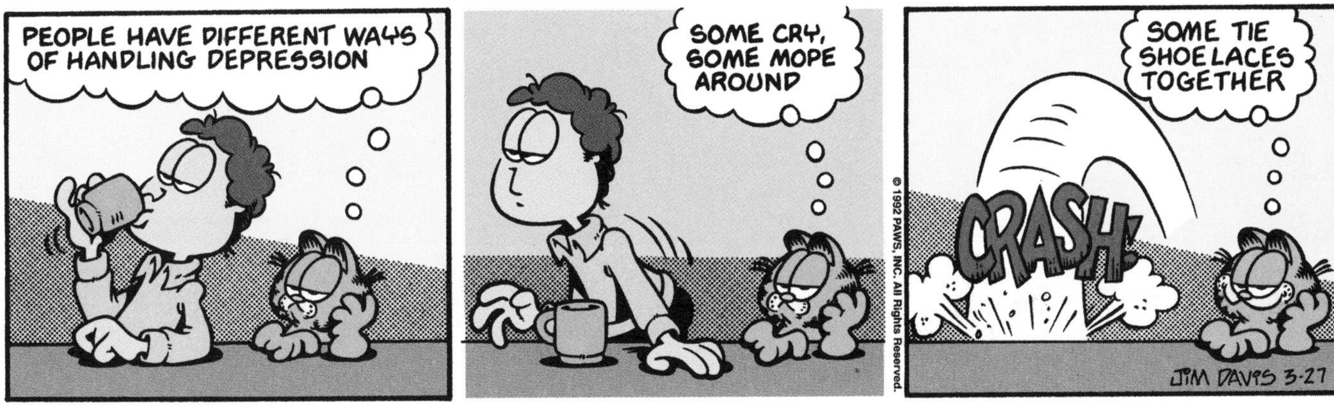
PEOPLE HAVE DIFFERENT WAYS OF HANDLING DEPRESSION
SOME CRY, SOME MOPE AROUND
© 1992 PAWS, INC. All Rights Reserved.
SOME TIE SHOELACES TOGETHER
CRASH!
JIM DAVIS 3-27

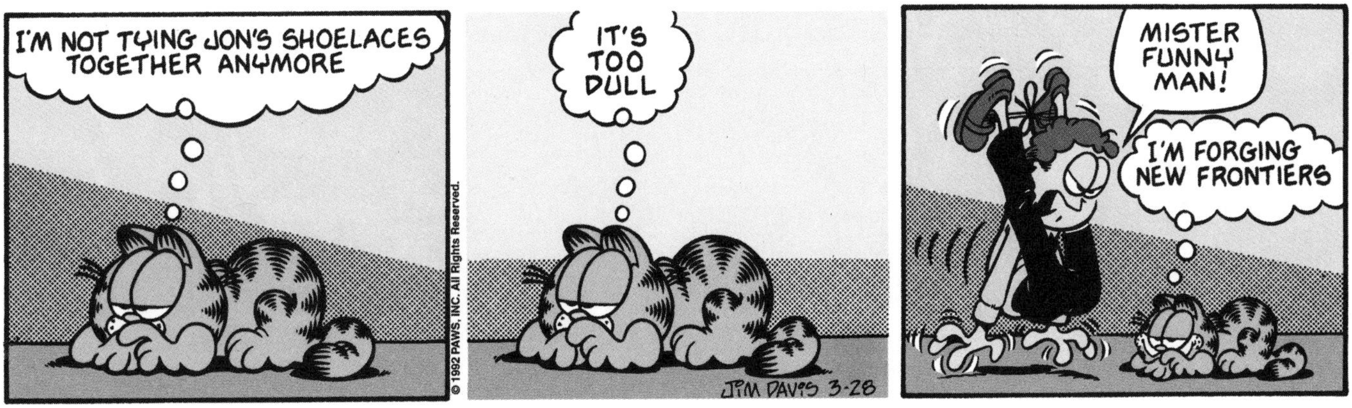
I'M NOT TYING JON'S SHOELACES TOGETHER ANYMORE
© 1992 PAWS, INC. All Rights Reserved.
IT'S TOO DULL
JIM DAVIS 3-28
MISTER FUNNY MAN!
I'M FORGING NEW FRONTIERS

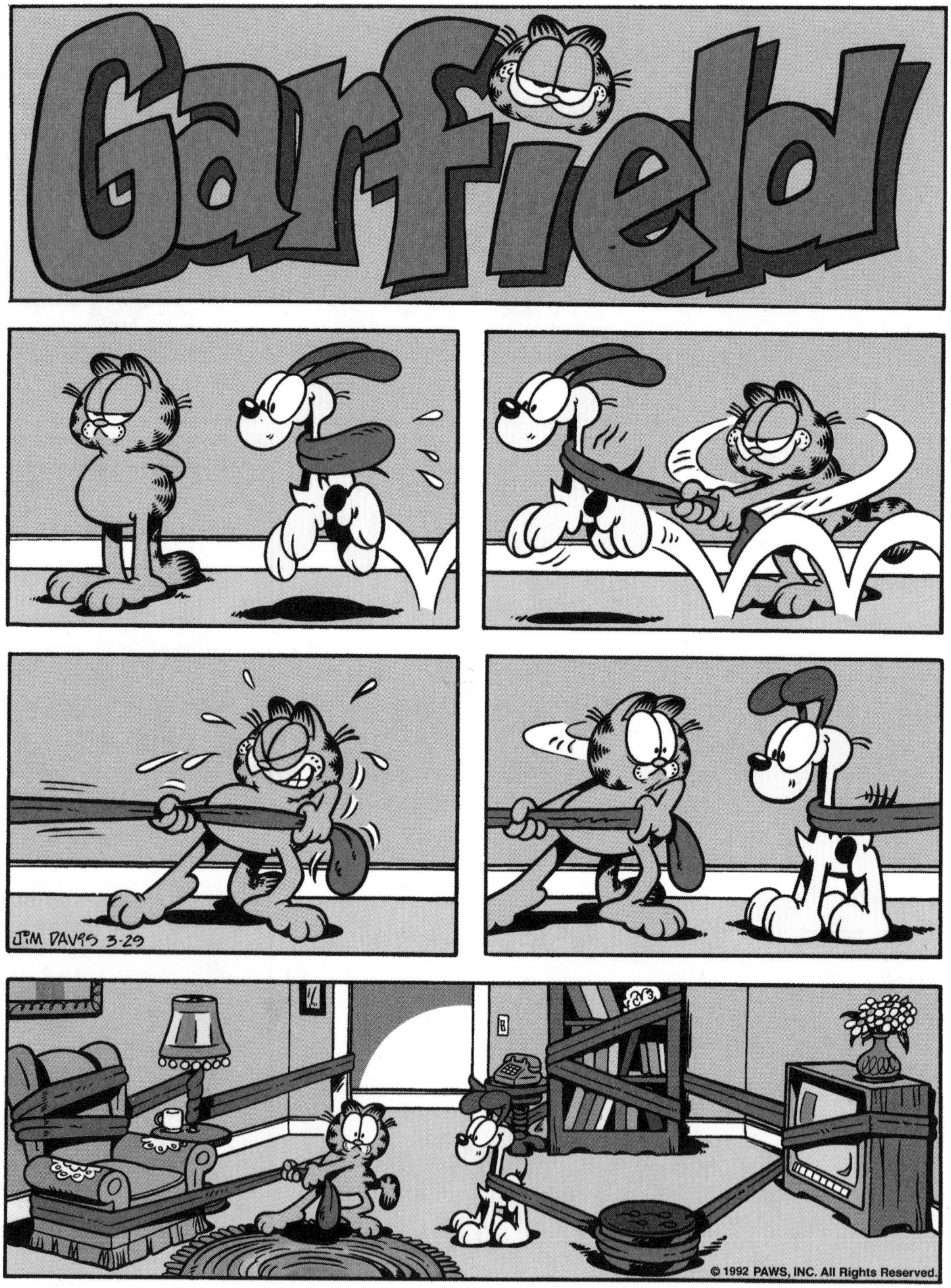
Garfield
JIM DAVIS 3-29
© 1992 PAWS, INC. All Rights Reserved.

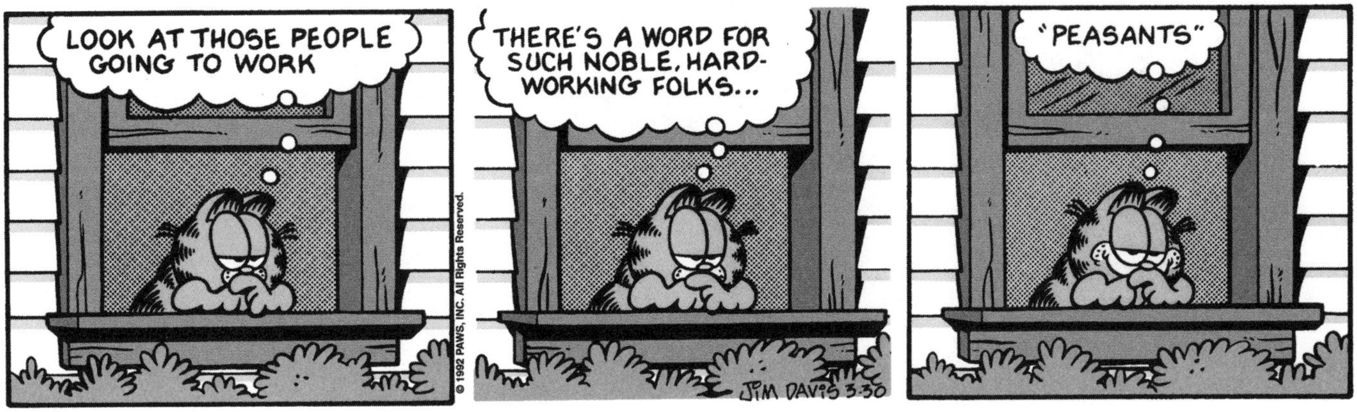
LOOK AT THOSE PEOPLE GOING TO WORK
THERE'S A WORD FOR SUCH NOBLE, HARD-WORKING FOLKS...
"PEASANTS"
© 1992 PAWS, INC. All Rights Reserved.
JIM DAVIS 3-30

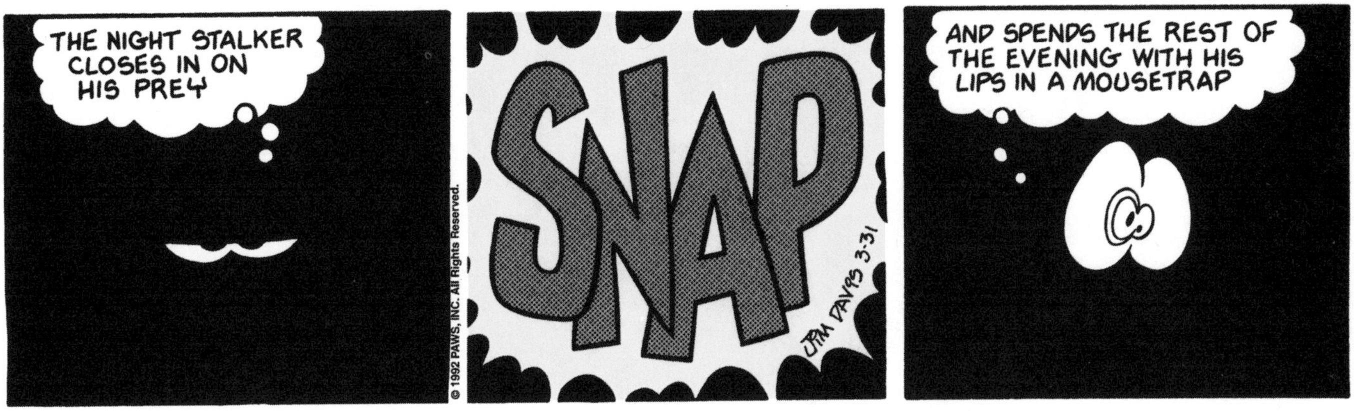
THE NIGHT STALKER CLOSES IN ON HIS PREY
SNAP
AND SPENDS THE REST OF THE EVENING WITH HIS LIPS IN A MOUSETRAP
© 1992 PAWS, INC. All Rights Reserved.
JIM DAVIS 3-31

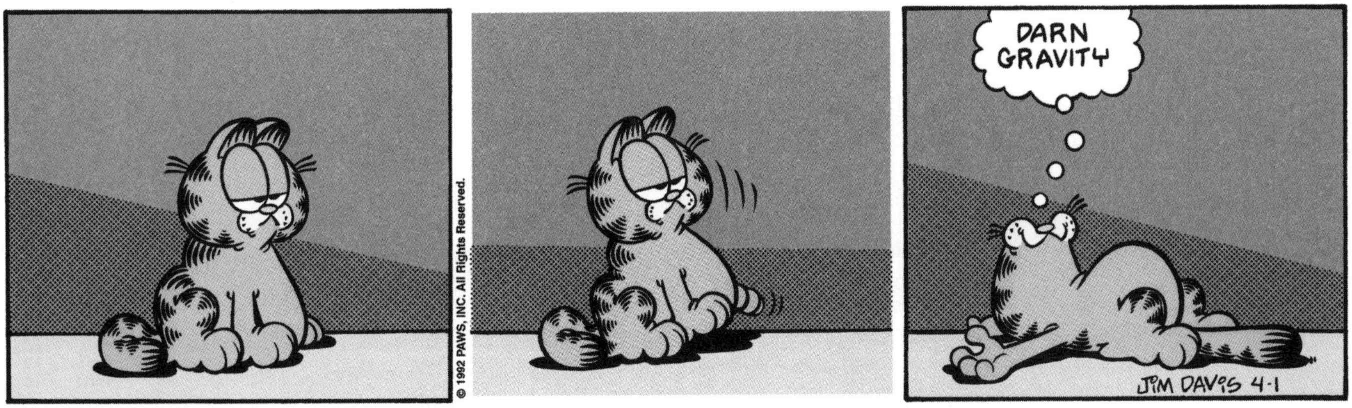
DARN GRAVITY
© 1992 PAWS, INC. All Rights Reserved.
JIM DAVIS 4-1

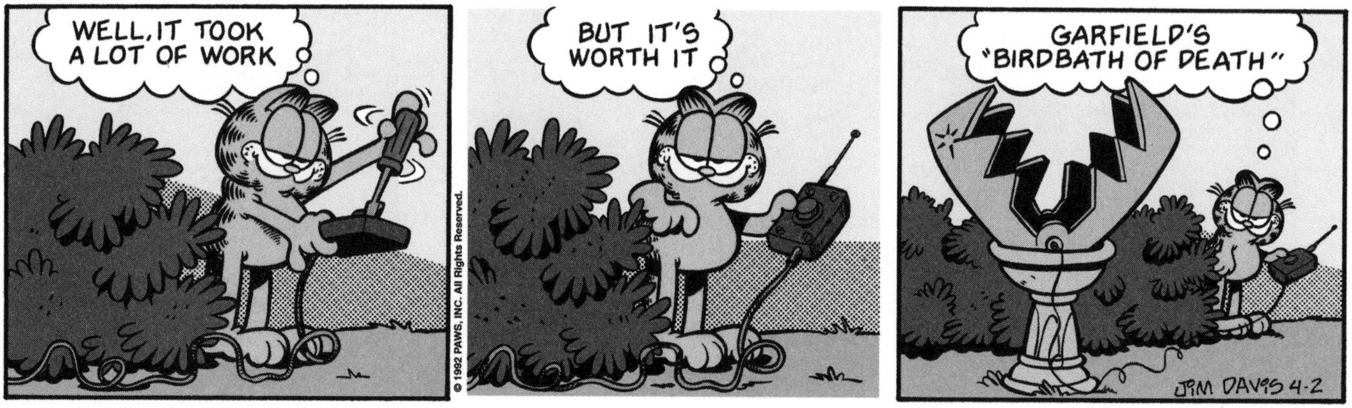
WELL, IT TOOK A LOT OF WORK
BUT IT'S WORTH IT
GARFIELD'S "BIRDBATH OF DEATH"
JIM DAVIS 4-2

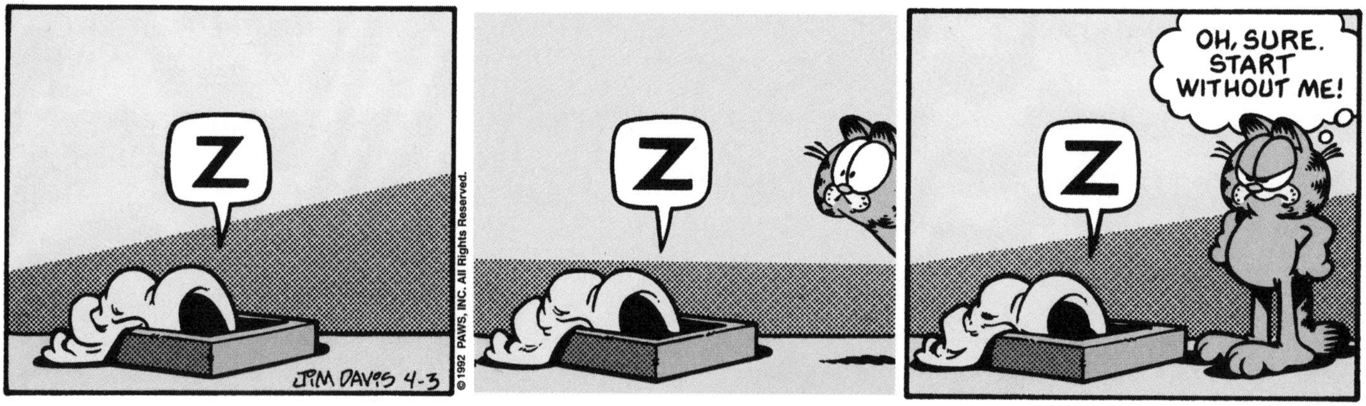
Z
JIM DAVIS 4-3
Z
Z
OH, SURE. START WITHOUT ME!

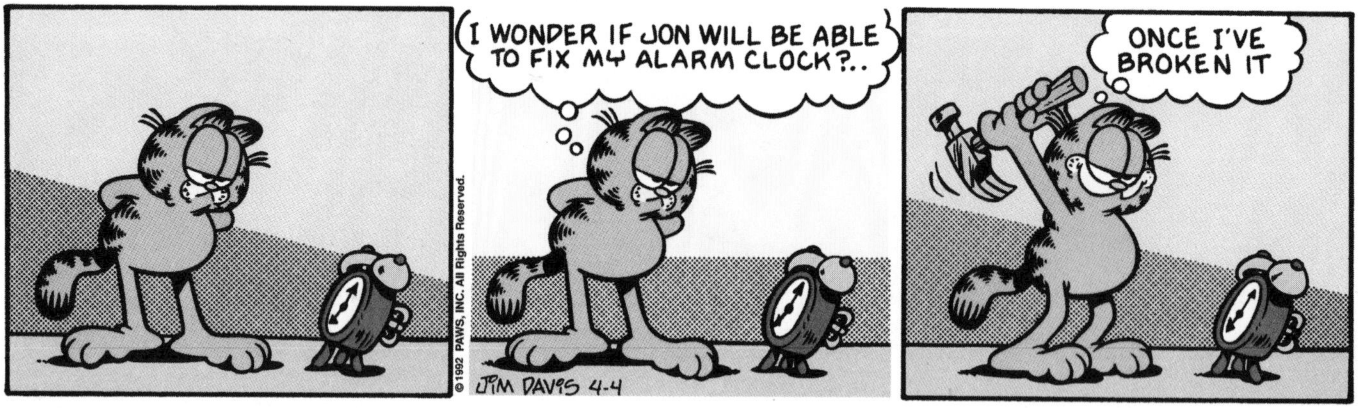
I WONDER IF JON WILL BE ABLE TO FIX MY ALARM CLOCK?..
JIM DAVIS 4-4
ONCE I'VE BROKEN IT

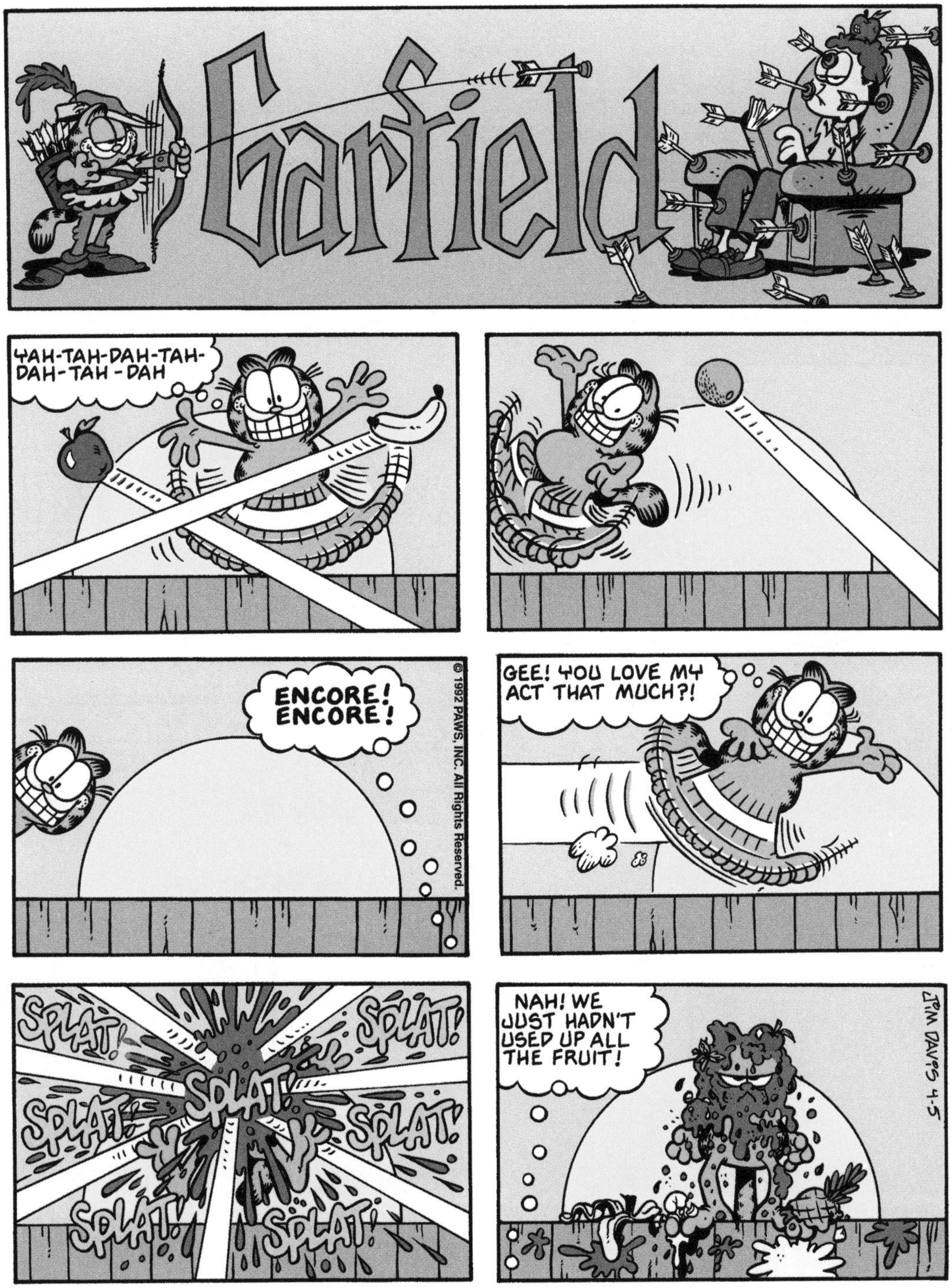
Garfield
YAH-TAH-DAH-TAH-DAH-TAH-DAH
ENCORE! ENCORE!
© 1992 PAWS, INC. All Rights Reserved.
GEE! YOU LOVE MY ACT THAT MUCH?!
SPLAT! SPLAT! SPLAT! SPLAT! SPLAT! SPLAT! SPLAT!
NAH! WE JUST HADN'T USED UP ALL THE FRUIT!
JIM DAVIS 4-5

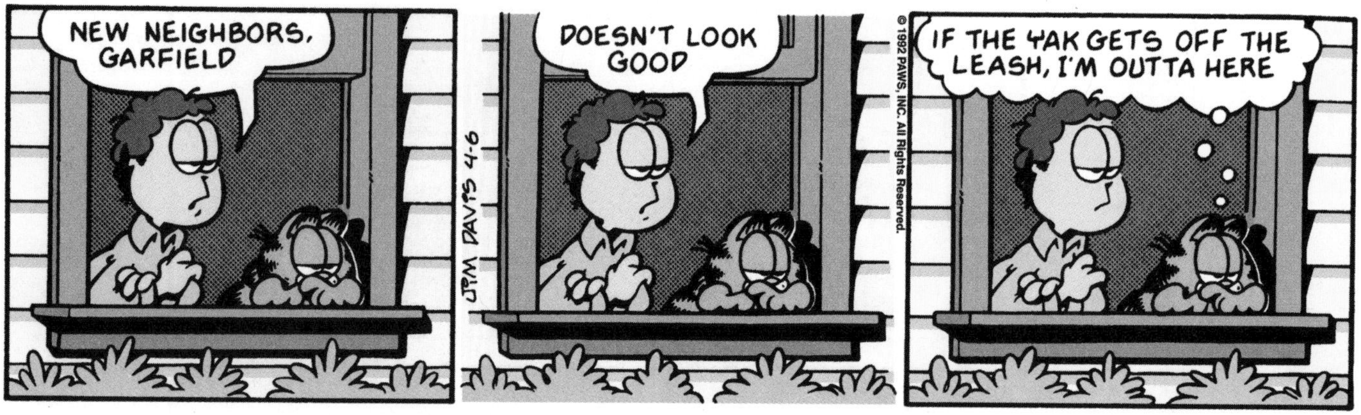
NEW NEIGHBORS, GARFIELD
JIM DAVIS 4-6
DOESN'T LOOK GOOD
© 1992 PAWS, INC. All Rights Reserved.
IF THE YAK GETS OFF THE LEASH, I'M OUTTA HERE

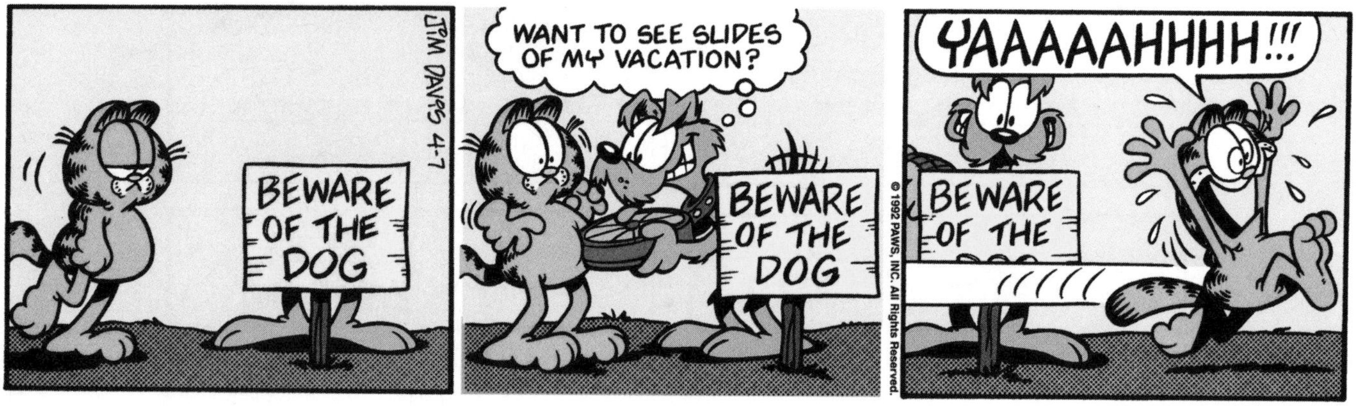
JIM DAVIS 4-7
BEWARE OF THE DOG
WANT TO SEE SLIDES OF MY VACATION?
BEWARE OF THE DOG
© 1992 PAWS, INC. All Rights Reserved.
YAAAAAHHHH!!!
BEWARE OF THE

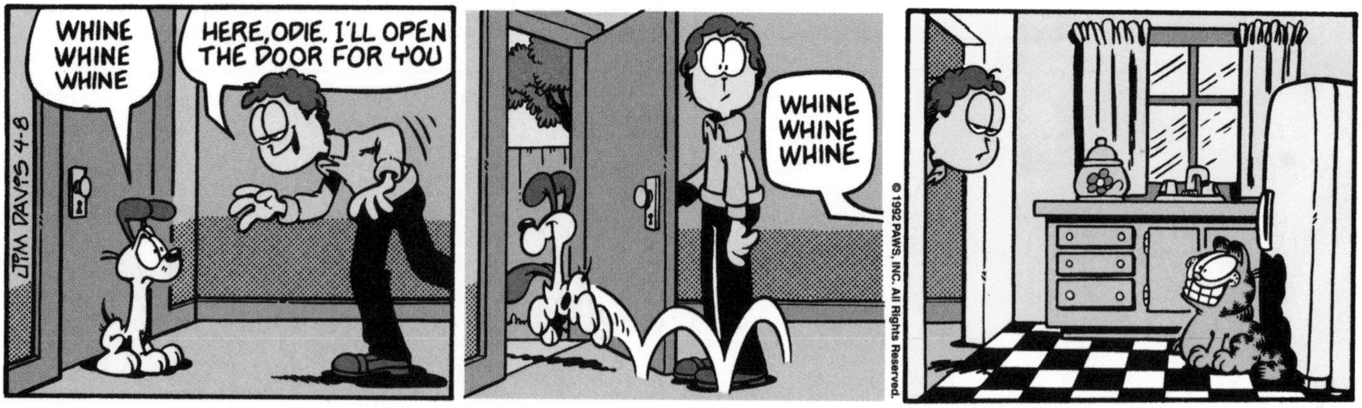
JIM DAVIS 4-8
WHINE WHINE WHINE
HERE, ODIE, I'LL OPEN THE DOOR FOR YOU
WHINE WHINE WHINE
© 1992 PAWS, INC. All Rights Reserved.

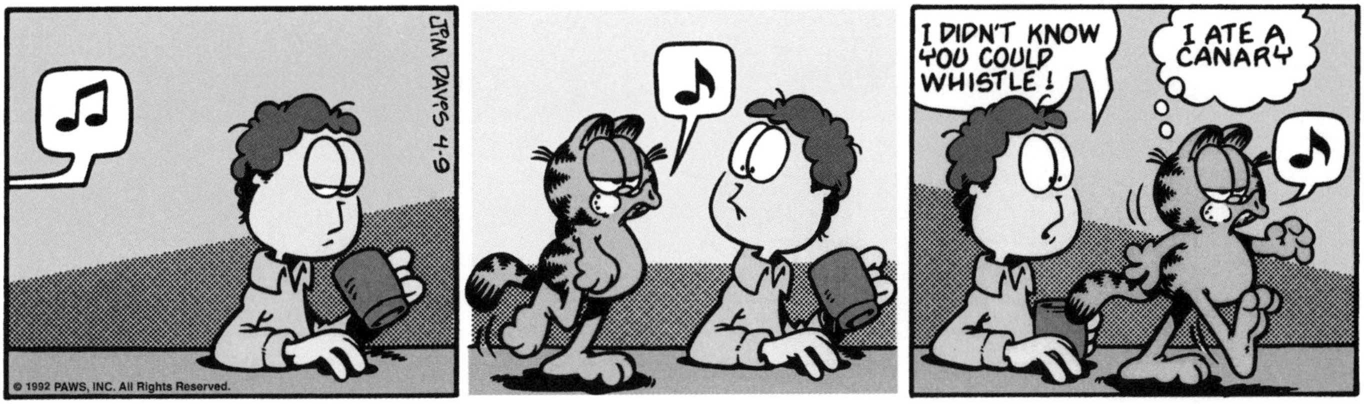
JIM DAVIS 4-9
© 1992 PAWS, INC. All Rights Reserved.
I DIDN'T KNOW YOU COULD WHISTLE!
I ATE A CANARY

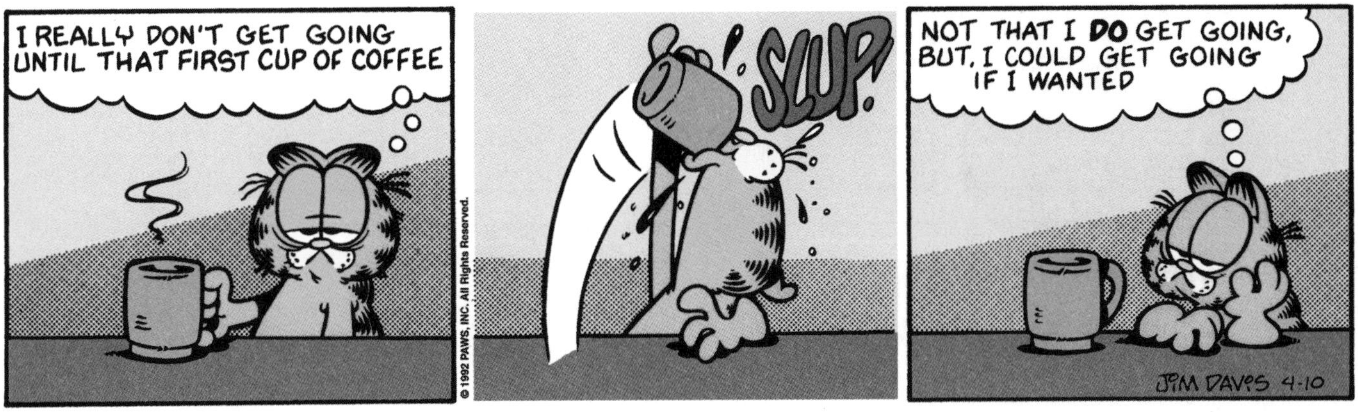
I REALLY DON'T GET GOING UNTIL THAT FIRST CUP OF COFFEE
© 1992 PAWS, INC. All Rights Reserved.
SLUP!
NOT THAT I **DO** GET GOING, BUT, I COULD GET GOING IF I WANTED
JIM DAVIS 4-10

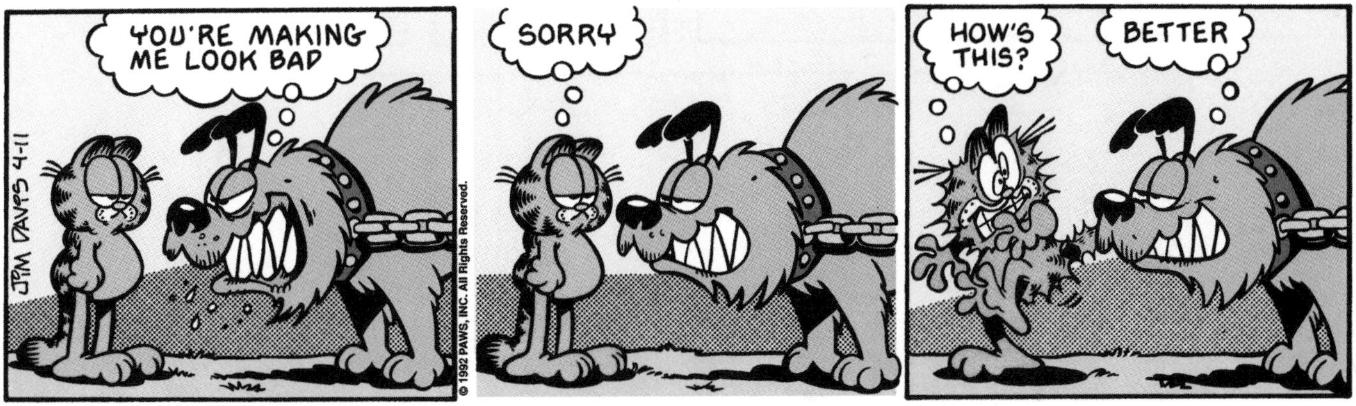
JIM DAVIS 4-11
YOU'RE MAKING ME LOOK BAD
© 1992 PAWS, INC. All Rights Reserved.
SORRY
HOW'S THIS?
BETTER

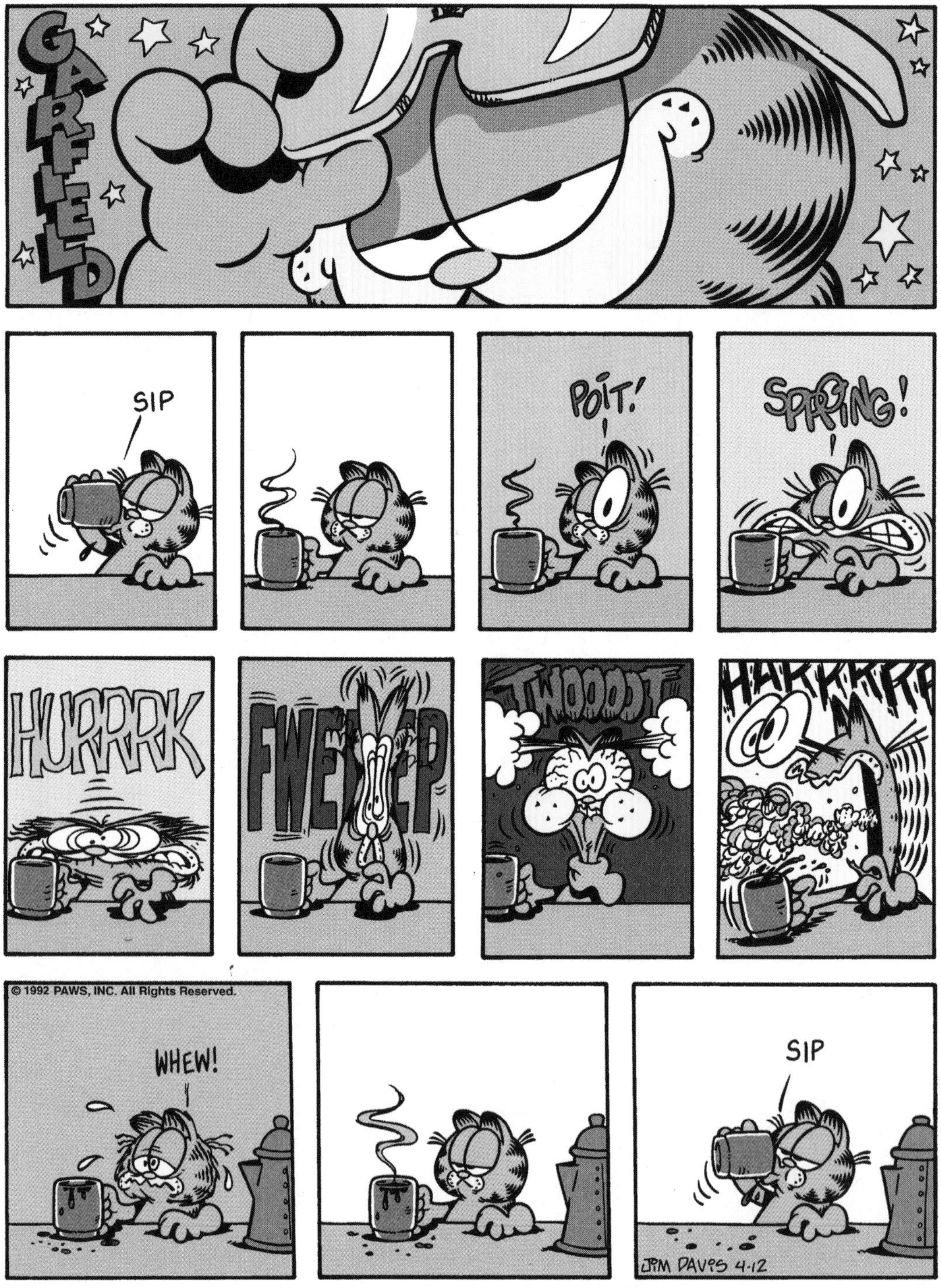
GARFIELD
SIP
POIT!
SPROING!
HURRRK
TWOOOOT
WHEW!
SIP
JIM DAVIS 4-12

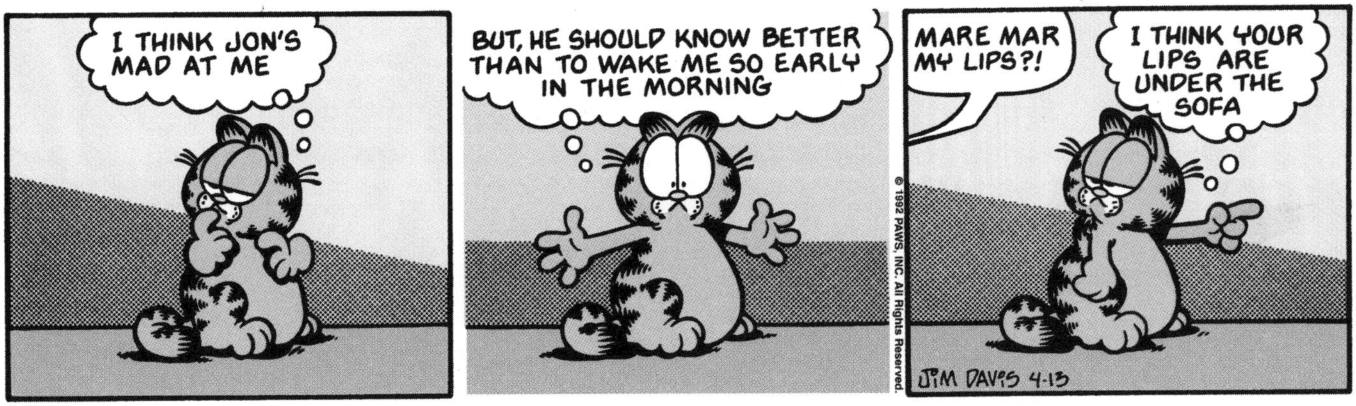
I THINK JON'S MAD AT ME
BUT, HE SHOULD KNOW BETTER THAN TO WAKE ME SO EARLY IN THE MORNING
© 1992 PAWS, INC. All Rights Reserved.
MARE MAR MY LIPS?!
I THINK YOUR LIPS ARE UNDER THE SOFA
JIM DAVIS 4-13

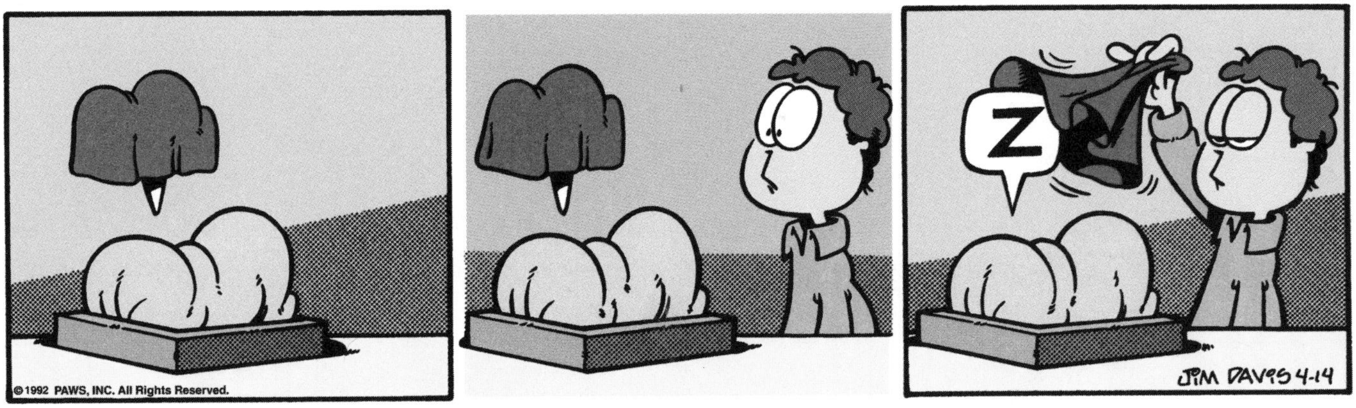
© 1992 PAWS, INC. All Rights Reserved.
Z
JIM DAVIS 4-14

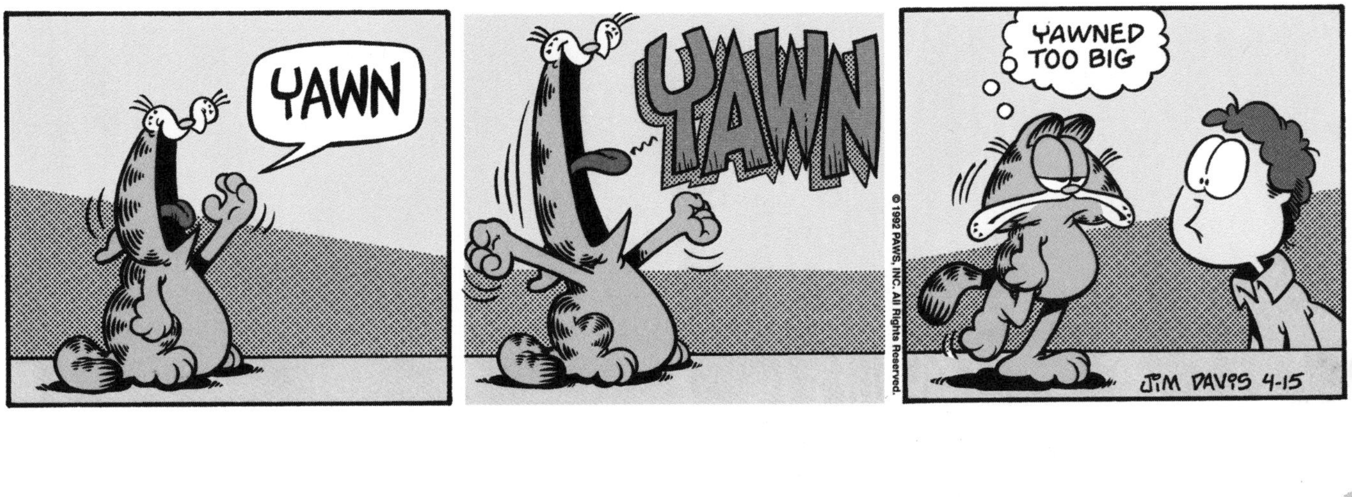
YAWN
YAWN
© 1992 PAWS, INC. All Rights Reserved.
YAWNED TOO BIG
JIM DAVIS 4-15

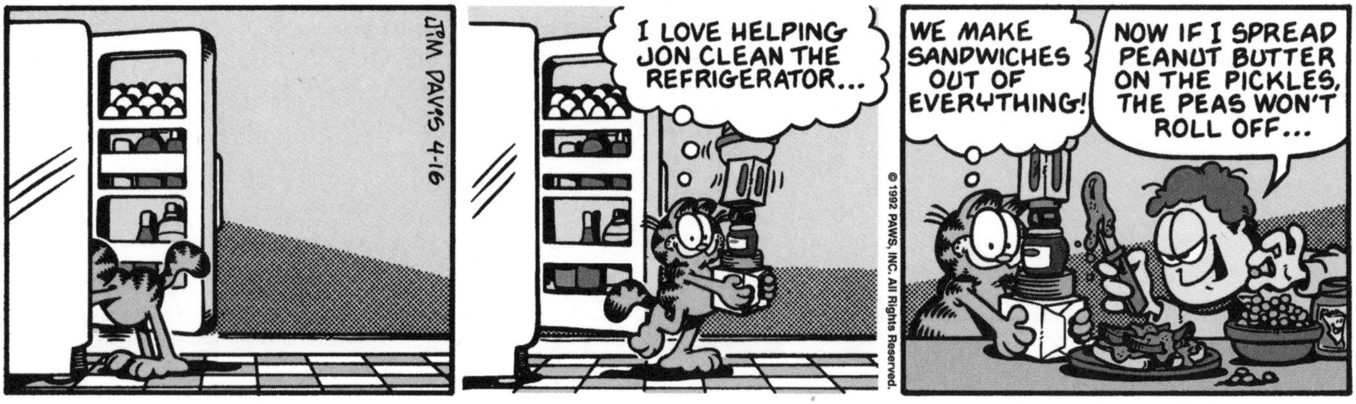
JIM DAVIS 4-16
I LOVE HELPING JON CLEAN THE REFRIGERATOR...
© 1992 PAWS, INC. All Rights Reserved.
WE MAKE SANDWICHES OUT OF EVERYTHING!
NOW IF I SPREAD PEANUT BUTTER ON THE PICKLES, THE PEAS WON'T ROLL OFF...

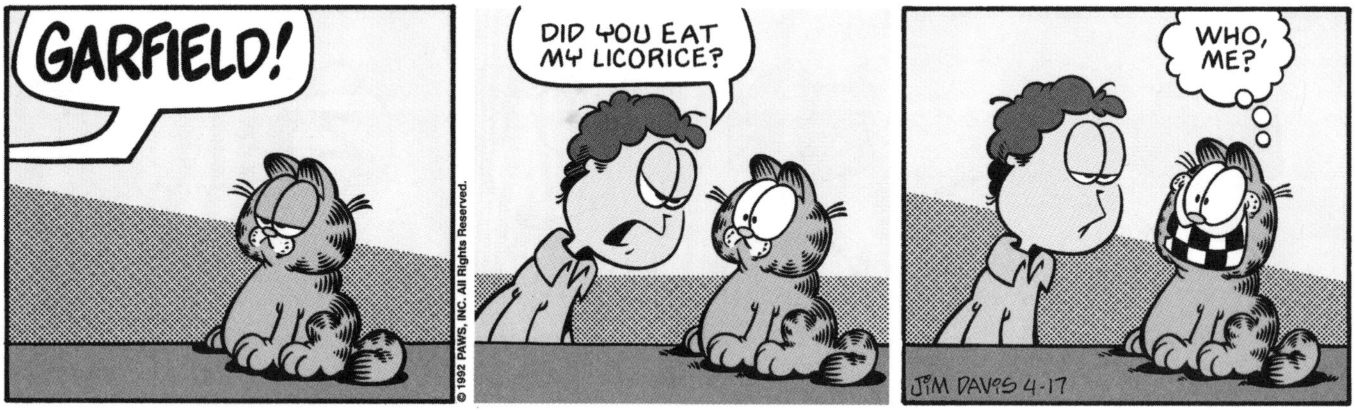
GARFIELD!
© 1992 PAWS, INC. All Rights Reserved.
DID YOU EAT MY LICORICE?
WHO, ME?
JIM DAVIS 4-17

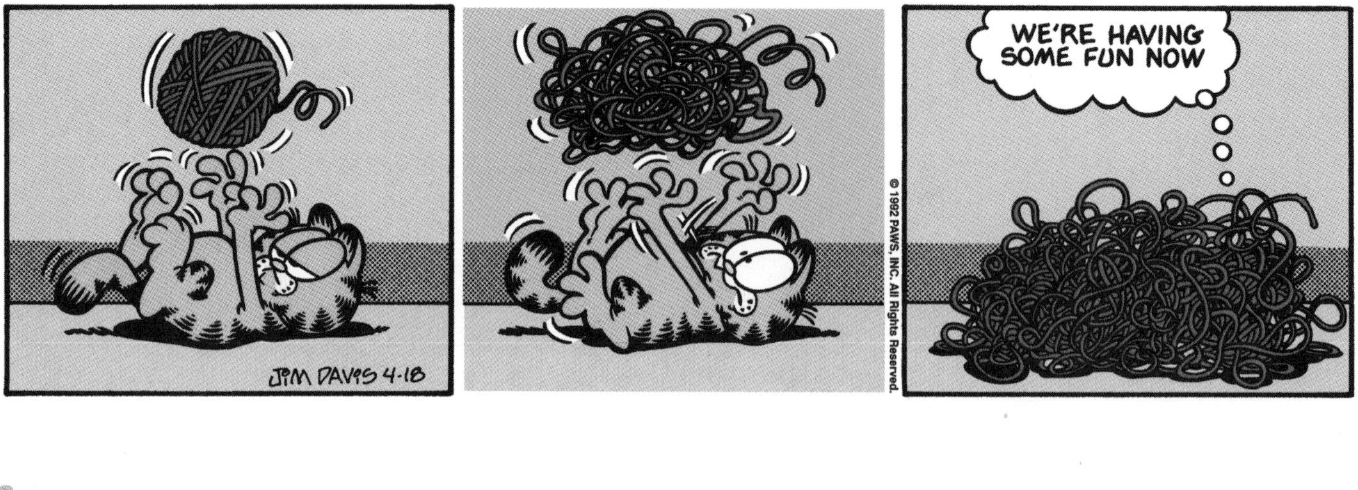
JIM DAVIS 4-18
© 1992 PAWS, INC. All Rights Reserved.
WE'RE HAVING SOME FUN NOW

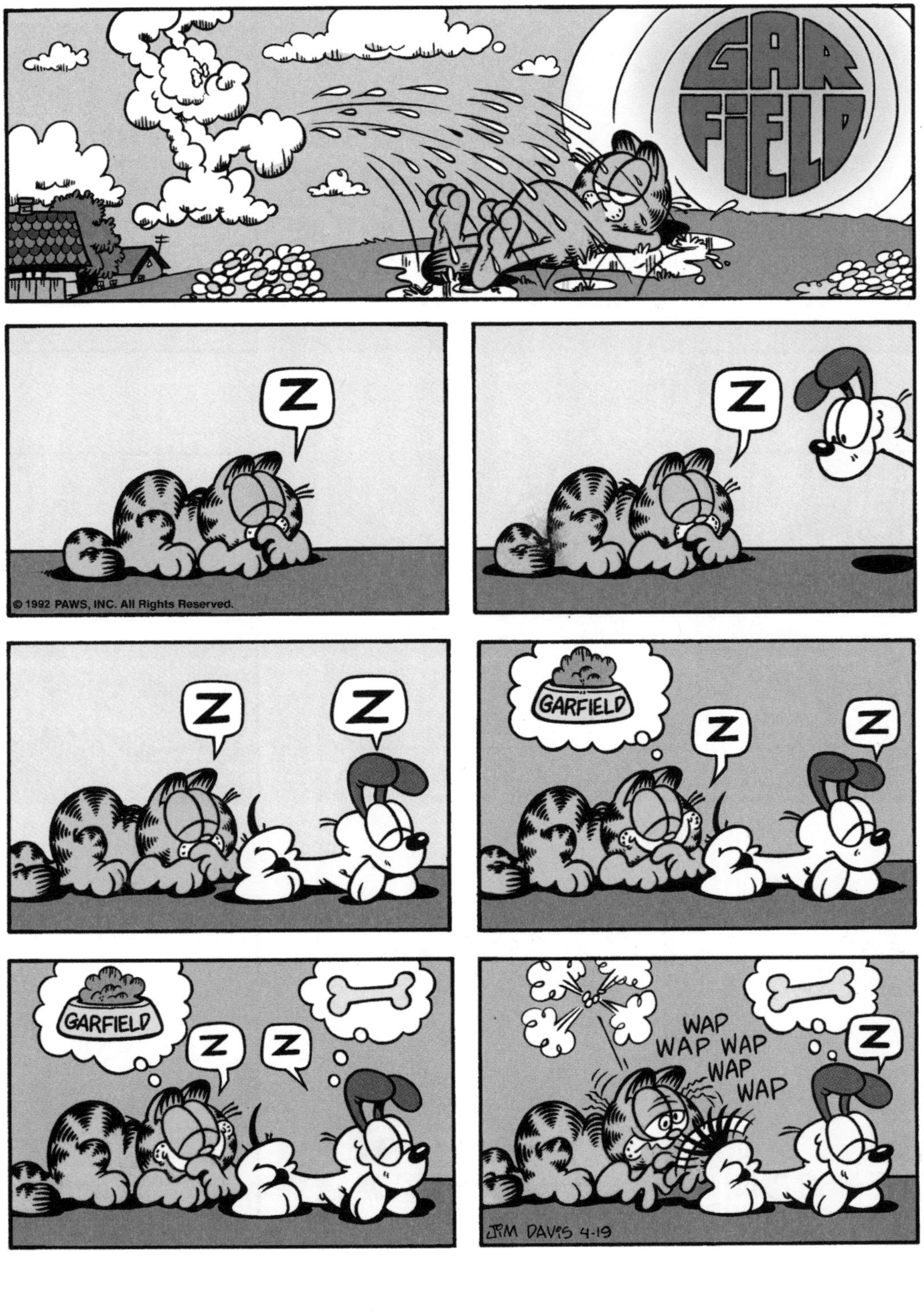
GARFIELD
© 1992 PAWS, INC. All Rights Reserved.
Z
Z
Z
Z
GARFIELD
Z
Z
GARFIELD
Z
Z
WAP
WAP WAP
WAP
WAP
Z
JIM DAVIS 4-19

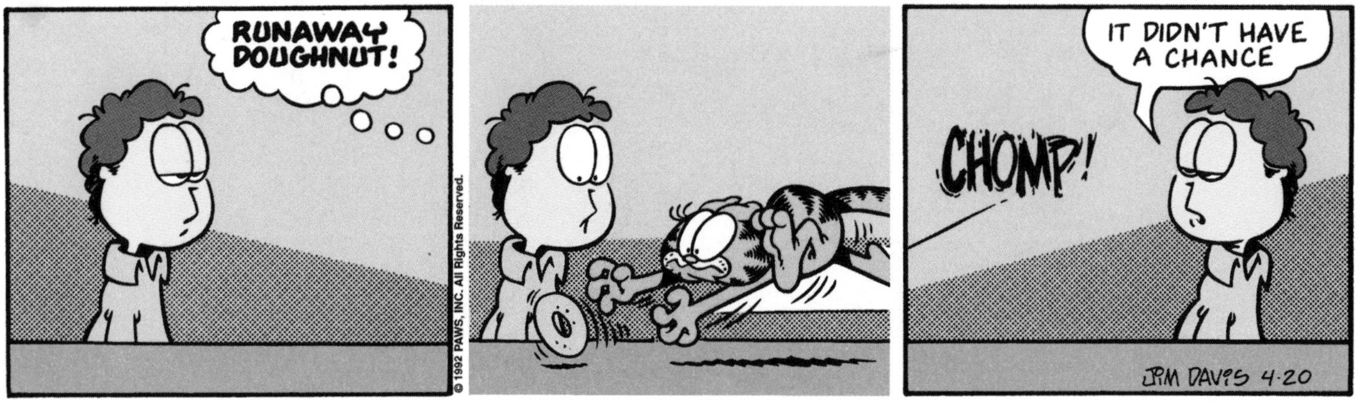
RUNAWAY DOUGHNUT!
© 1992 PAWS, INC. All Rights Reserved.
CHOMP!
IT DIDN'T HAVE A CHANCE
JIM DAVIS 4·20

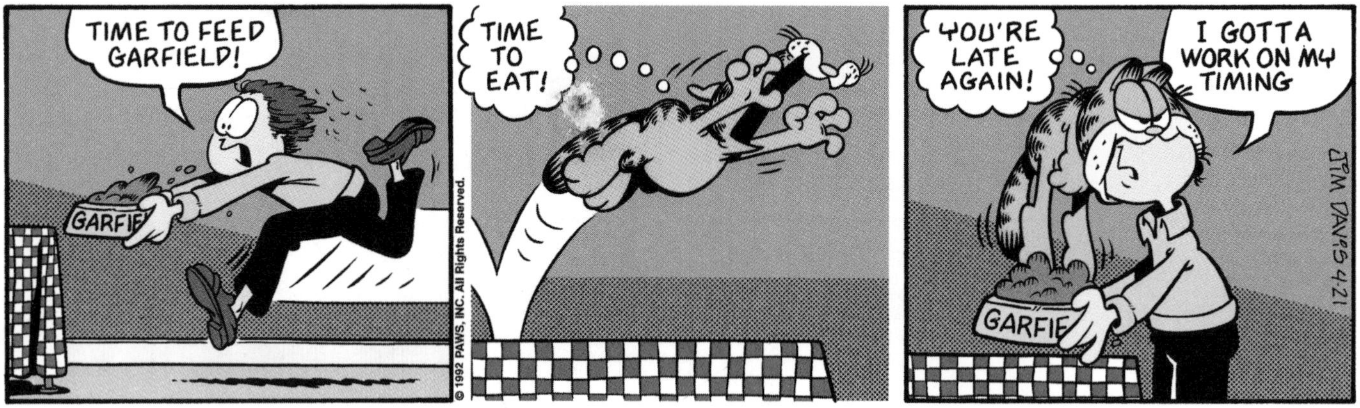
TIME TO FEED GARFIELD!
GARFIE
© 1992 PAWS, INC. All Rights Reserved.
TIME TO EAT!
YOU'RE LATE AGAIN!
I GOTTA WORK ON MY TIMING
GARFIE
JIM DAVIS 4·21

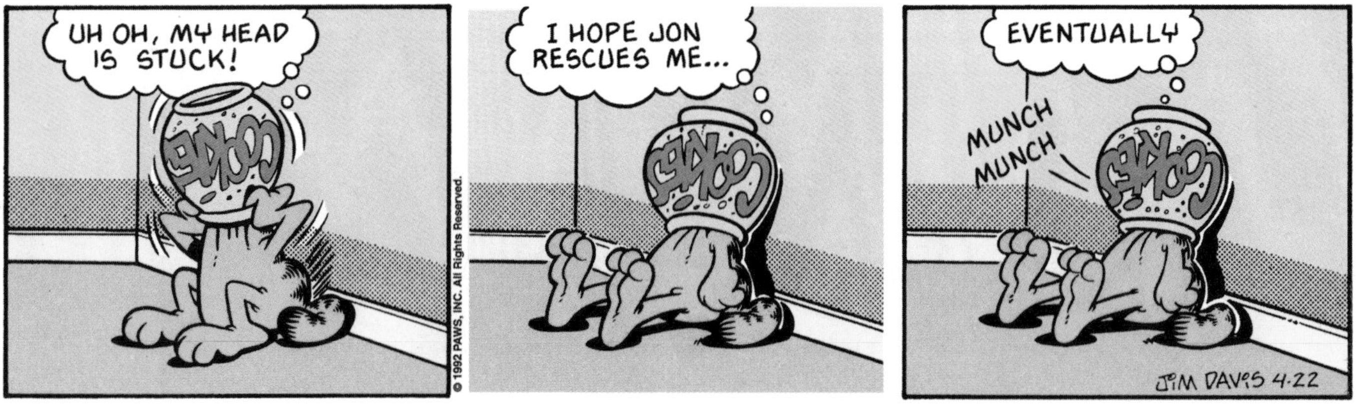
UH OH, MY HEAD IS STUCK!
© 1992 PAWS, INC. All Rights Reserved.
I HOPE JON RESCUES ME...
EVENTUALLY
MUNCH MUNCH
JIM DAVIS 4·22

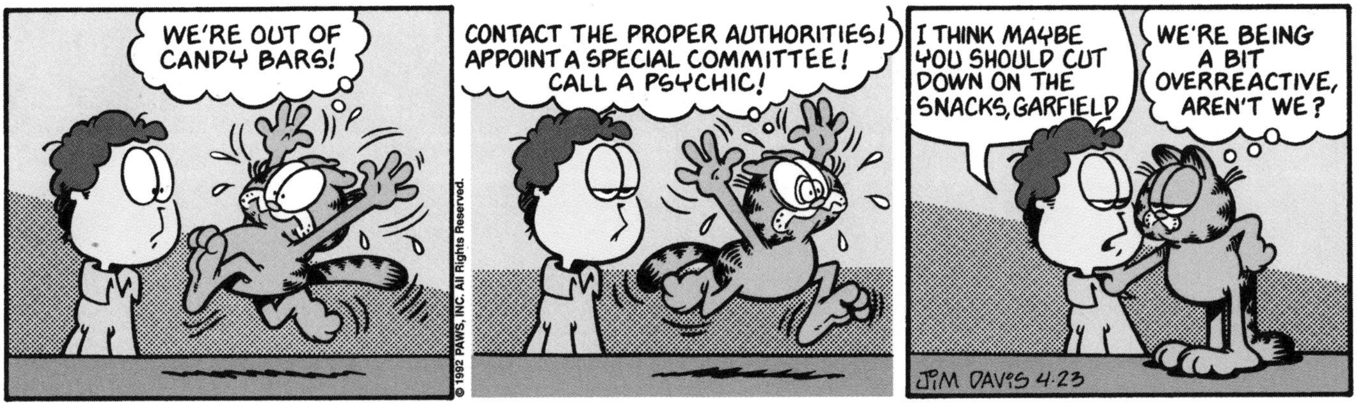
WE'RE OUT OF CANDY BARS!
CONTACT THE PROPER AUTHORITIES! APPOINT A SPECIAL COMMITTEE! CALL A PSYCHIC!
I THINK MAYBE YOU SHOULD CUT DOWN ON THE SNACKS, GARFIELD
WE'RE BEING A BIT OVERREACTIVE, AREN'T WE?
© 1992 PAWS, INC. All Rights Reserved.
JIM DAVIS 4·23

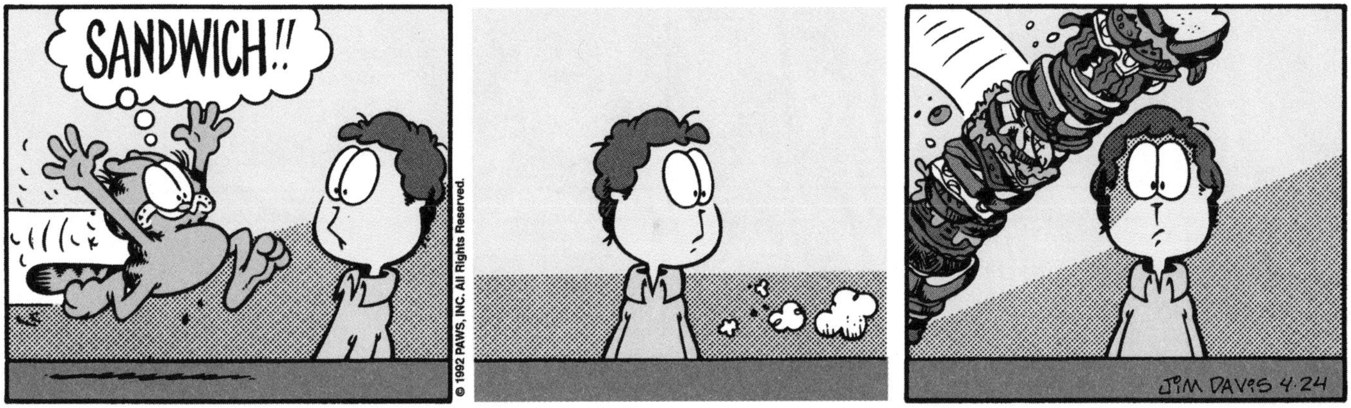
SANDWICH!!
© 1992 PAWS, INC. All Rights Reserved.
JIM DAVIS 4·24

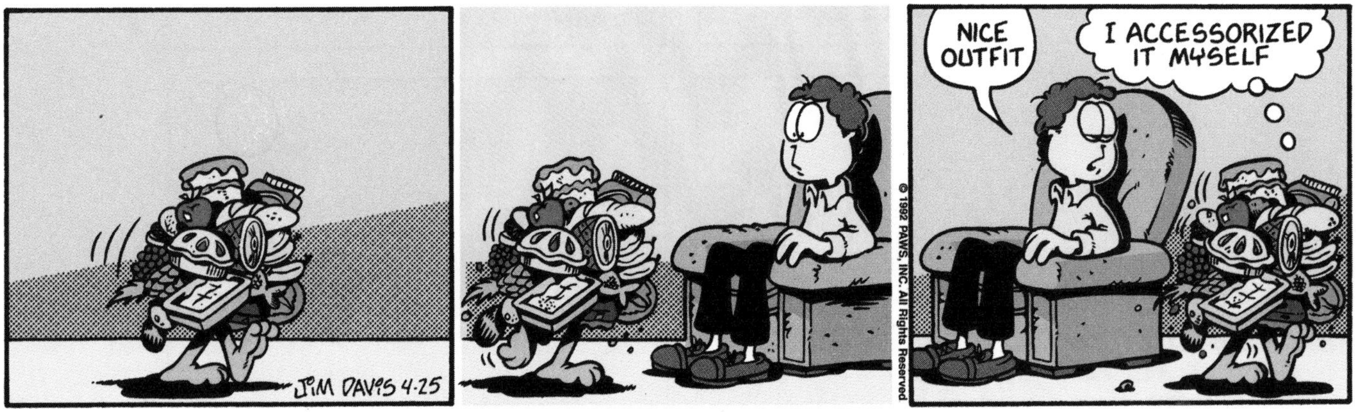
JIM DAVIS 4·25
NICE OUTFIT
I ACCESSORIZED IT MYSELF
© 1992 PAWS, INC. All Rights Reserved.

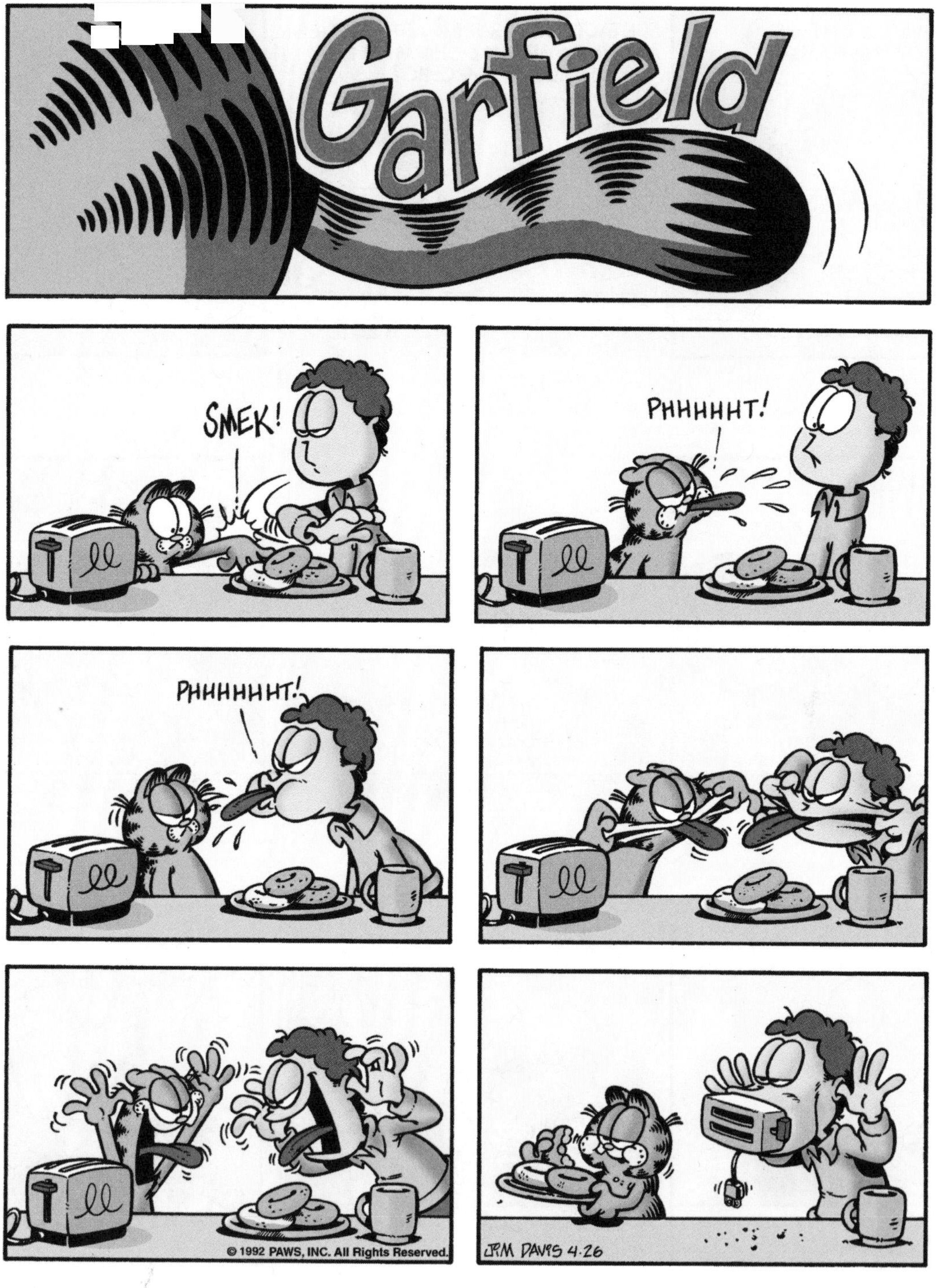
Garfield
SMEK!
PHHHHHT!
PHHHHHHT!
© 1992 PAWS, INC. All Rights Reserved.
JIM DAVIS 4-26

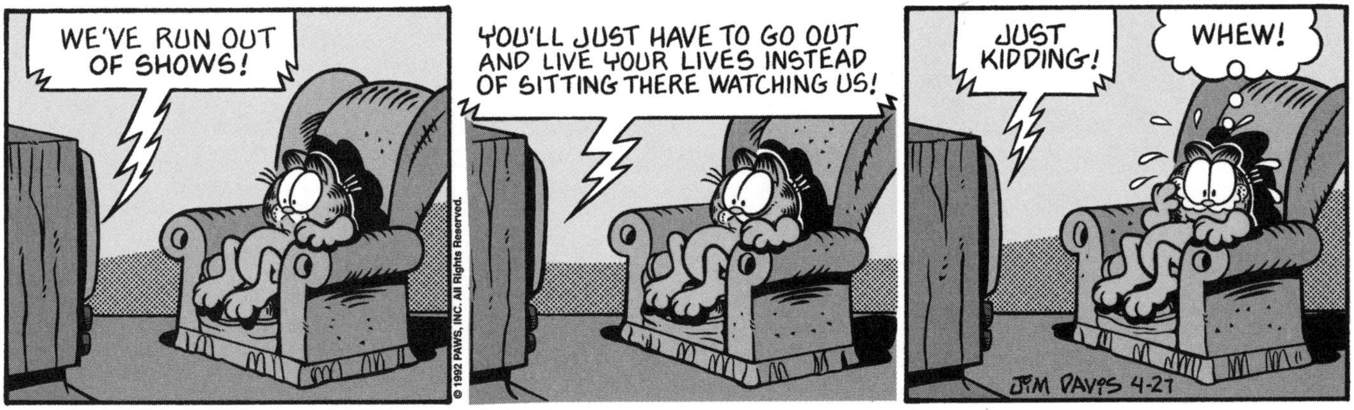
WE'VE RUN OUT OF SHOWS!
© 1992 PAWS, INC. All Rights Reserved.
YOU'LL JUST HAVE TO GO OUT AND LIVE YOUR LIVES INSTEAD OF SITTING THERE WATCHING US!
JUST KIDDING!
WHEW!
JIM DAVIS 4-27

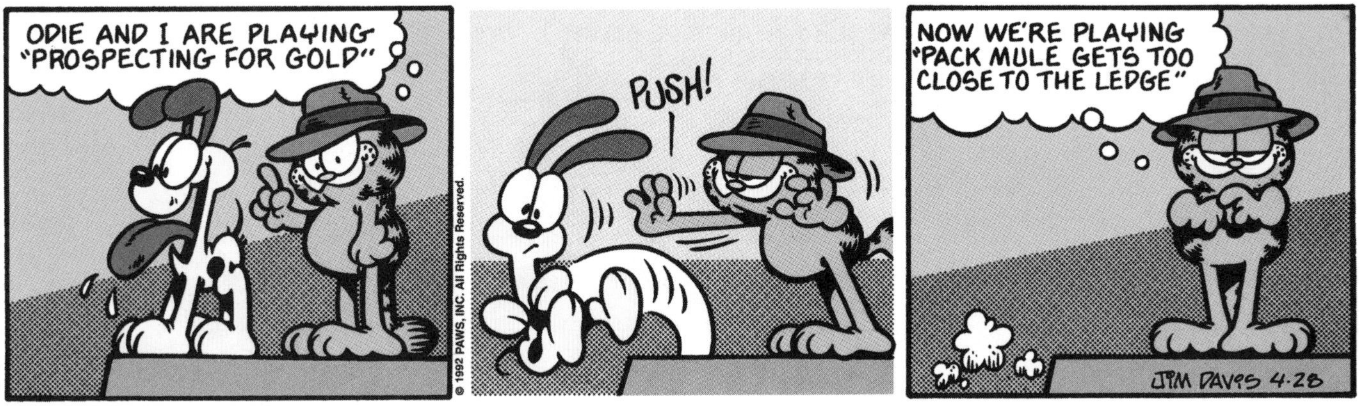
ODIE AND I ARE PLAYING "PROSPECTING FOR GOLD"
© 1992 PAWS, INC. All Rights Reserved.
PUSH!
NOW WE'RE PLAYING "PACK MULE GETS TOO CLOSE TO THE LEDGE"
JIM DAVIS 4-28

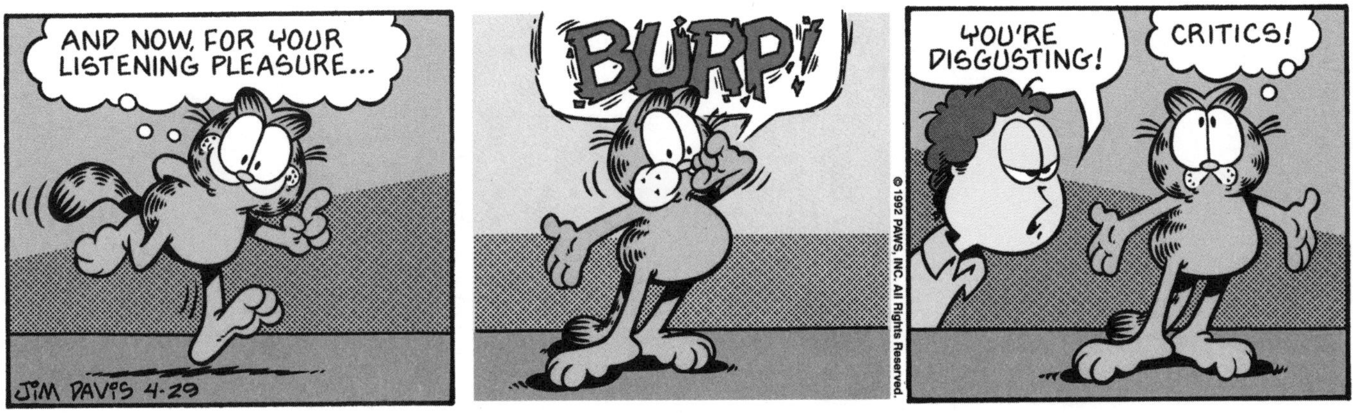
AND NOW, FOR YOUR LISTENING PLEASURE...
JIM DAVIS 4-29
BURP!
© 1992 PAWS, INC. All Rights Reserved.
YOU'RE DISGUSTING!
CRITICS!

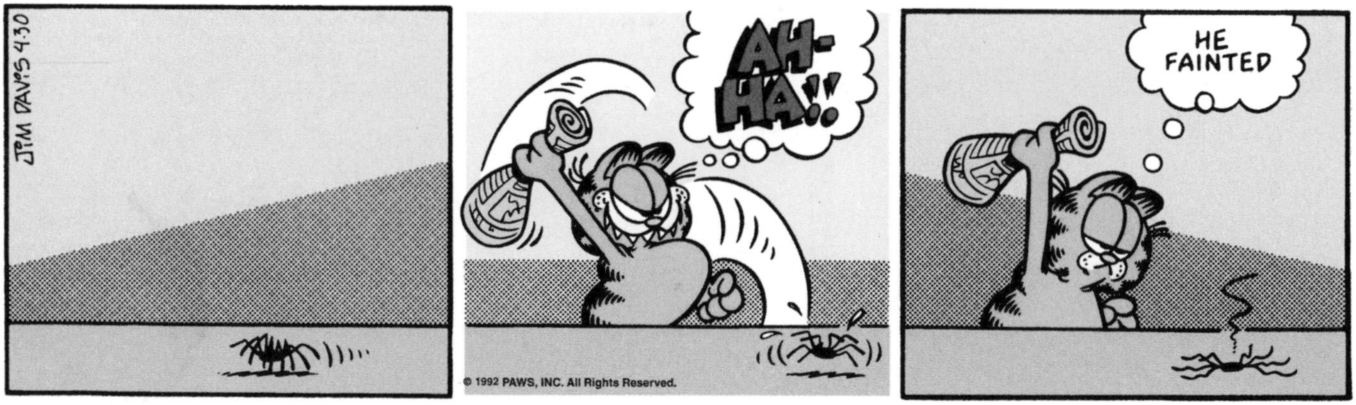
JIM DAVIS 4-30
AH-HA!!
HE FAINTED
© 1992 PAWS, INC. All Rights Reserved.

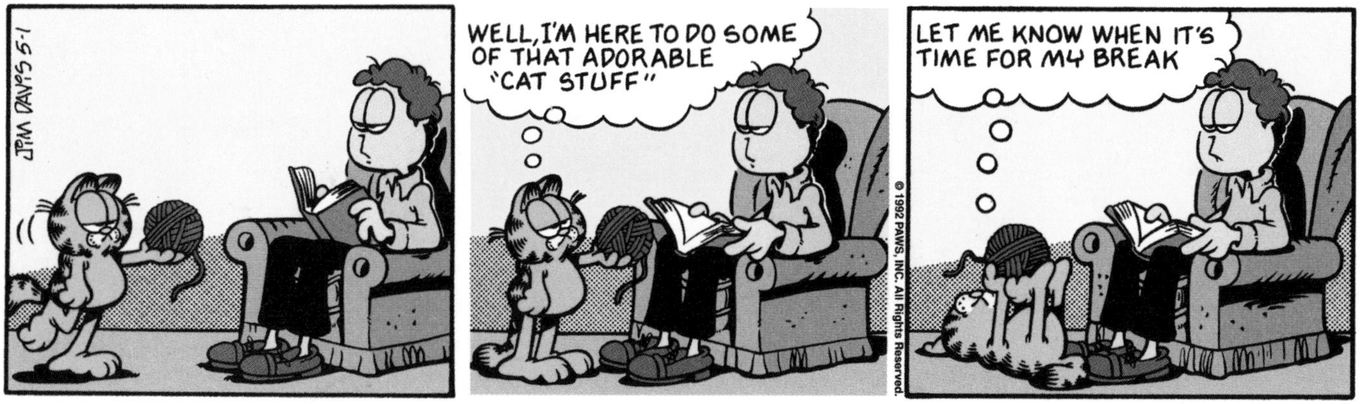
JIM DAVIS 5-1
WELL, I'M HERE TO DO SOME OF THAT ADORABLE "CAT STUFF"
LET ME KNOW WHEN IT'S TIME FOR MY BREAK
© 1992 PAWS, INC. All Rights Reserved.

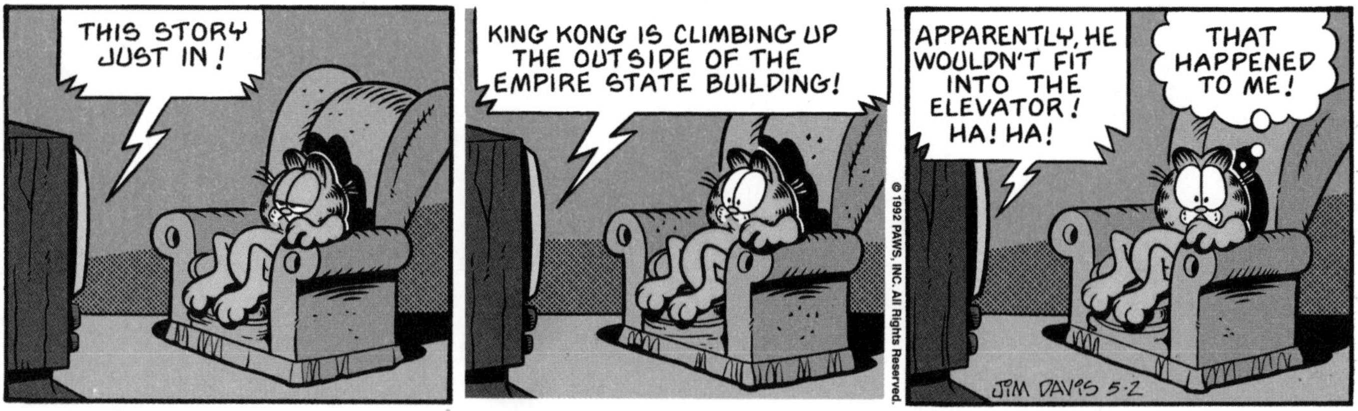
THIS STORY JUST IN!
KING KONG IS CLIMBING UP THE OUTSIDE OF THE EMPIRE STATE BUILDING!
APPARENTLY, HE WOULDN'T FIT INTO THE ELEVATOR! HA! HA!
THAT HAPPENED TO ME!
JIM DAVIS 5-2
© 1992 PAWS, INC. All Rights Reserved.

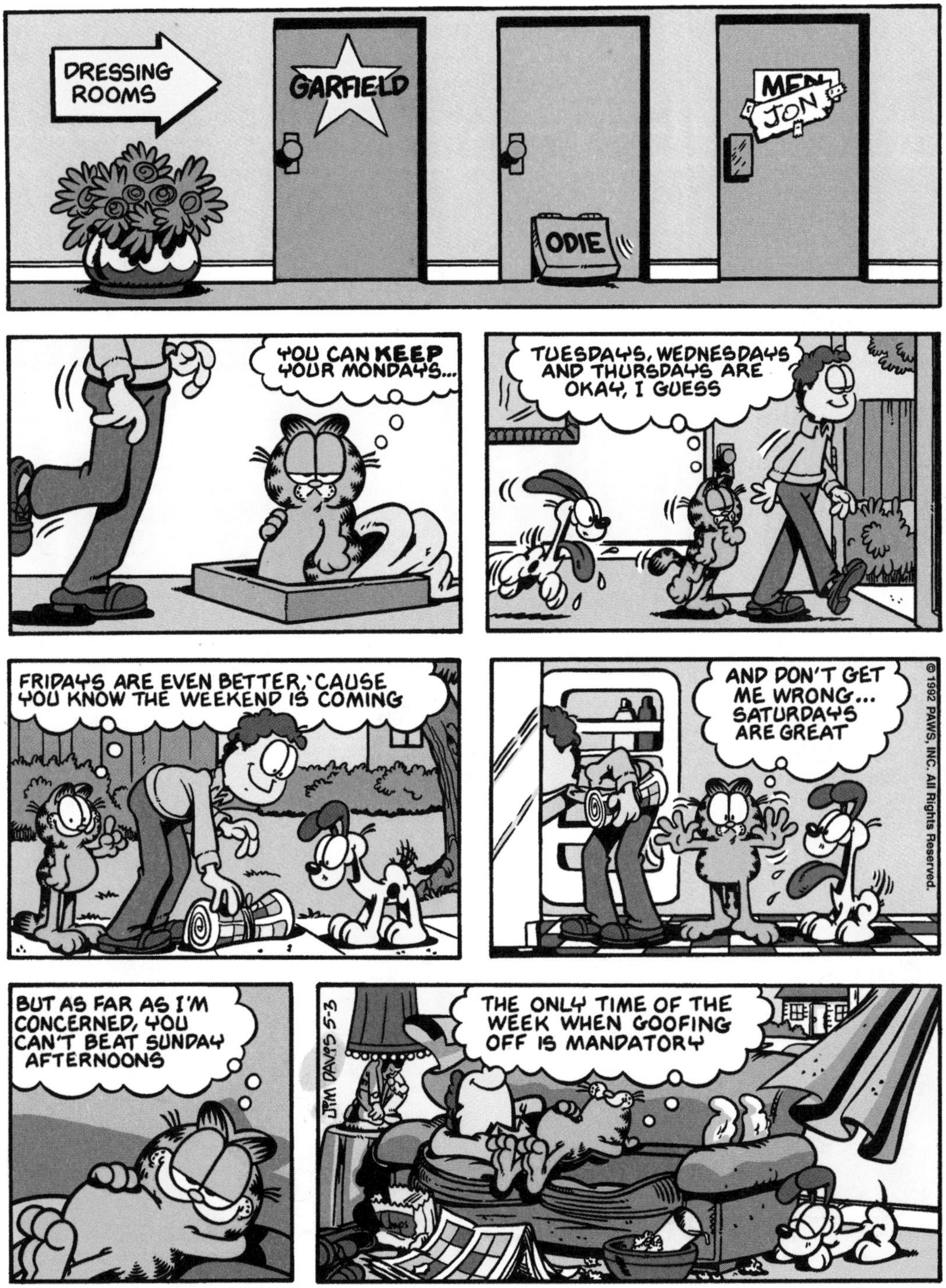
DRESSING ROOMS
GARFIELD
MEN
JON
ODIE
YOU CAN KEEP YOUR MONDAYS...
TUESDAYS, WEDNESDAYS AND THURSDAYS ARE OKAY, I GUESS
FRIDAYS ARE EVEN BETTER, 'CAUSE YOU KNOW THE WEEKEND IS COMING
AND DON'T GET ME WRONG... SATURDAYS ARE GREAT
© 1992 PAWS, INC. All Rights Reserved.
BUT AS FAR AS I'M CONCERNED, YOU CAN'T BEAT SUNDAY AFTERNOONS
JIM DAVIS 5-3
THE ONLY TIME OF THE WEEK WHEN GOOFING OFF IS MANDATORY

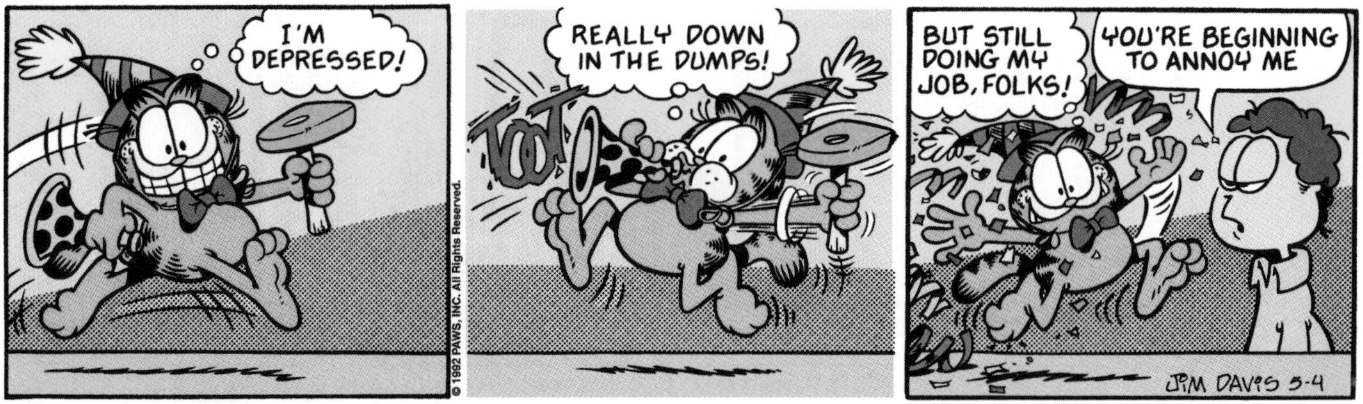
I'M DEPRESSED!
REALLY DOWN IN THE DUMPS!
TOOT
BUT STILL DOING MY JOB, FOLKS!
YOU'RE BEGINNING TO ANNOY ME
© 1992 PAWS, INC. All Rights Reserved.
JIM DAVIS 5-4

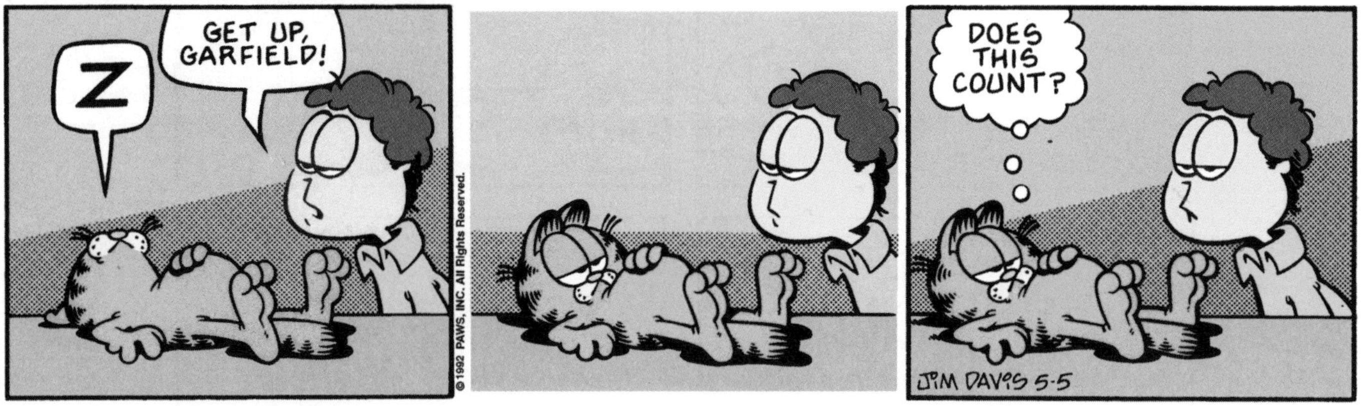
Z
GET UP, GARFIELD!
DOES THIS COUNT?
© 1992 PAWS, INC. All Rights Reserved.
JIM DAVIS 5-5

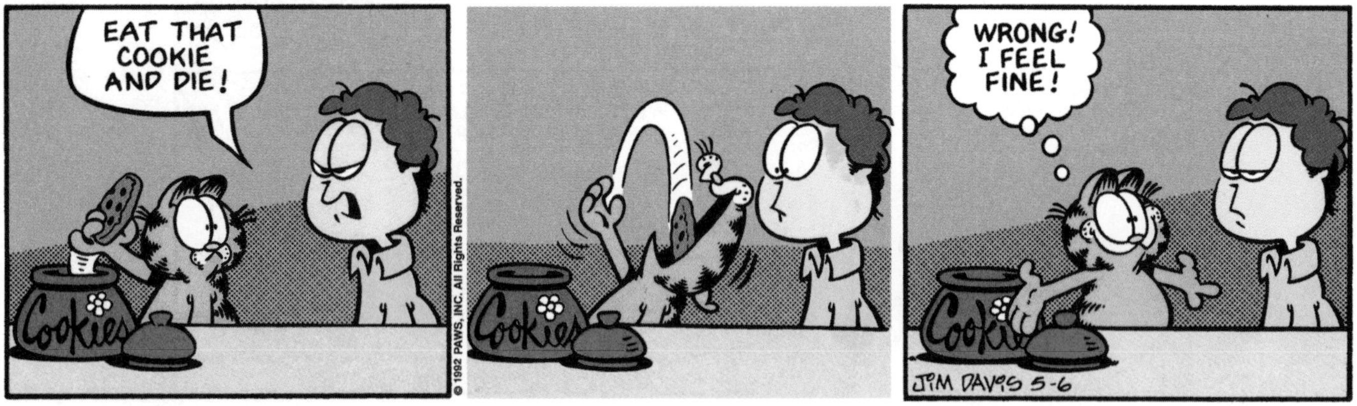
EAT THAT COOKIE AND DIE!
Cookies
WRONG! I FEEL FINE!
© 1992 PAWS, INC. All Rights Reserved.
JIM DAVIS 5-6

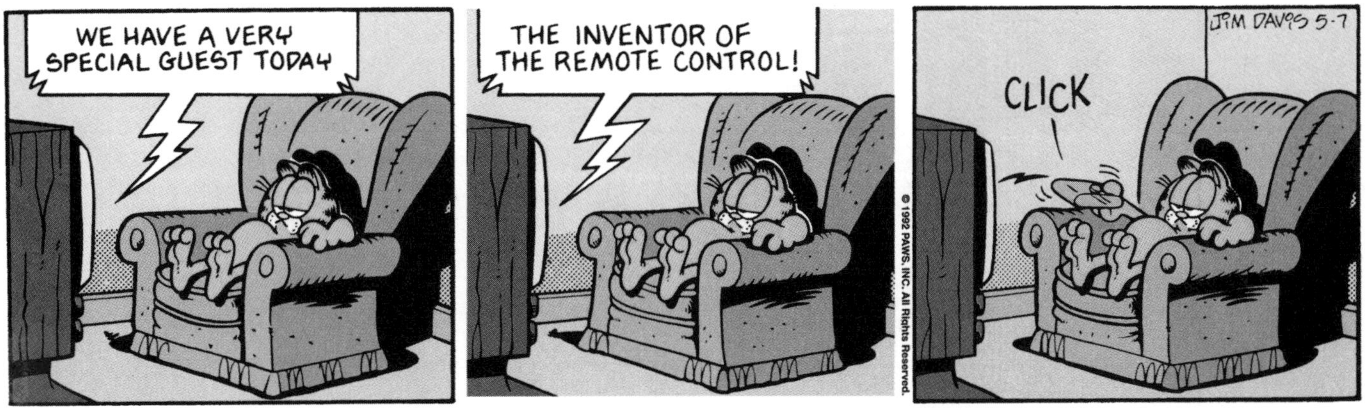
WE HAVE A VERY SPECIAL GUEST TODAY
THE INVENTOR OF THE REMOTE CONTROL!
CLICK
JIM DAVIS 5-7
© 1992 PAWS, INC. All Rights Reserved.

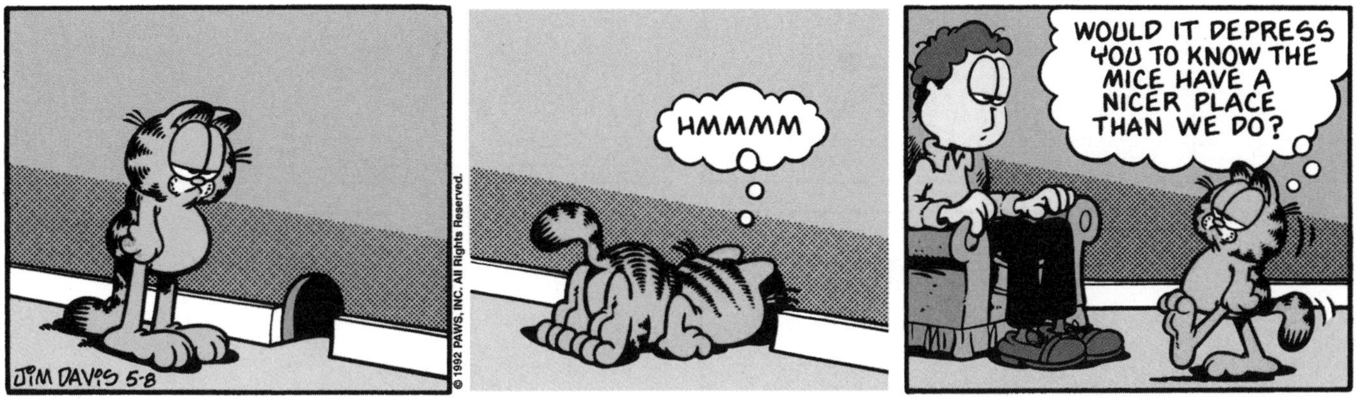
JIM DAVIS 5-8
© 1992 PAWS, INC. All Rights Reserved.
HMMMM
WOULD IT DEPRESS YOU TO KNOW THE MICE HAVE A NICER PLACE THAN WE DO?

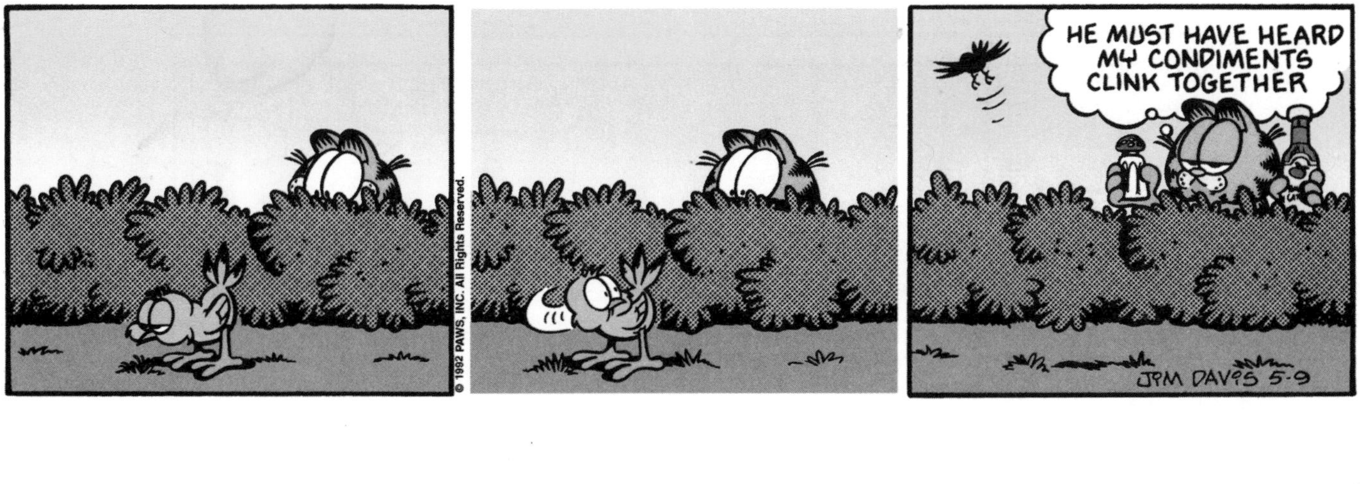
© 1992 PAWS, INC. All Rights Reserved.
HE MUST HAVE HEARD MY CONDIMENTS CLINK TOGETHER
JIM DAVIS 5-9

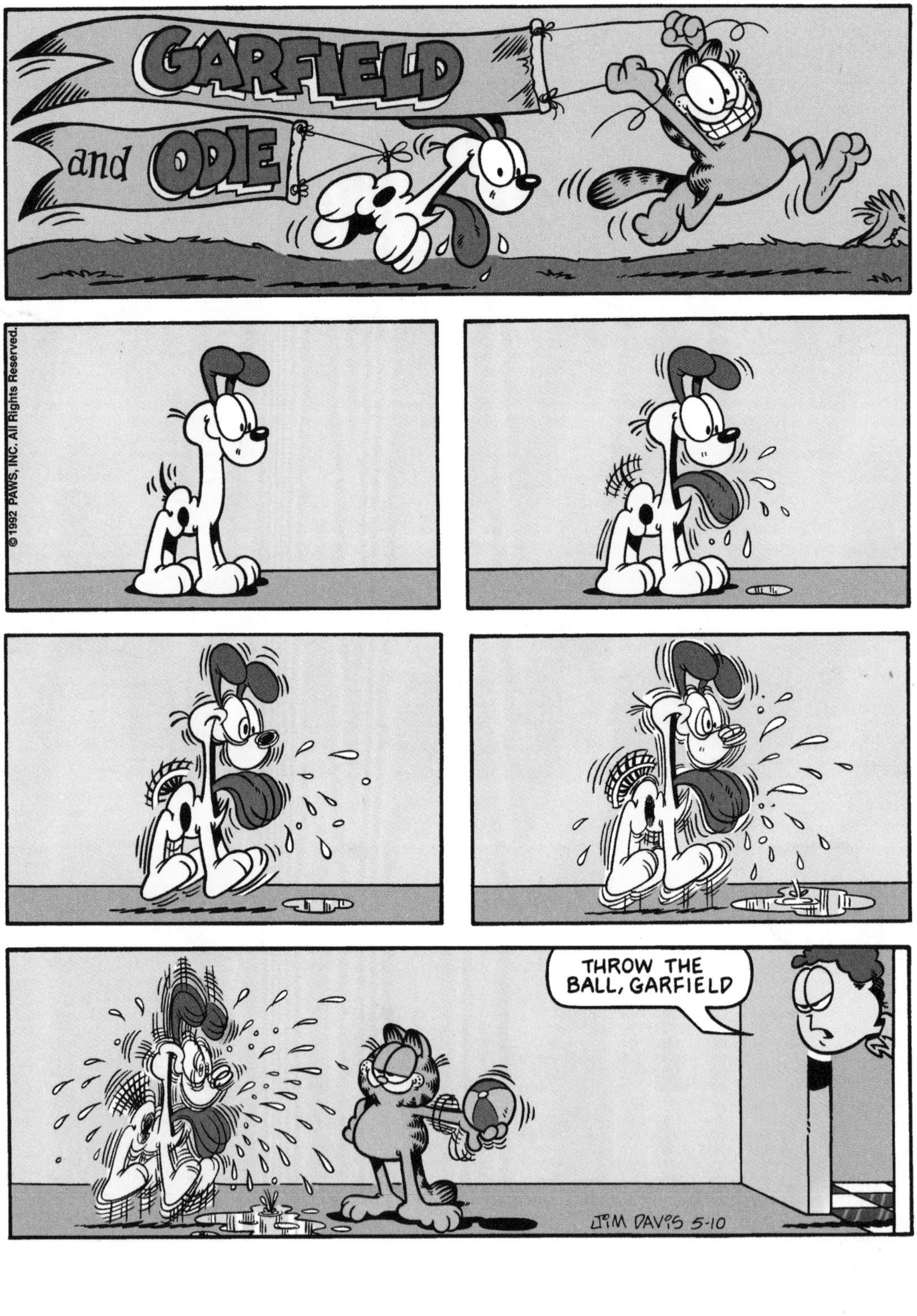
GARFIELD
and ODIE
THROW THE BALL, GARFIELD
JIM DAVIS 5-10

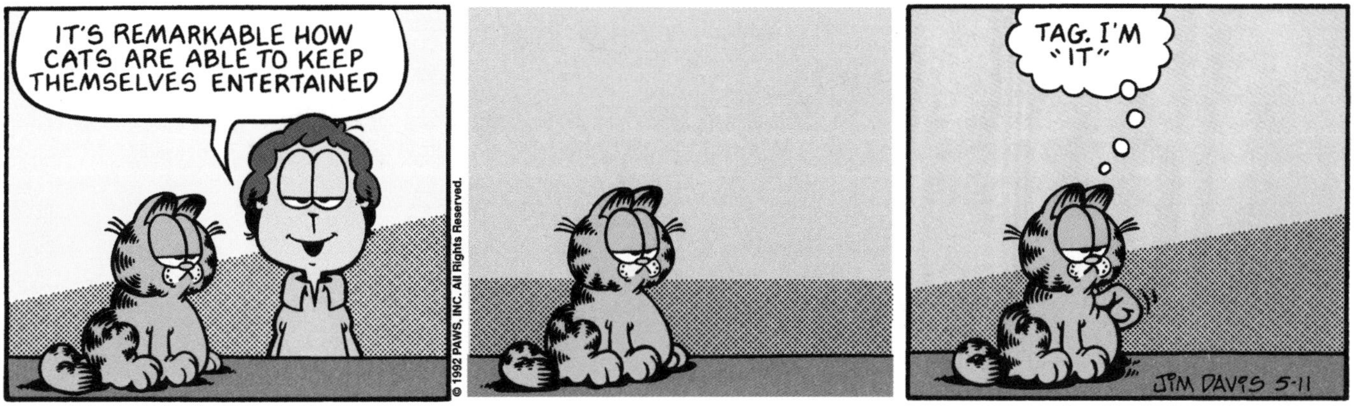
IT'S REMARKABLE HOW CATS ARE ABLE TO KEEP THEMSELVES ENTERTAINED
© 1992 PAWS, INC. All Rights Reserved.
TAG. I'M "IT"
JIM DAVIS 5-11

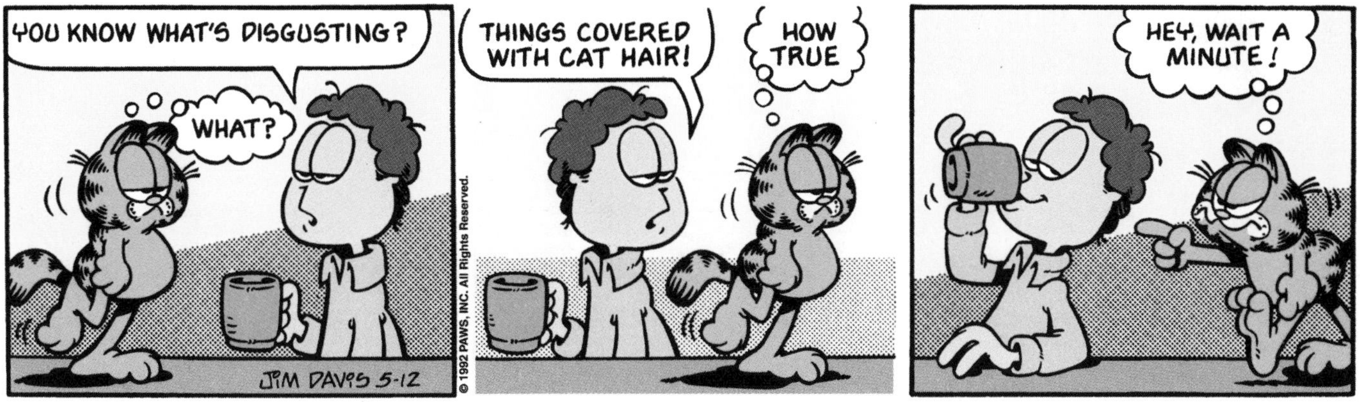
YOU KNOW WHAT'S DISGUSTING?
WHAT?
JIM DAVIS 5-12
© 1992 PAWS, INC. All Rights Reserved.
THINGS COVERED WITH CAT HAIR!
HOW TRUE
HEY, WAIT A MINUTE!

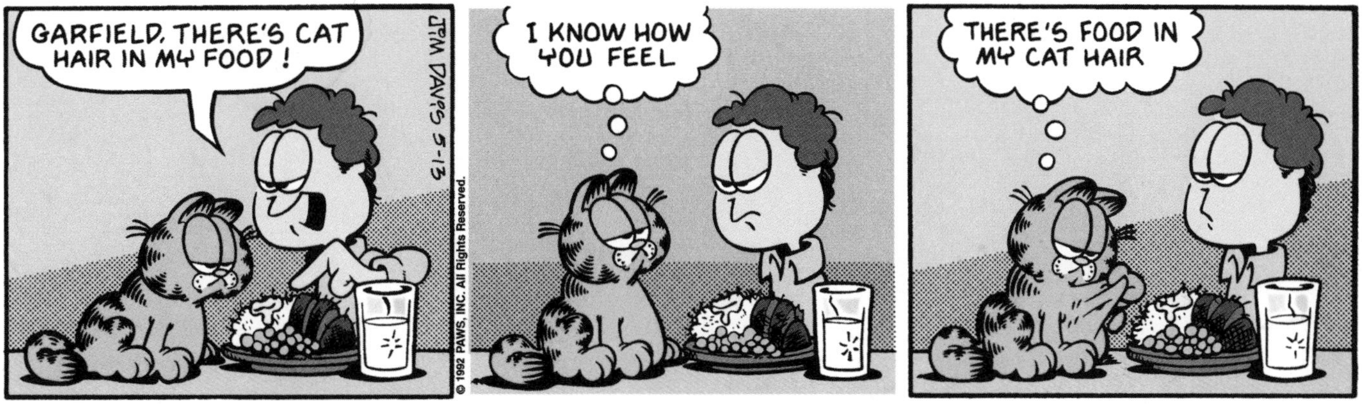
GARFIELD, THERE'S CAT HAIR IN MY FOOD!
JIM DAVIS 5-13
© 1992 PAWS, INC. All Rights Reserved.
I KNOW HOW YOU FEEL
THERE'S FOOD IN MY CAT HAIR

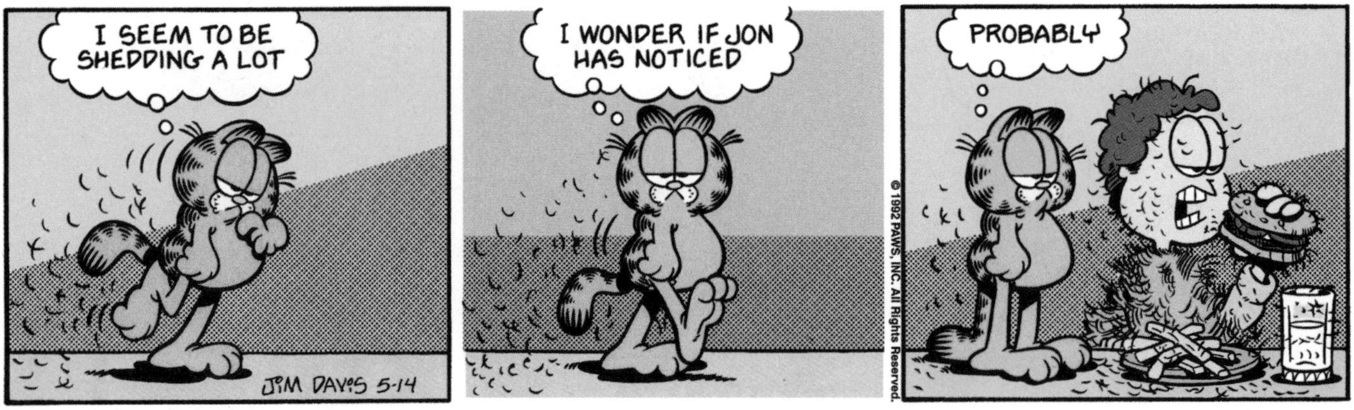
I SEEM TO BE SHEDDING A LOT
JIM DAVIS 5-14
I WONDER IF JON HAS NOTICED
© 1992 PAWS, INC. All Rights Reserved.
PROBABLY

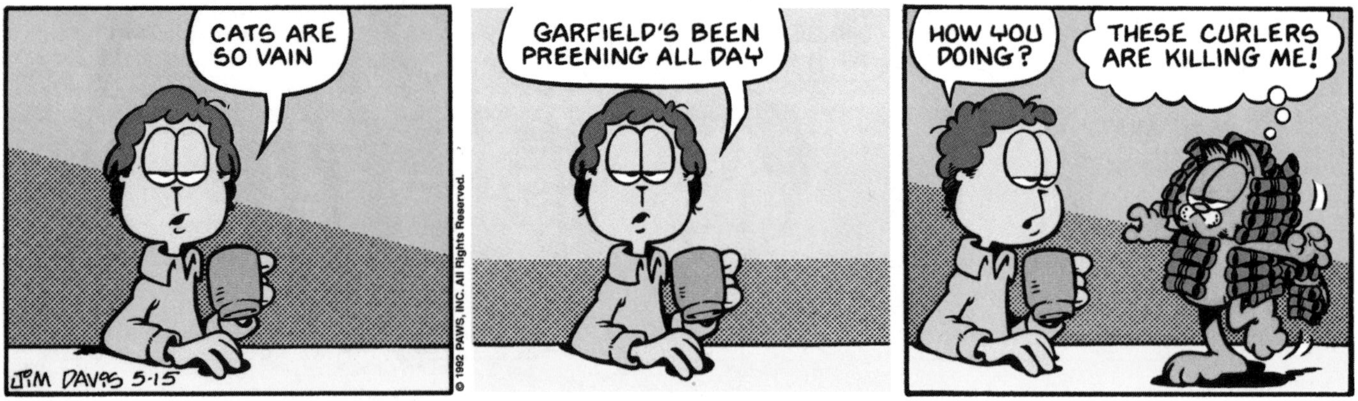
CATS ARE SO VAIN
JIM DAVIS 5-15
© 1992 PAWS, INC. All Rights Reserved.
GARFIELD'S BEEN PREENING ALL DAY
HOW YOU DOING?
THESE CURLERS ARE KILLING ME!

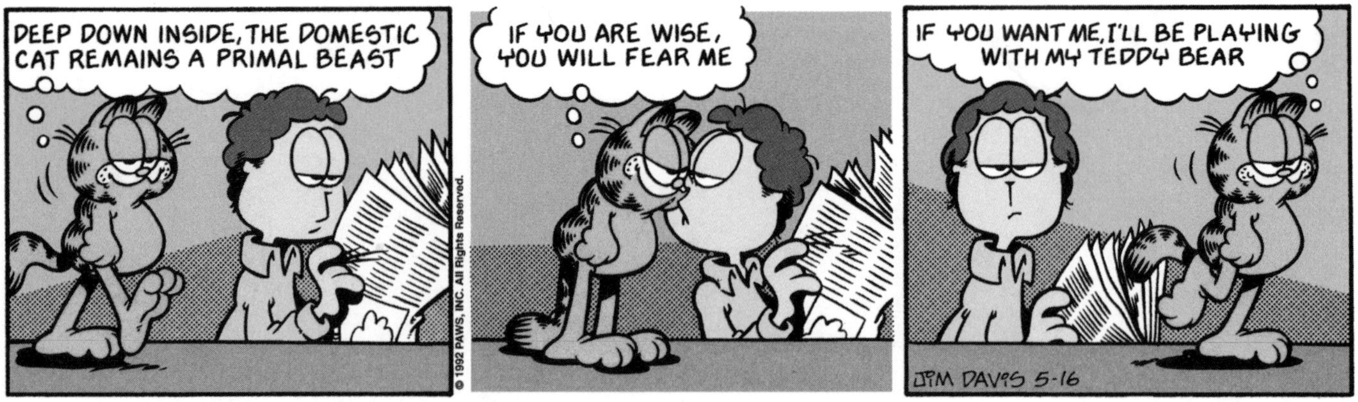
DEEP DOWN INSIDE, THE DOMESTIC CAT REMAINS A PRIMAL BEAST
© 1992 PAWS, INC. All Rights Reserved.
IF YOU ARE WISE, YOU WILL FEAR ME
IF YOU WANT ME, I'LL BE PLAYING WITH MY TEDDY BEAR
JIM DAVIS 5-16

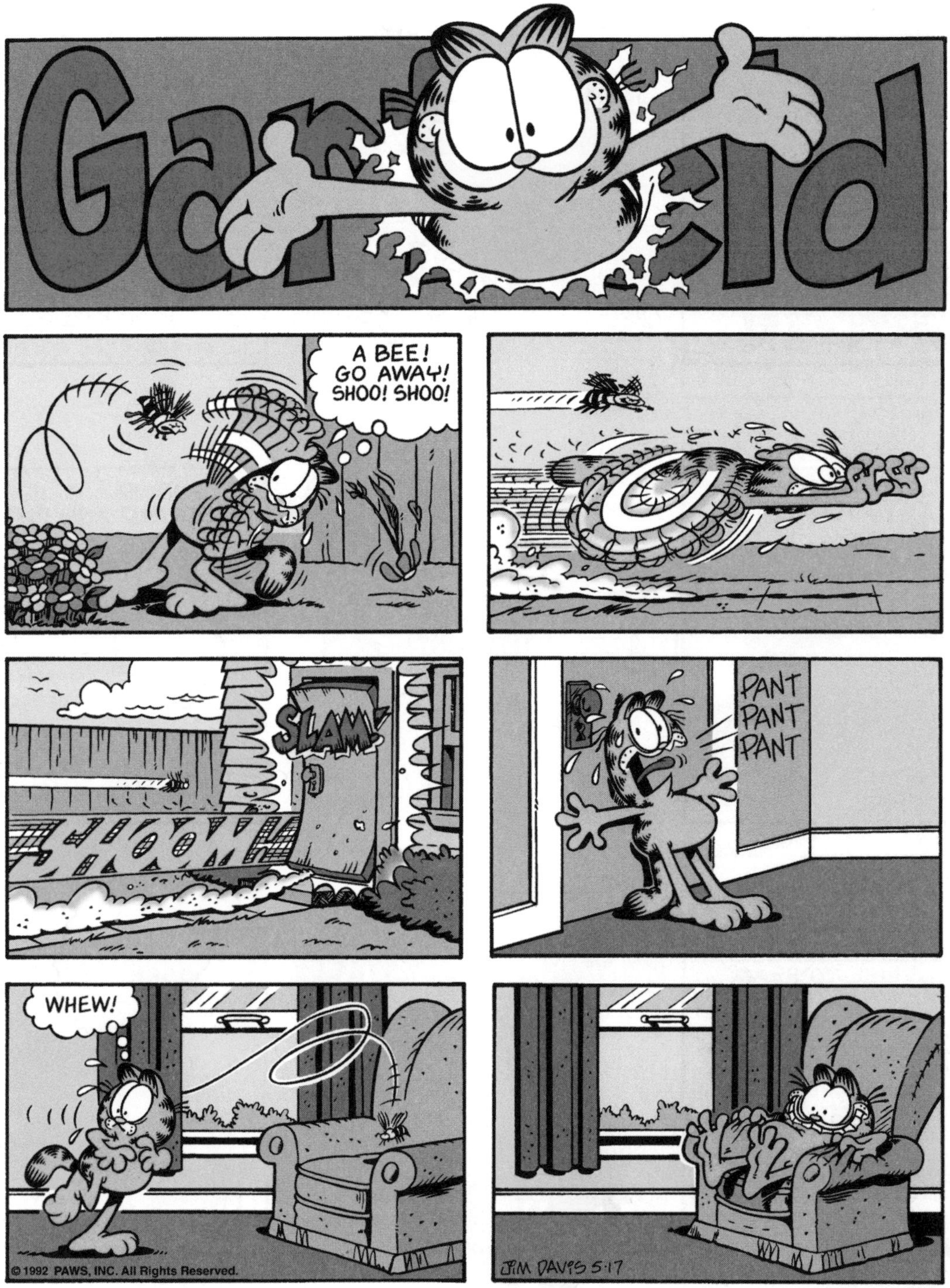
Garfield
A BEE! GO AWAY! SHOO! SHOO!
SLAM
SHOOM
PANT PANT PANT
WHEW!
© 1992 PAWS, INC. All Rights Reserved.
JIM DAVIS 5-17

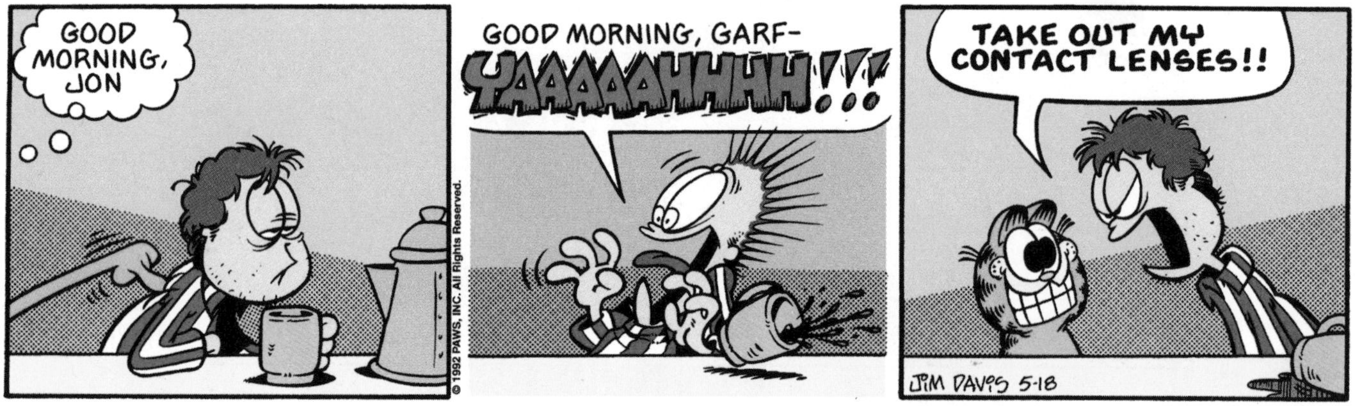
GOOD MORNING, JON
GOOD MORNING, GARF-
YAAAAAHHHH!!!
TAKE OUT MY CONTACT LENSES!!
© 1992 PAWS, INC. All Rights Reserved.
JIM DAVIS 5-18

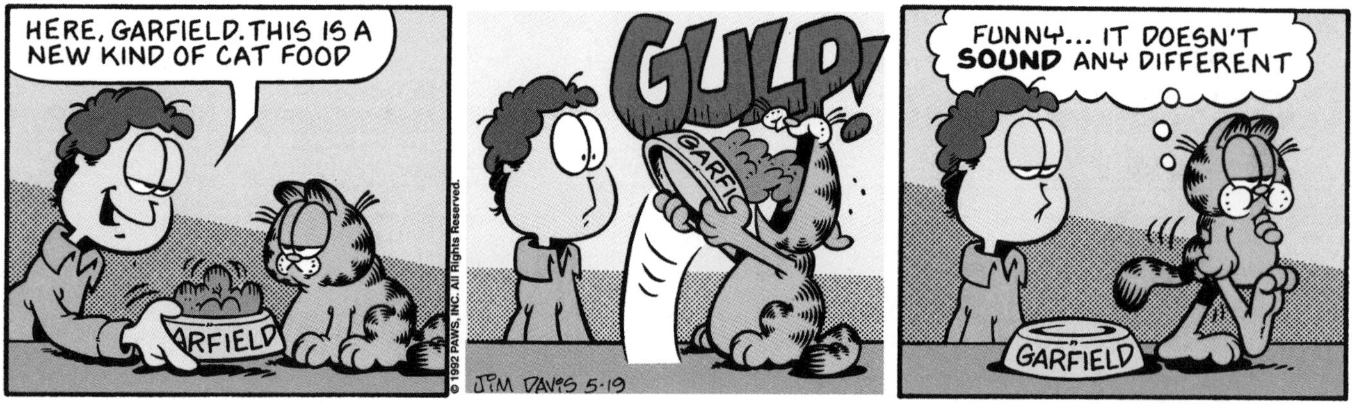
HERE, GARFIELD. THIS IS A NEW KIND OF CAT FOOD
ARFIELD
GULP
GARFI
FUNNY... IT DOESN'T **SOUND** ANY DIFFERENT
GARFIELD
© 1992 PAWS, INC. All Rights Reserved.
JIM DAVIS 5-19

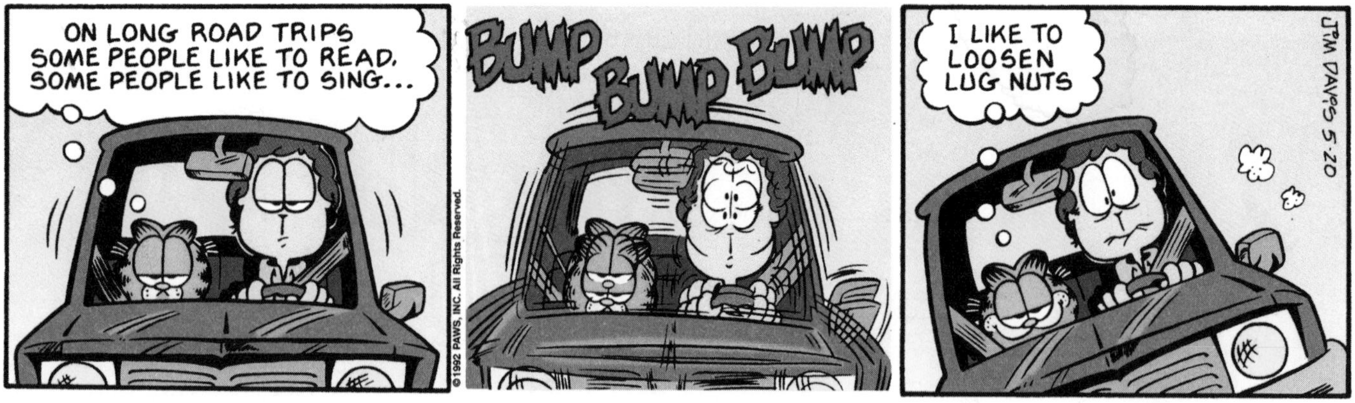
ON LONG ROAD TRIPS SOME PEOPLE LIKE TO READ, SOME PEOPLE LIKE TO SING...
BUMP BUMP BUMP
I LIKE TO LOOSEN LUG NUTS
© 1992 PAWS, INC. All Rights Reserved.
JIM DAVIS 5-20

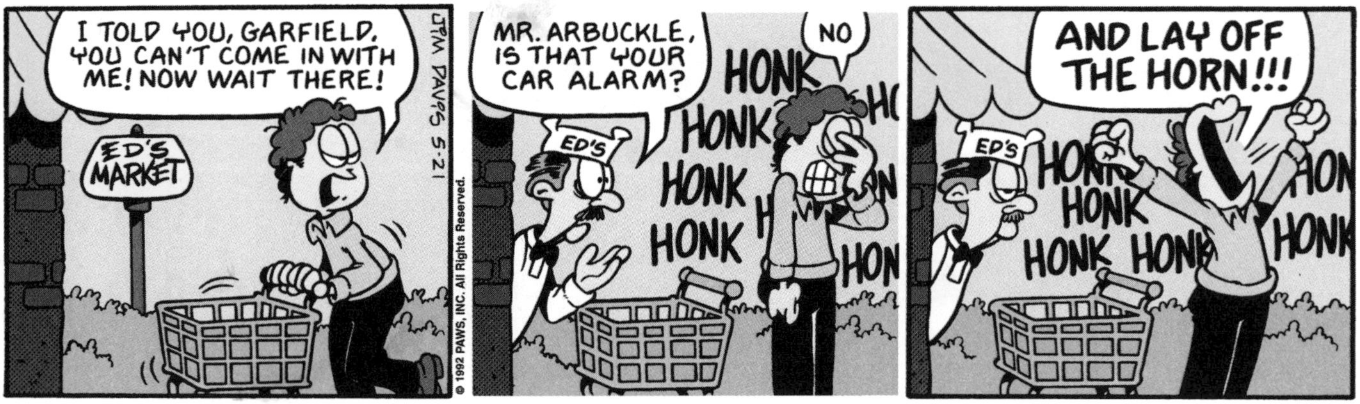
I TOLD YOU, GARFIELD. YOU CAN'T COME IN WITH ME! NOW WAIT THERE!
ED'S MARKET
JIM DAVIS 5-21
© 1992 PAWS, INC. All Rights Reserved.
MR. ARBUCKLE, IS THAT YOUR CAR ALARM?
ED'S
NO
HONK HONK HONK HONK
AND LAY OFF THE HORN!!!
ED'S
HONK HONK HONK HONK

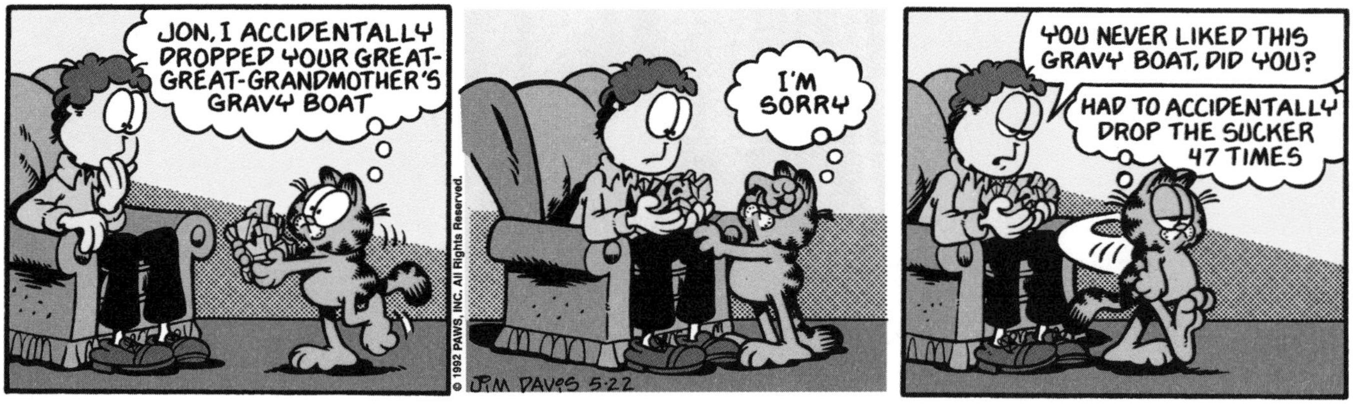
JON, I ACCIDENTALLY DROPPED YOUR GREAT-GREAT-GRANDMOTHER'S GRAVY BOAT
© 1992 PAWS, INC. All Rights Reserved.
I'M SORRY
JIM DAVIS 5-22
YOU NEVER LIKED THIS GRAVY BOAT, DID YOU?
HAD TO ACCIDENTALLY DROP THE SUCKER 47 TIMES

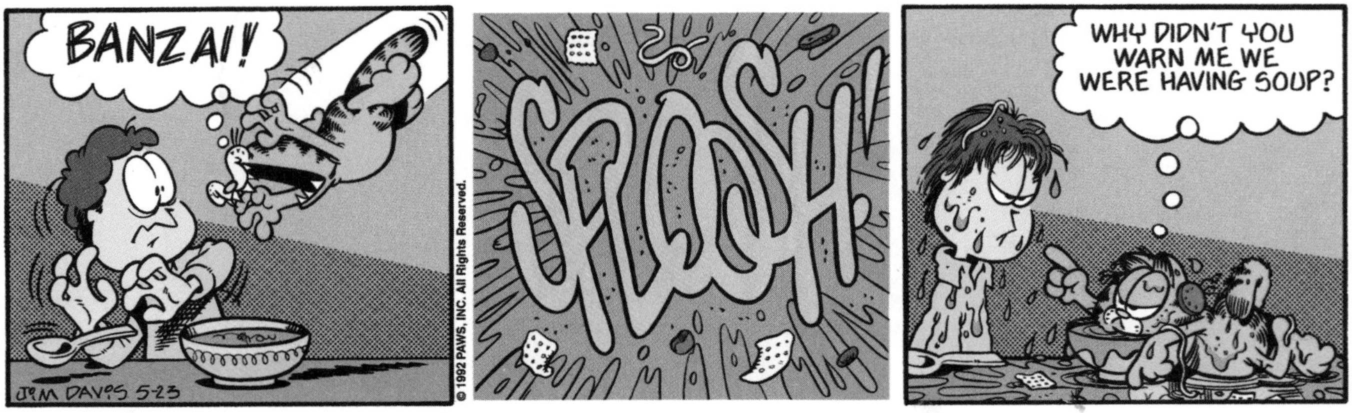
BANZAI!
JIM DAVIS 5-23
© 1992 PAWS, INC. All Rights Reserved.
SPLOOSH!
WHY DIDN'T YOU WARN ME WE WERE HAVING SOUP?

DINGLE
DINGLE
BOINK!
SCREEe
PLOP
DINGLE
GARFIELD
?
AHHHH...
PAT
PAT
PAT
GARFIELD
DINGLE
DINGLE
DINGLE
GARFIELD
DINGLE
DINGLE
DINGLE
JIM DAVIS 5-24

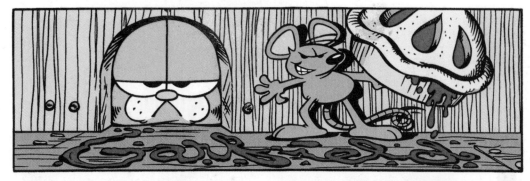

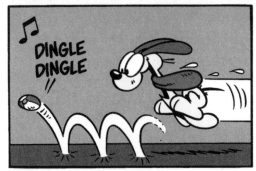

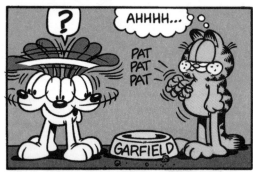

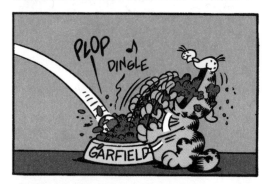

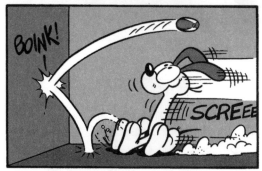

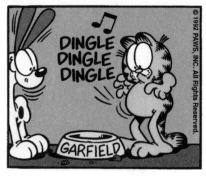

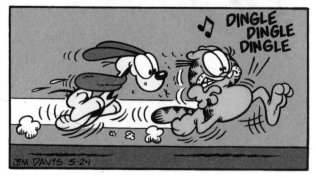

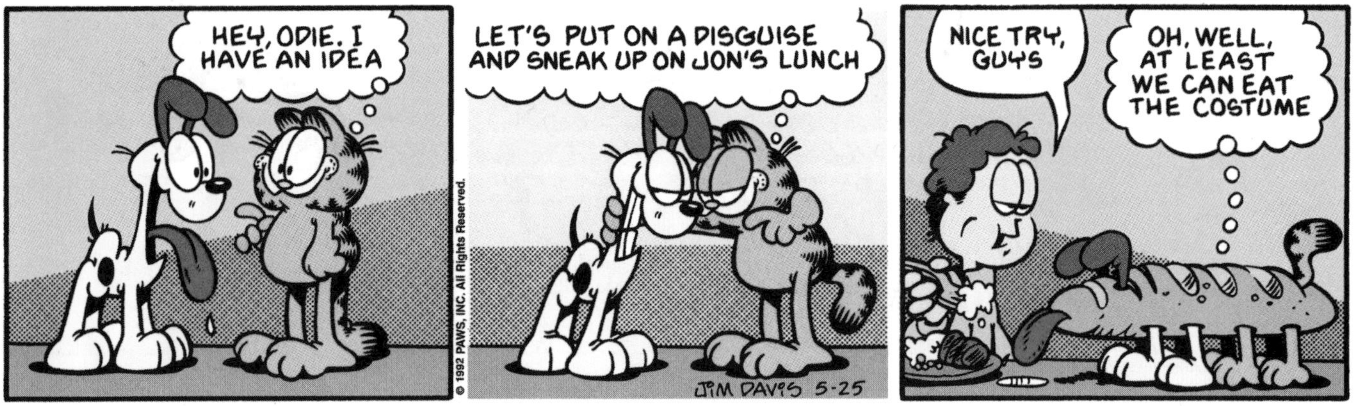
HEY, ODIE. I HAVE AN IDEA
LET'S PUT ON A DISGUISE AND SNEAK UP ON JON'S LUNCH
© 1992 PAWS, INC. All Rights Reserved.
JIM DAVIS 5-25
NICE TRY, GUYS
OH, WELL, AT LEAST WE CAN EAT THE COSTUME

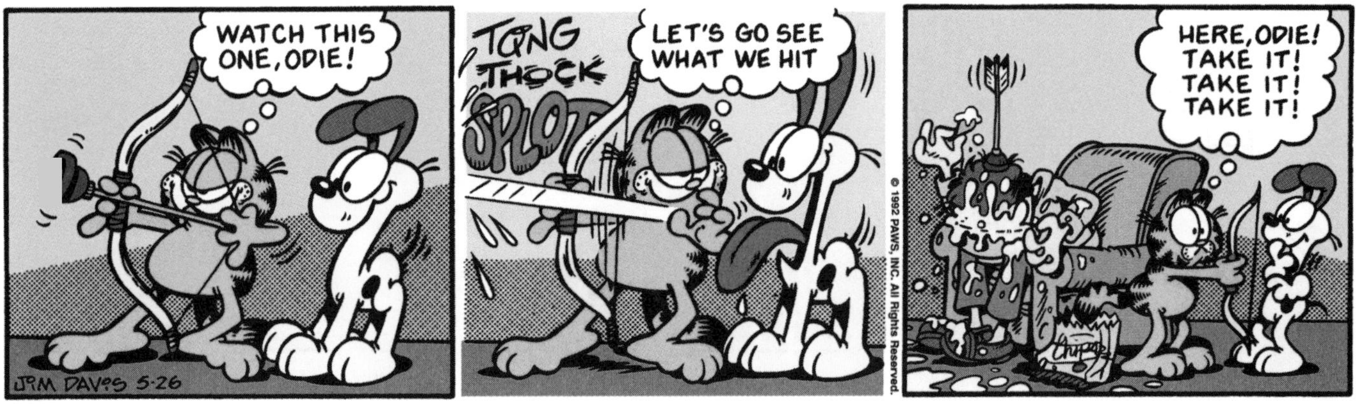
WATCH THIS ONE, ODIE!
JIM DAVIS 5-26
TWANG
THOCK
SPLOT
LET'S GO SEE WHAT WE HIT
© 1992 PAWS, INC. All Rights Reserved.
HERE, ODIE! TAKE IT! TAKE IT! TAKE IT!

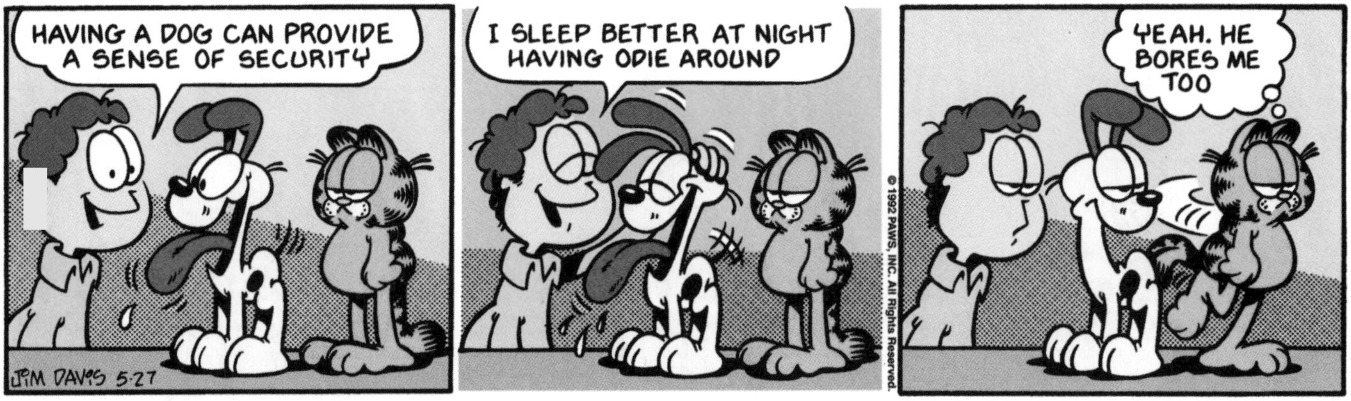
HAVING A DOG CAN PROVIDE A SENSE OF SECURITY
JIM DAVIS 5-27
I SLEEP BETTER AT NIGHT HAVING ODIE AROUND
© 1992 PAWS, INC. All Rights Reserved.
YEAH. HE BORES ME TOO

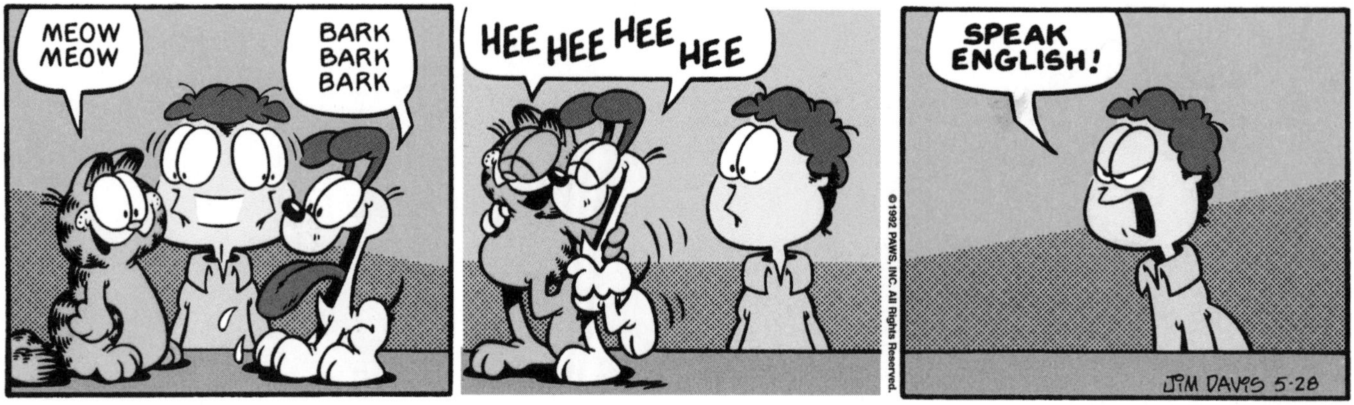
MEOW MEOW
BARK BARK BARK
HEE HEE HEE HEE
SPEAK ENGLISH!
© 1992 PAWS, INC. All Rights Reserved.
JIM DAVIS 5-28

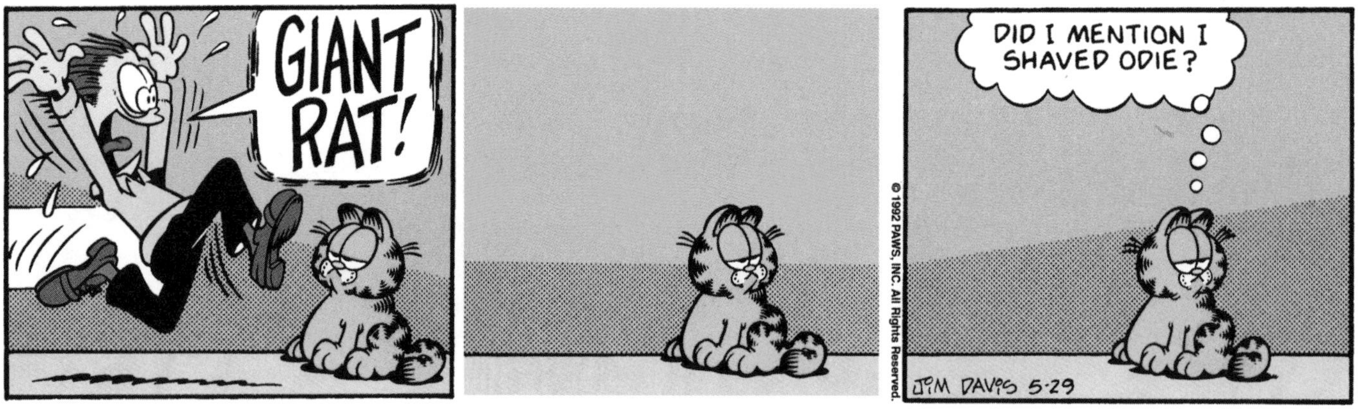
GIANT RAT!
DID I MENTION I SHAVED ODIE?
© 1992 PAWS, INC. All Rights Reserved.
JIM DAVIS 5-29

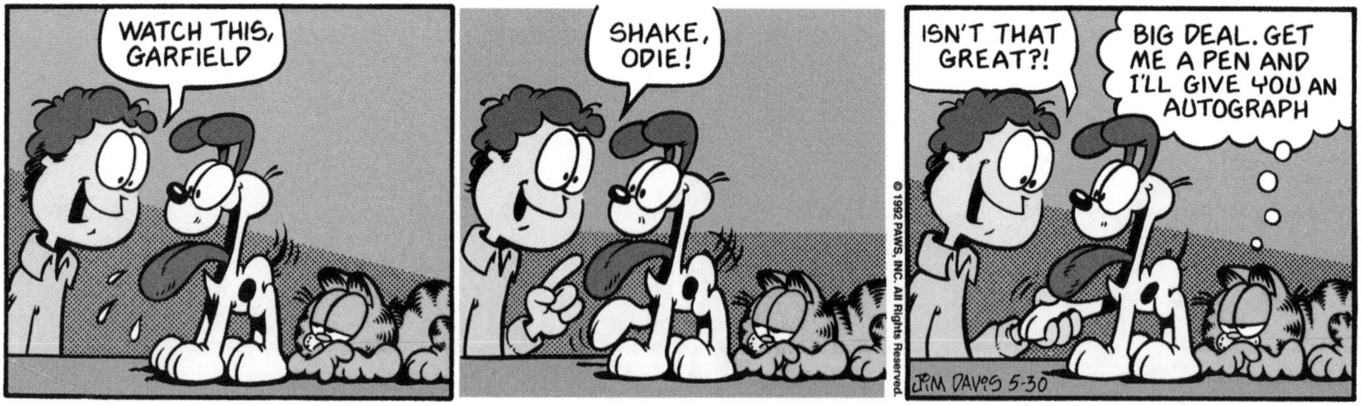
WATCH THIS, GARFIELD
SHAKE, ODIE!
ISN'T THAT GREAT?!
BIG DEAL. GET ME A PEN AND I'LL GIVE YOU AN AUTOGRAPH
© 1992 PAWS, INC. All Rights Reserved.
JIM DAVIS 5-30

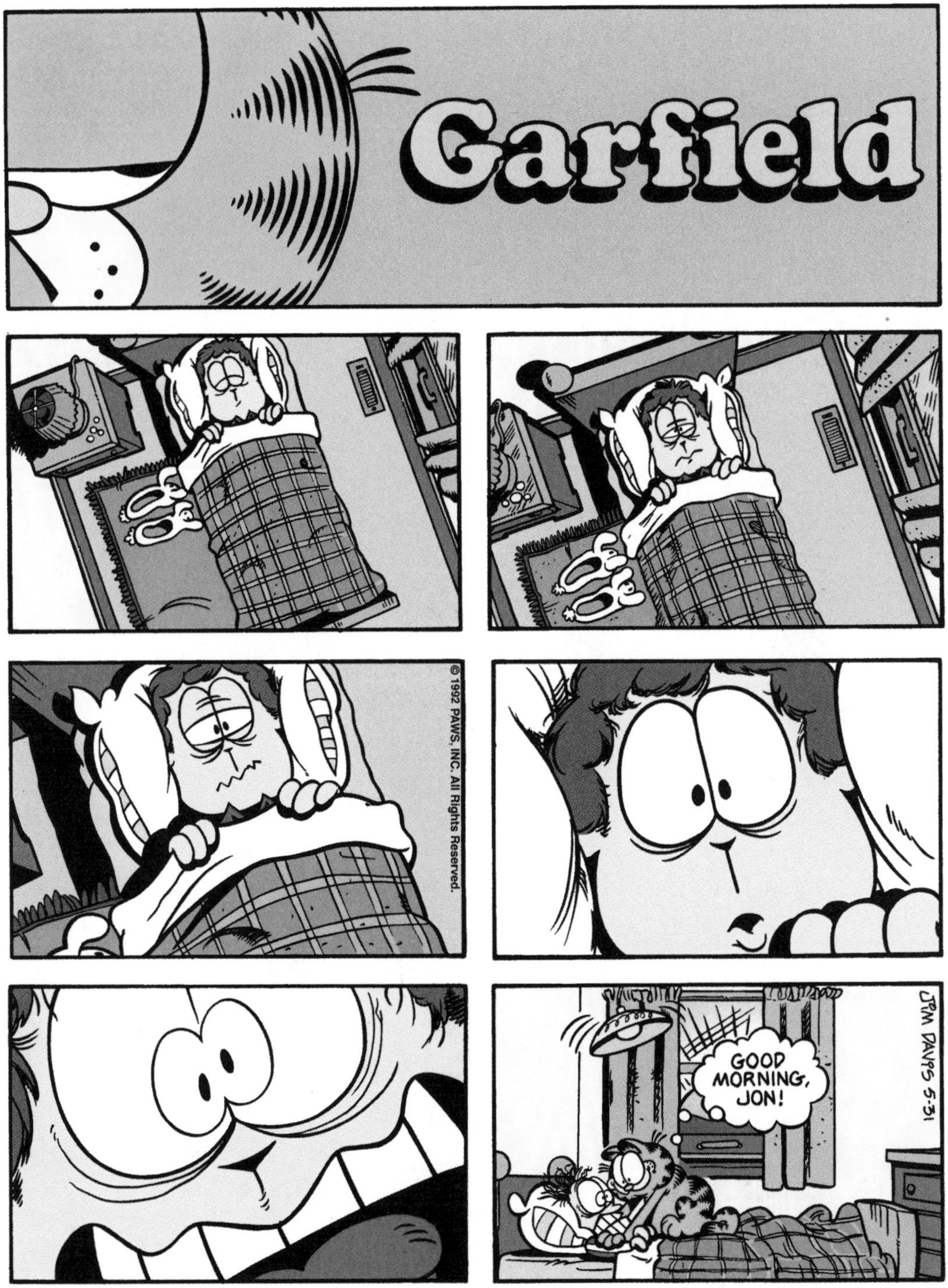
Garfield
© 1992 PAWS, INC. All Rights Reserved.
GOOD MORNING, JON!
JIM DAVIS 5-31

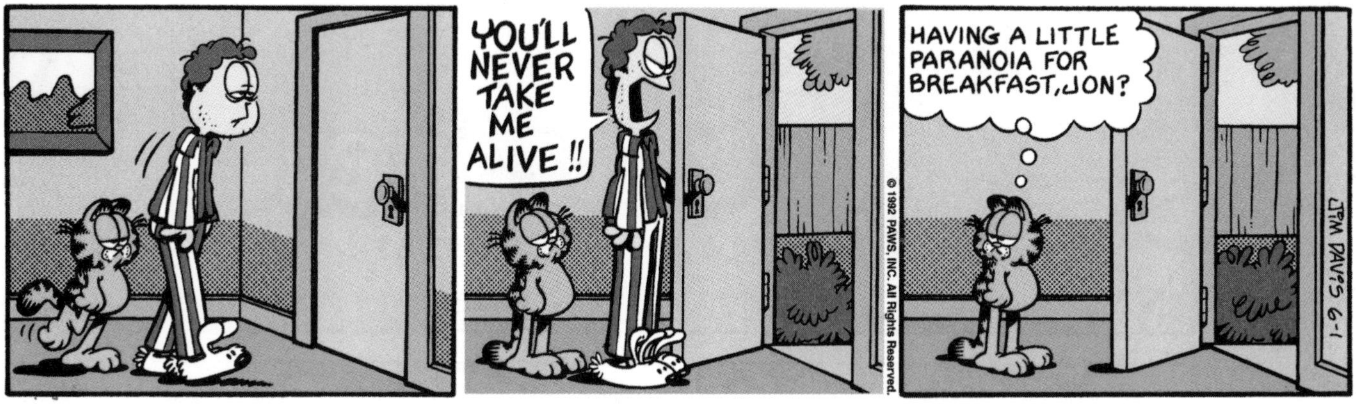
YOU'LL NEVER TAKE ME ALIVE !!
HAVING A LITTLE PARANOIA FOR BREAKFAST, JON?
© 1992 PAWS, INC. All Rights Reserved.
JIM DAVIS 6-1

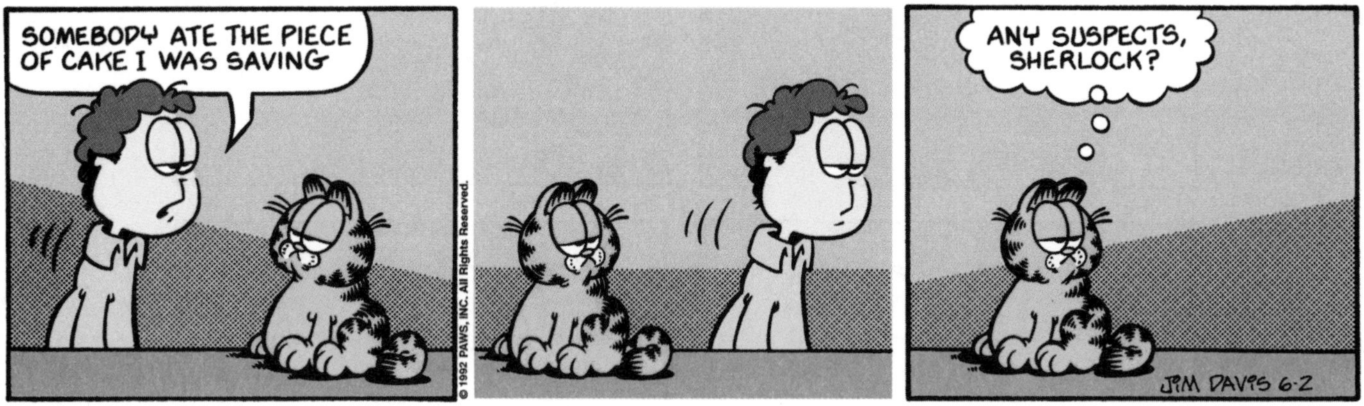
SOMEBODY ATE THE PIECE OF CAKE I WAS SAVING
ANY SUSPECTS, SHERLOCK?
© 1992 PAWS, INC. All Rights Reserved.
JIM DAVIS 6-2

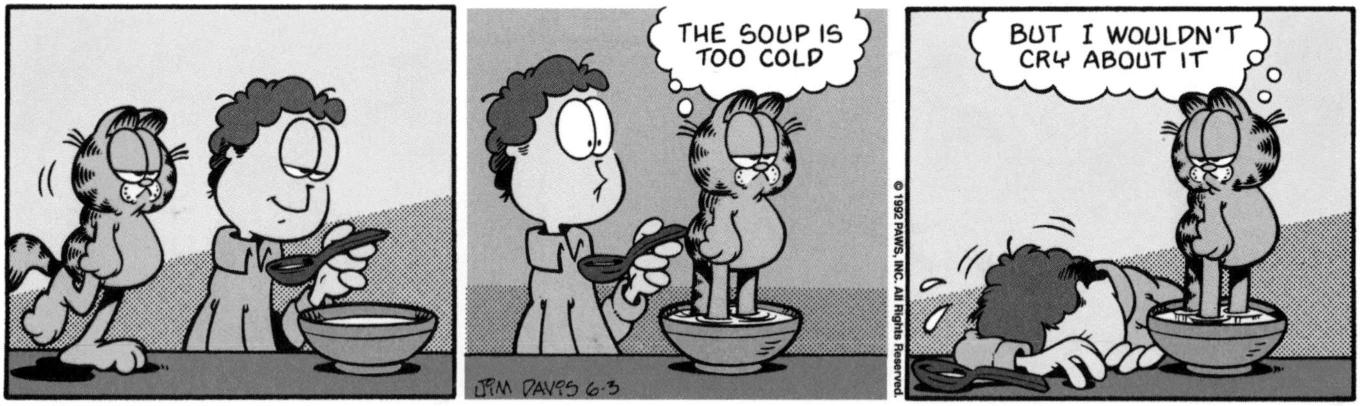
THE SOUP IS TOO COLD
BUT I WOULDN'T CRY ABOUT IT
JIM DAVIS 6-3
© 1992 PAWS, INC. All Rights Reserved.

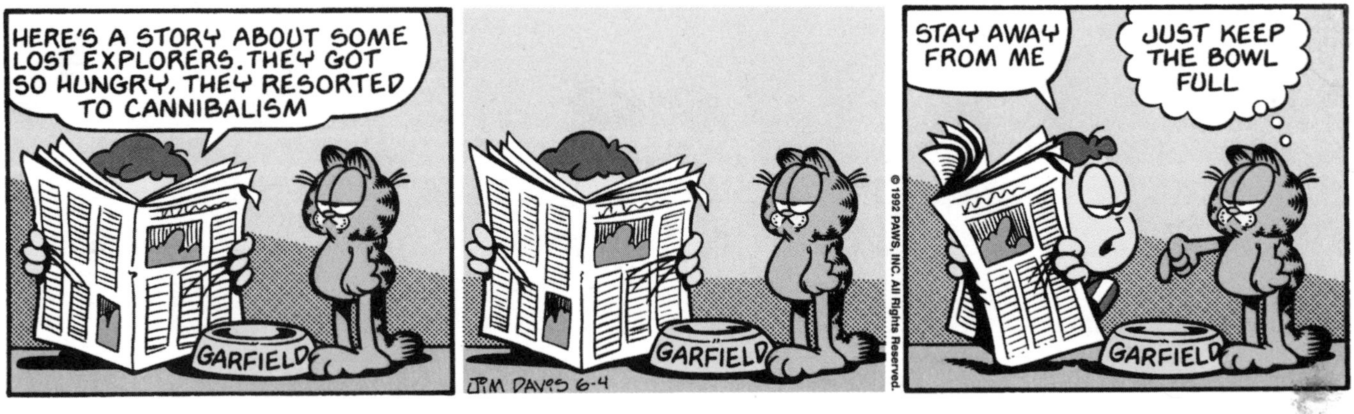
HERE'S A STORY ABOUT SOME LOST EXPLORERS. THEY GOT SO HUNGRY, THEY RESORTED TO CANNIBALISM
GARFIELD
GARFIELD
JIM DAVIS 6-4
© 1992 PAWS, INC. All Rights Reserved.
STAY AWAY FROM ME
JUST KEEP THE BOWL FULL
GARFIELD

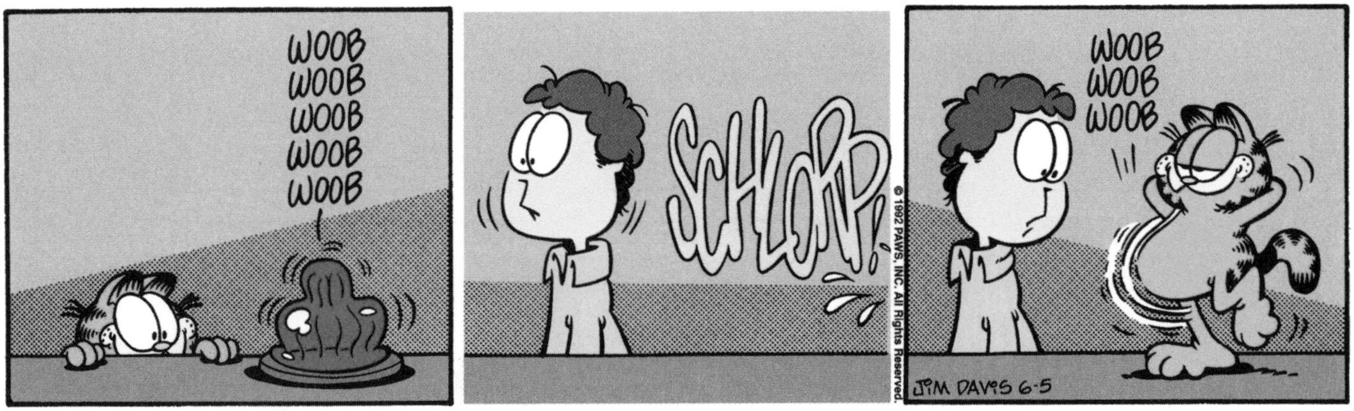
WOOB WOOB WOOB WOOB WOOB
SCHLORP!
© 1992 PAWS, INC. All Rights Reserved.
WOOB WOOB WOOB
JIM DAVIS 6-5

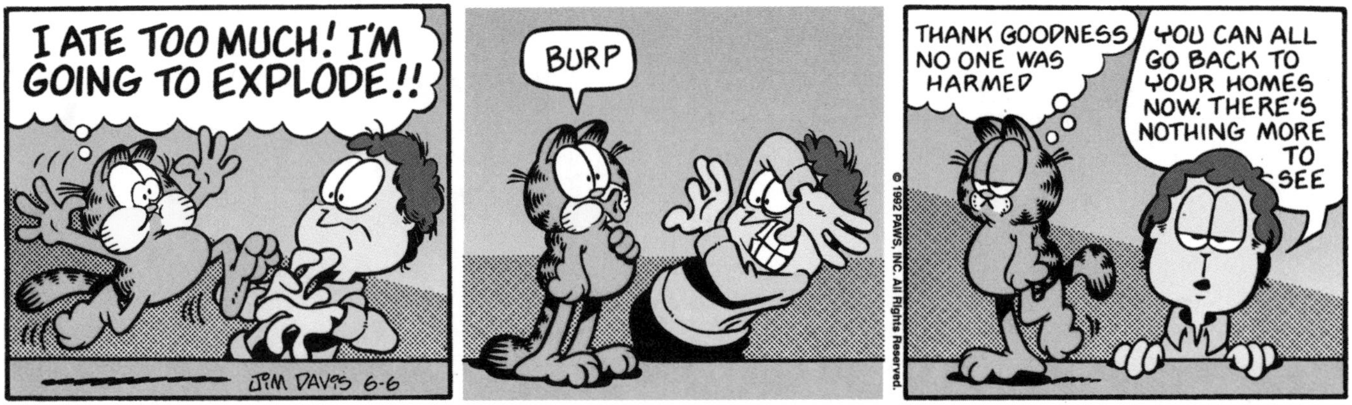
I ATE TOO MUCH! I'M GOING TO EXPLODE!!
JIM DAVIS 6-6
BURP
© 1992 PAWS, INC. All Rights Reserved.
THANK GOODNESS NO ONE WAS HARMED
YOU CAN ALL GO BACK TO YOUR HOMES NOW. THERE'S NOTHING MORE TO SEE

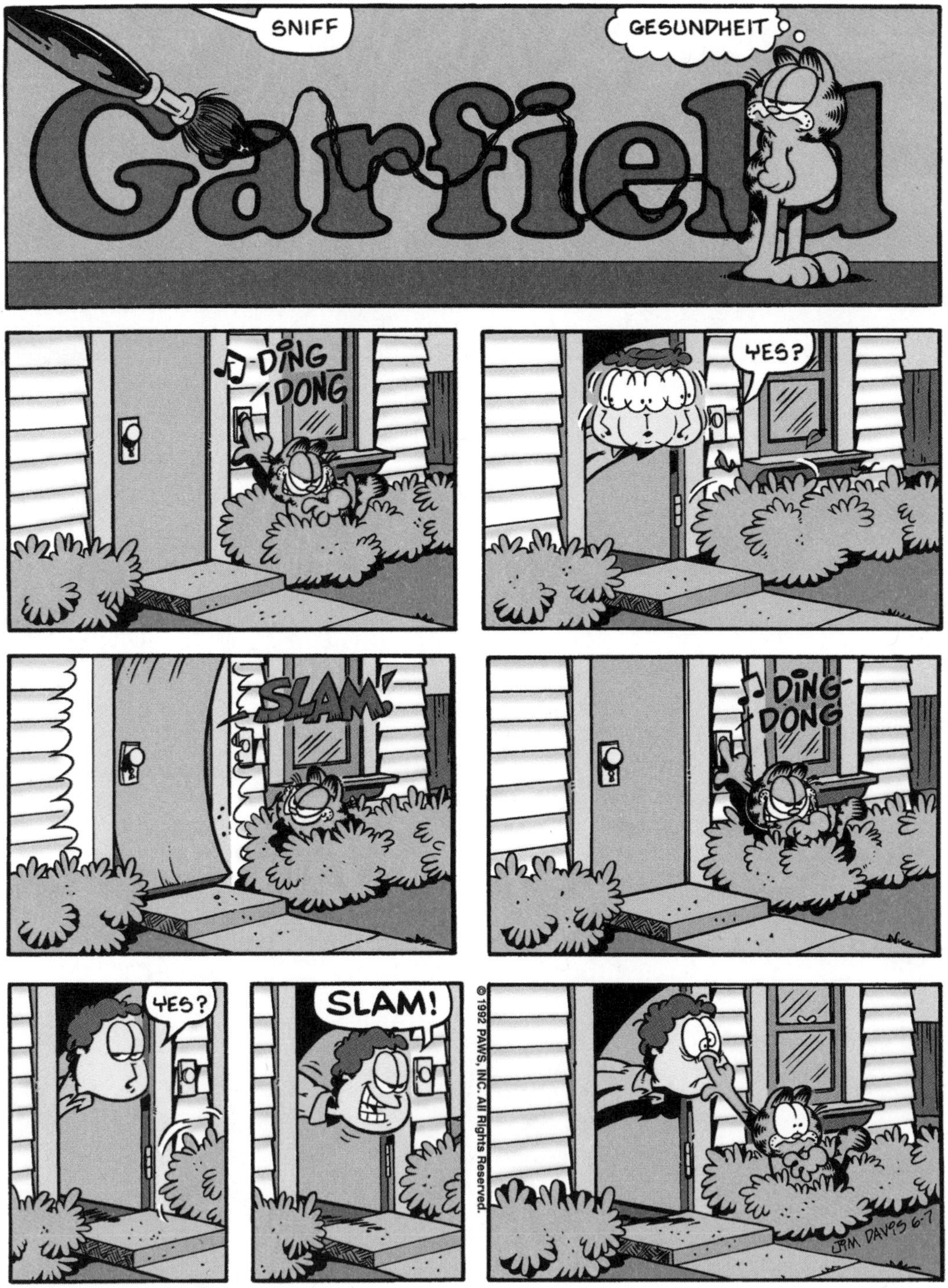
SNIFF
GESUNDHEIT
Garfield
DING DONG
YES?
SLAM
DING-DONG
YES?
SLAM!
© 1992 PAWS, INC. All Rights Reserved.
JIM DAVIS 6-7

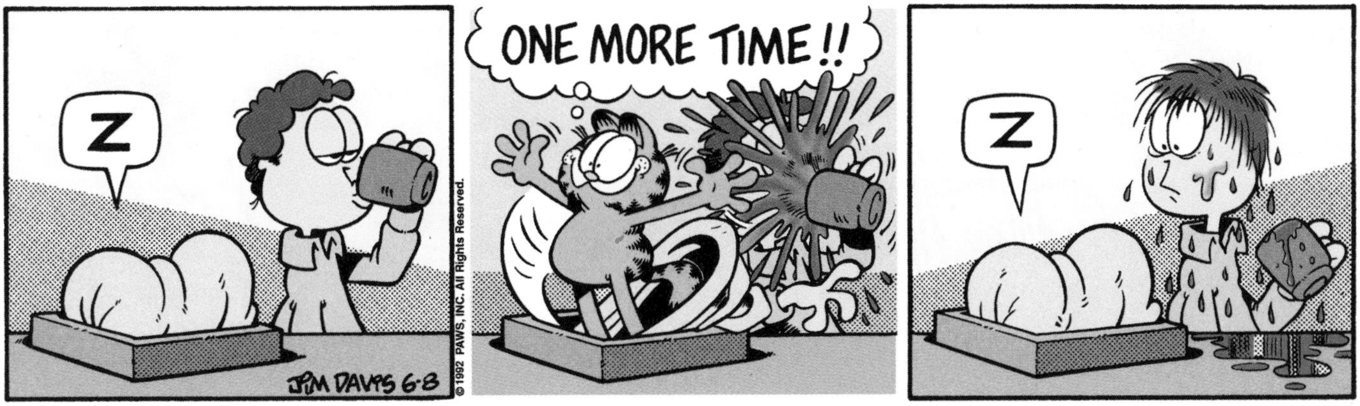
Z
JIM DAVIS 6-8
© 1992 PAWS, INC. All Rights Reserved.
ONE MORE TIME!!
Z

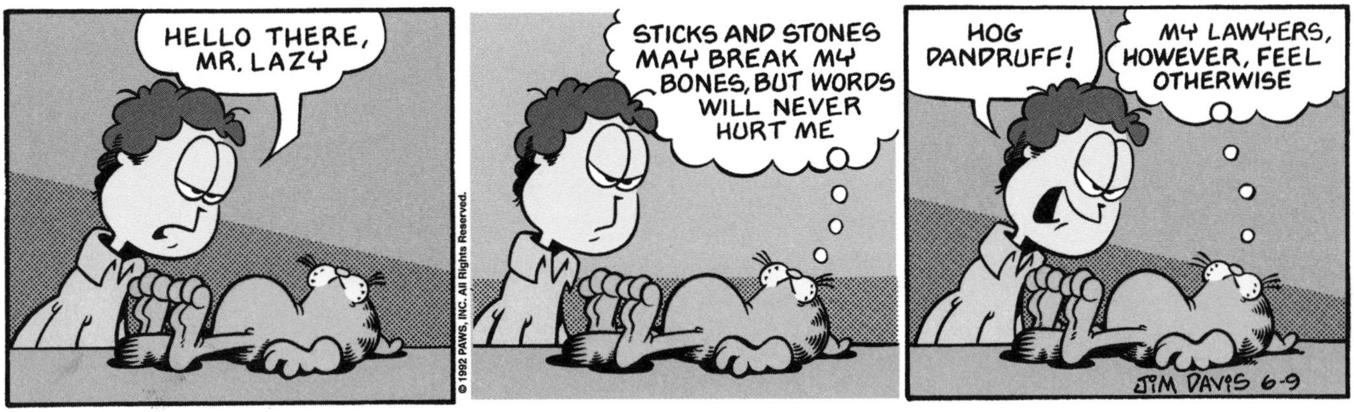
HELLO THERE, MR. LAZY
© 1992 PAWS, INC. All Rights Reserved.
STICKS AND STONES MAY BREAK MY BONES, BUT WORDS WILL NEVER HURT ME
HOG DANDRUFF!
MY LAWYERS, HOWEVER, FEEL OTHERWISE
JIM DAVIS 6-9

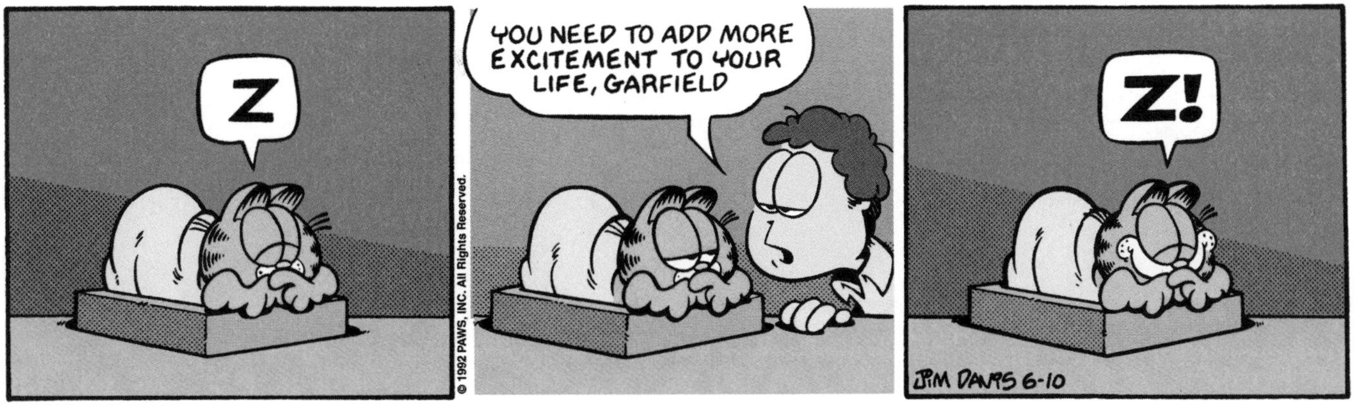
Z
© 1992 PAWS, INC. All Rights Reserved.
YOU NEED TO ADD MORE EXCITEMENT TO YOUR LIFE, GARFIELD
Z!
JIM DAVIS 6-10

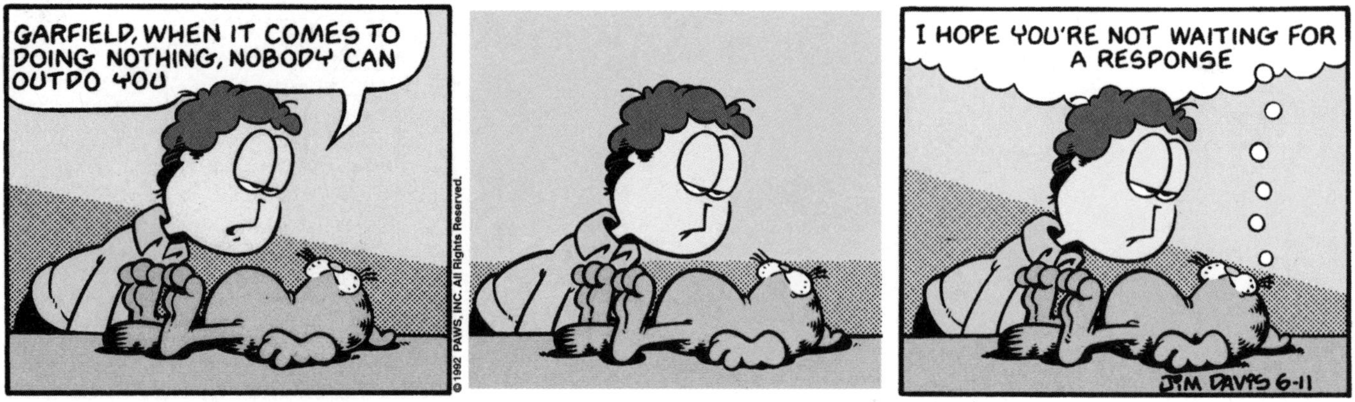
GARFIELD, WHEN IT COMES TO DOING NOTHING, NOBODY CAN OUTDO YOU
© 1992 PAWS, INC. All Rights Reserved.
I HOPE YOU'RE NOT WAITING FOR A RESPONSE
JIM DAVIS 6-11

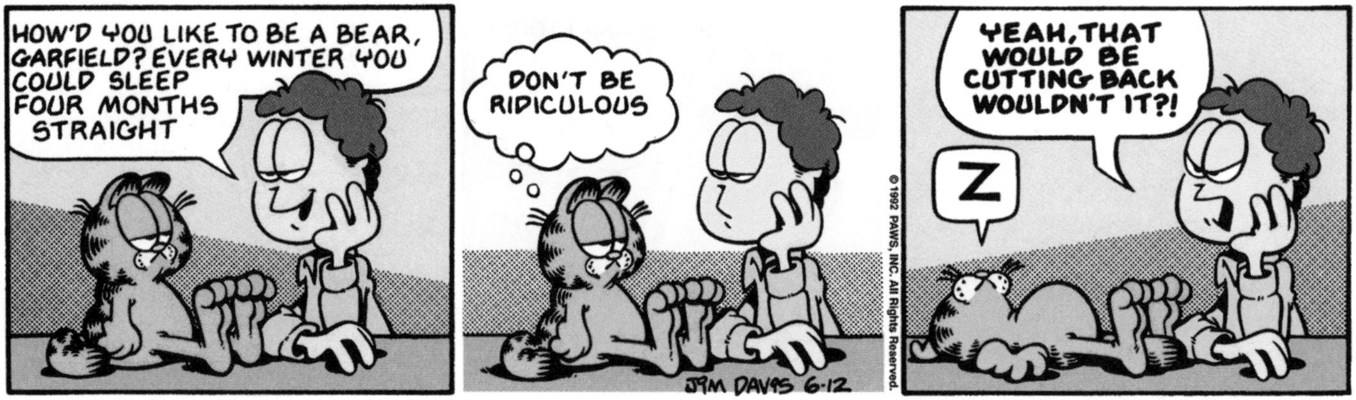
HOW'D YOU LIKE TO BE A BEAR, GARFIELD? EVERY WINTER YOU COULD SLEEP FOUR MONTHS STRAIGHT
DON'T BE RIDICULOUS
JIM DAVIS 6-12
© 1992 PAWS, INC. All Rights Reserved.
Z
YEAH, THAT WOULD BE CUTTING BACK WOULDN'T IT?!

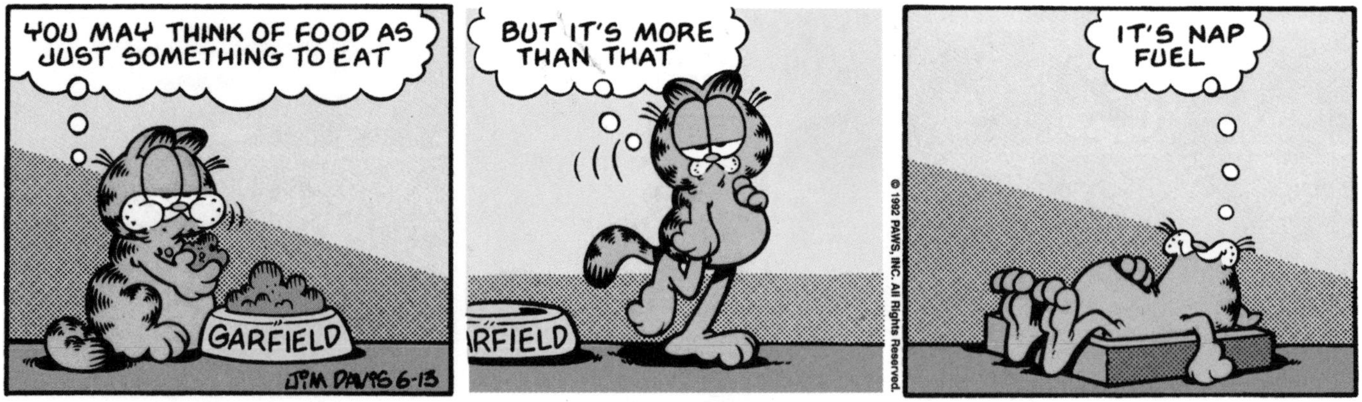
YOU MAY THINK OF FOOD AS JUST SOMETHING TO EAT
GARFIELD
JIM DAVIS 6-13
BUT IT'S MORE THAN THAT
RFIELD
© 1992 PAWS, INC. All Rights Reserved.
IT'S NAP FUEL

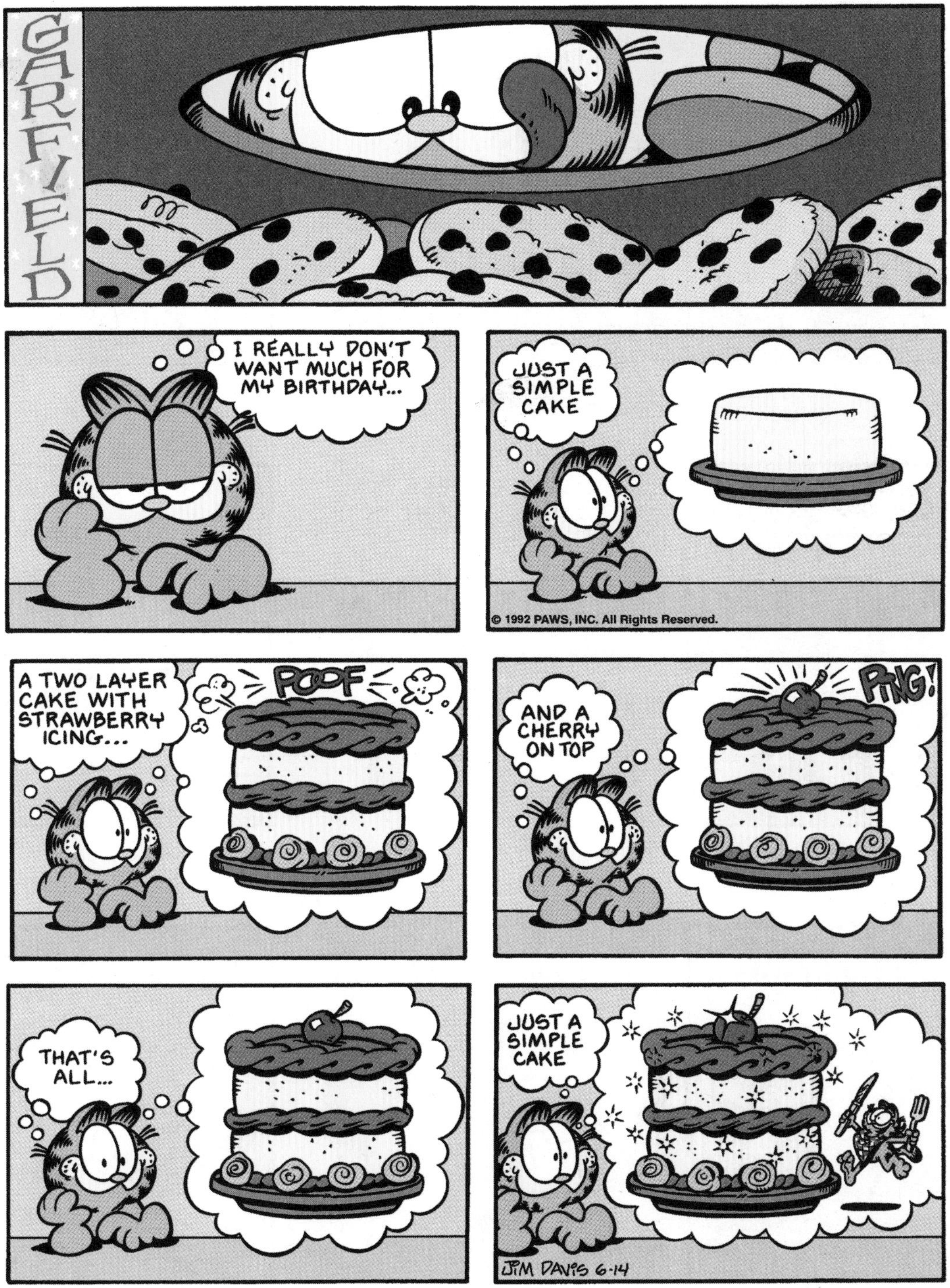
GARFIELD
I REALLY DON'T WANT MUCH FOR MY BIRTHDAY...
JUST A SIMPLE CAKE
© 1992 PAWS, INC. All Rights Reserved.
A TWO LAYER CAKE WITH STRAWBERRY ICING...
POOF
AND A CHERRY ON TOP
PING!
THAT'S ALL...
JUST A SIMPLE CAKE
JIM DAVIS 6-14

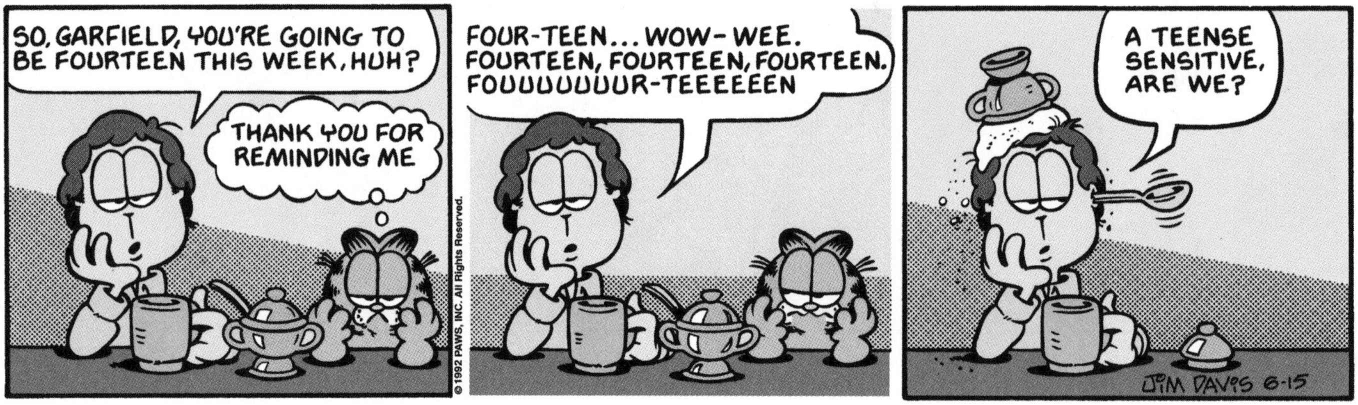
SO, GARFIELD, YOU'RE GOING TO BE FOURTEEN THIS WEEK, HUH?
THANK YOU FOR REMINDING ME
© 1992 PAWS, INC. All Rights Reserved.
FOUR-TEEN... WOW-WEE. FOURTEEN, FOURTEEN, FOURTEEN. FOUUUUUUUR-TEEEEEEN
A TEENSE SENSITIVE, ARE WE?
JIM DAVIS 6-15

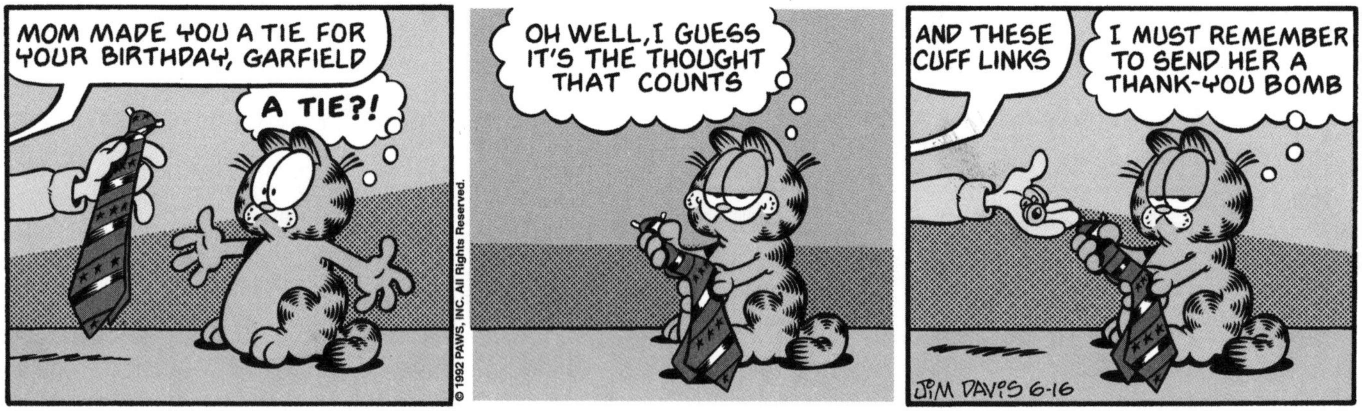
MOM MADE YOU A TIE FOR YOUR BIRTHDAY, GARFIELD
A TIE?!
© 1992 PAWS, INC. All Rights Reserved.
OH WELL, I GUESS IT'S THE THOUGHT THAT COUNTS
AND THESE CUFF LINKS
I MUST REMEMBER TO SEND HER A THANK-YOU BOMB
JIM DAVIS 6-16

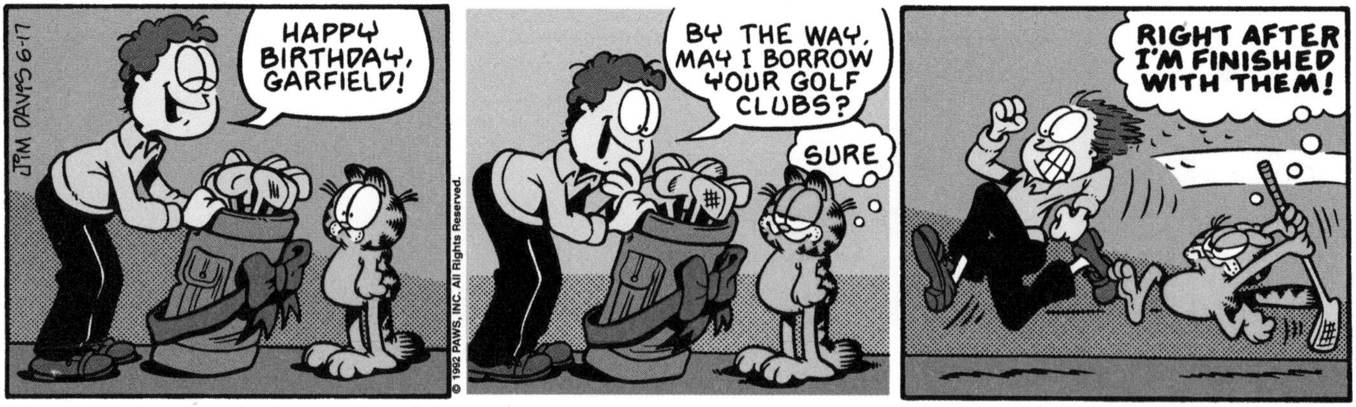
JIM DAVIS 6-17
HAPPY BIRTHDAY, GARFIELD!
© 1992 PAWS, INC. All Rights Reserved.
BY THE WAY, MAY I BORROW YOUR GOLF CLUBS?
SURE
RIGHT AFTER I'M FINISHED WITH THEM!

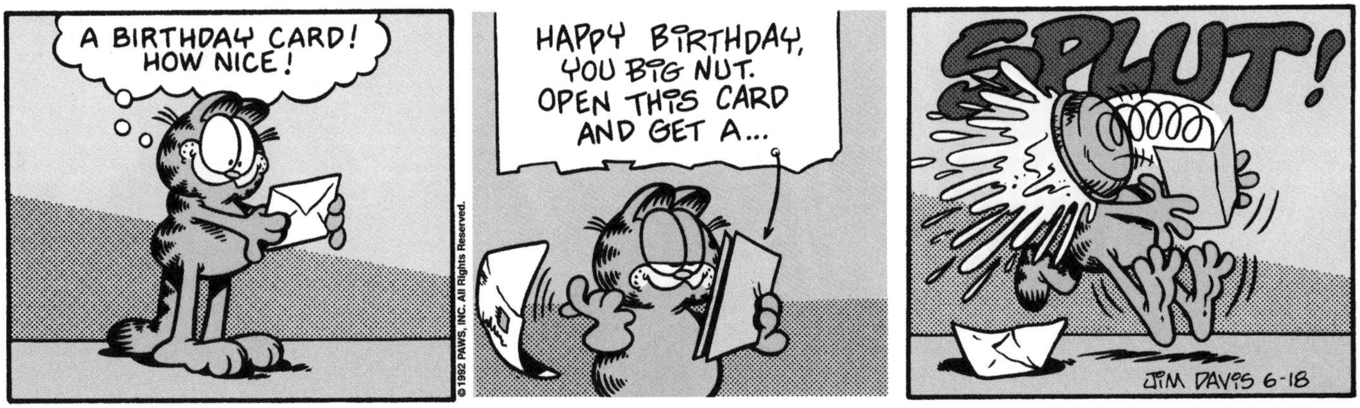
A BIRTHDAY CARD! HOW NICE!
HAPPY BIRTHDAY, YOU BIG NUT. OPEN THIS CARD AND GET A...
SPLUT!
JIM DAVIS 6-18
© 1992 PAWS, INC. All Rights Reserved.

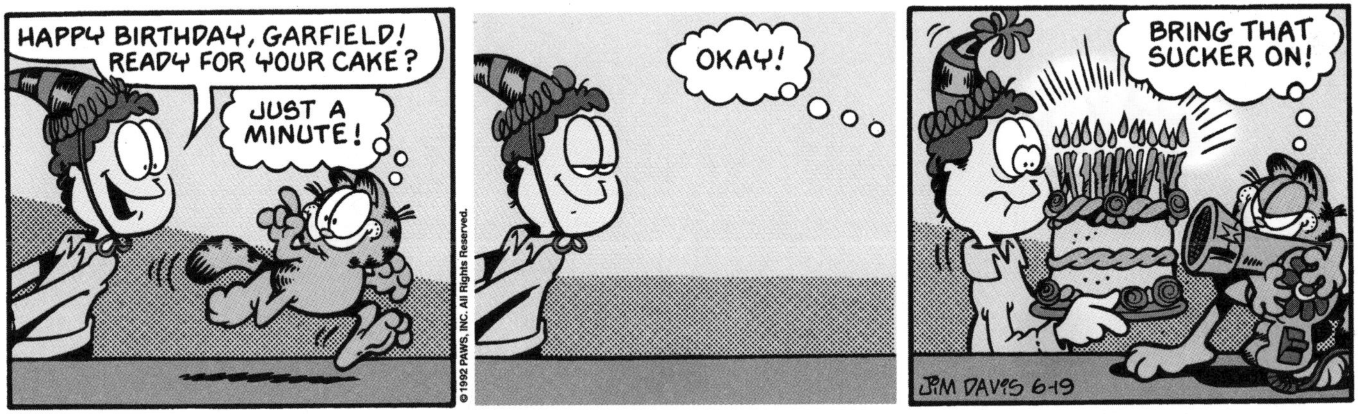
HAPPY BIRTHDAY, GARFIELD! READY FOR YOUR CAKE?
JUST A MINUTE!
OKAY!
BRING THAT SUCKER ON!
JIM DAVIS 6-19
© 1992 PAWS, INC. All Rights Reserved.

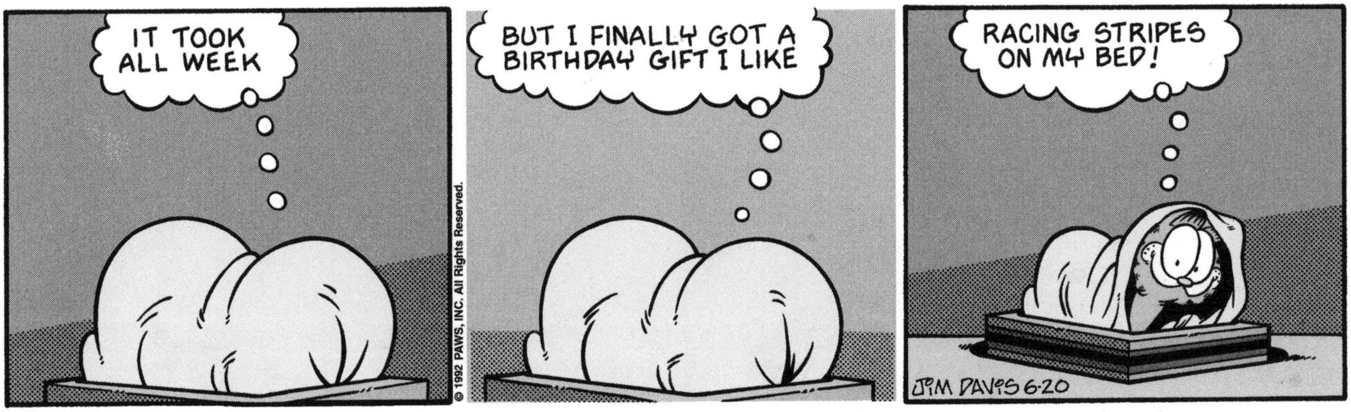
IT TOOK ALL WEEK
BUT I FINALLY GOT A BIRTHDAY GIFT I LIKE
RACING STRIPES ON MY BED!
JIM DAVIS 6-20
© 1992 PAWS, INC. All Rights Reserved.

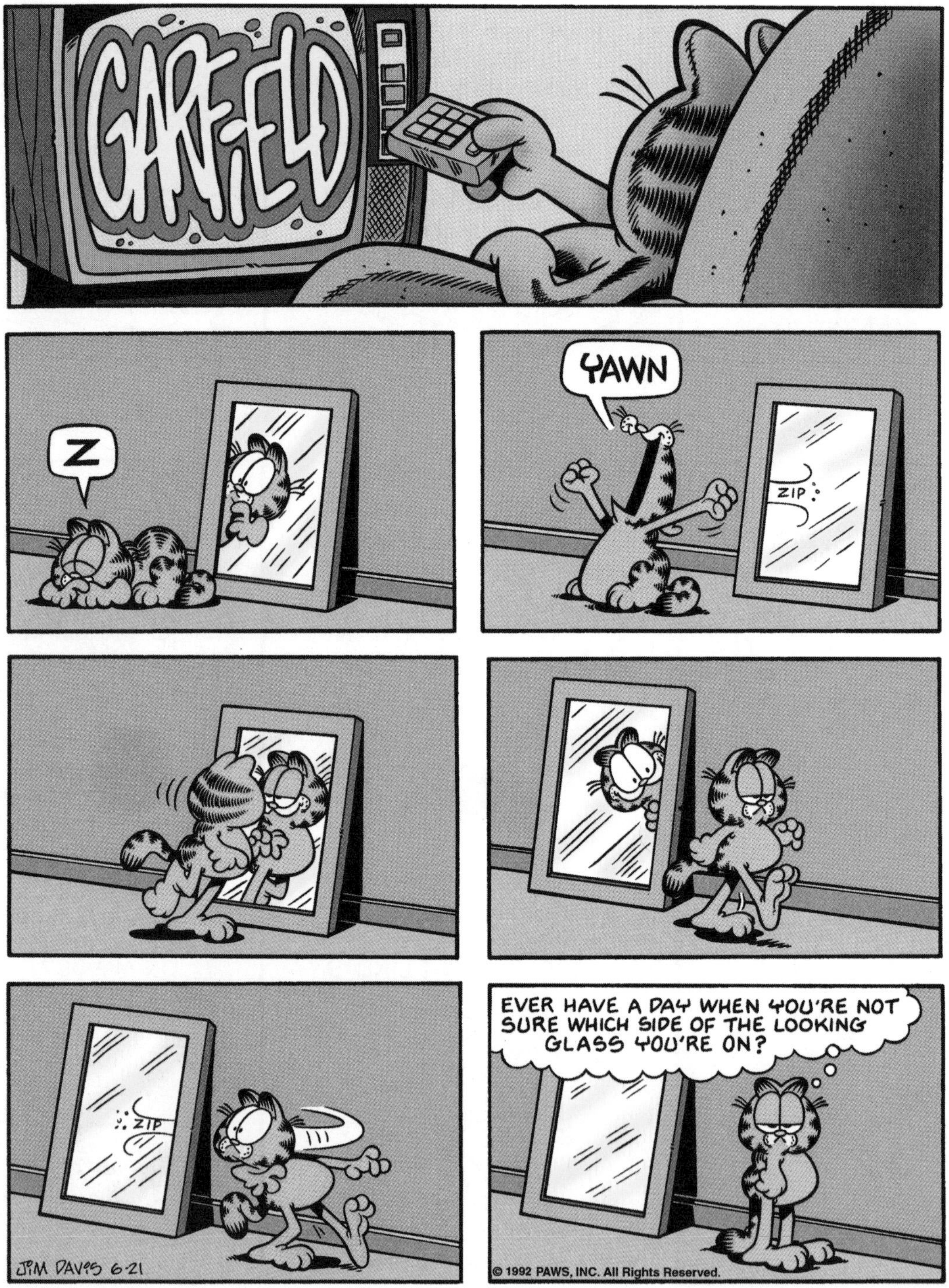
GARFIELD
Z
YAWN
ZIP
ZIP
JIM DAVIS 6-21
EVER HAVE A DAY WHEN YOU'RE NOT SURE WHICH SIDE OF THE LOOKING GLASS YOU'RE ON?
© 1992 PAWS, INC. All Rights Reserved.

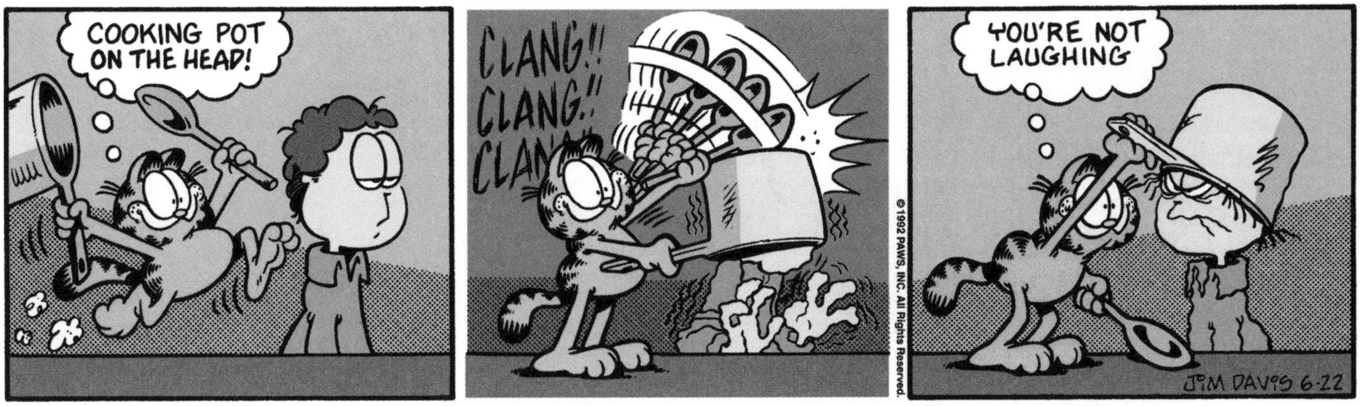
COOKING POT ON THE HEAD!
CLANG!!
CLANG!!
© 1992 PAWS, INC. All Rights Reserved.
YOU'RE NOT LAUGHING
JIM DAVIS 6-22

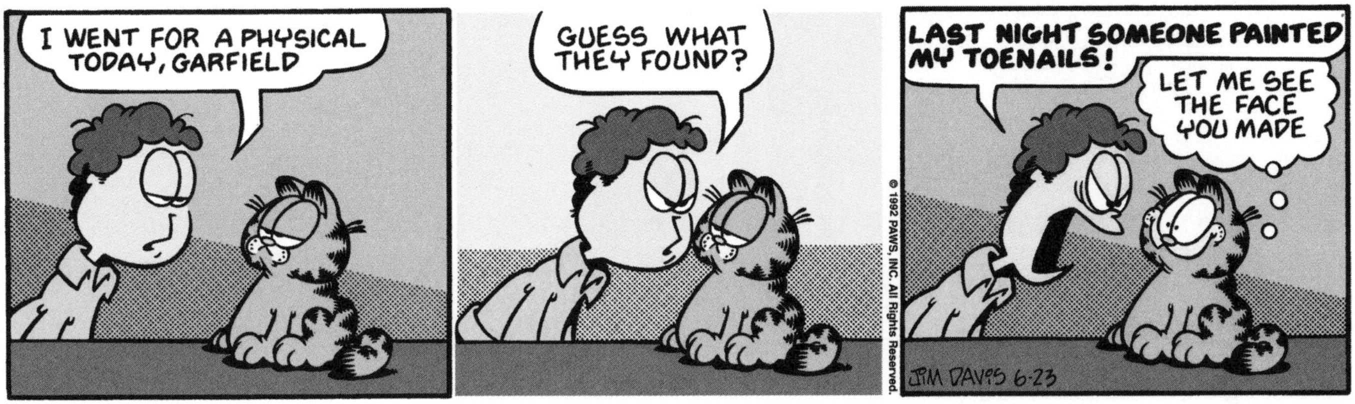
I WENT FOR A PHYSICAL TODAY, GARFIELD
GUESS WHAT THEY FOUND?
© 1992 PAWS, INC. All Rights Reserved.
LAST NIGHT SOMEONE PAINTED MY TOENAILS!
LET ME SEE THE FACE YOU MADE
JIM DAVIS 6-23

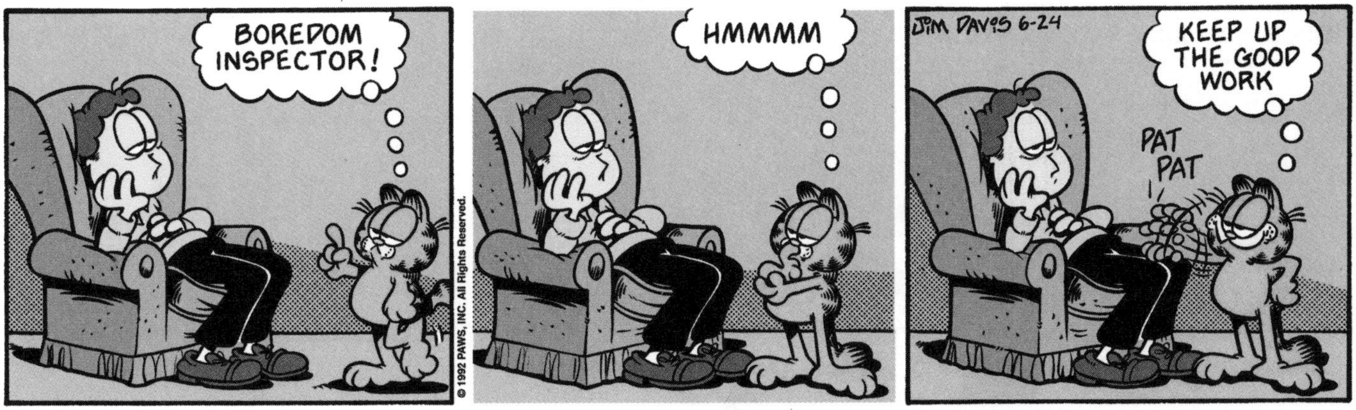
BOREDOM INSPECTOR!
© 1992 PAWS, INC. All Rights Reserved.
HMMMM
JIM DAVIS 6-24
KEEP UP THE GOOD WORK
PAT PAT

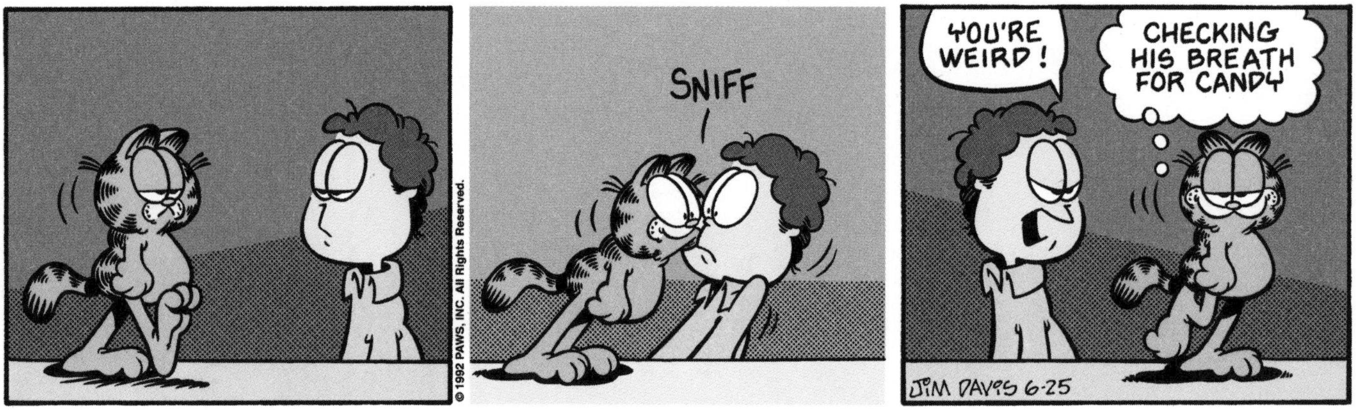
© 1992 PAWS, INC. All Rights Reserved.
SNIFF
YOU'RE WEIRD!
CHECKING HIS BREATH FOR CANDY
JIM DAVIS 6-25

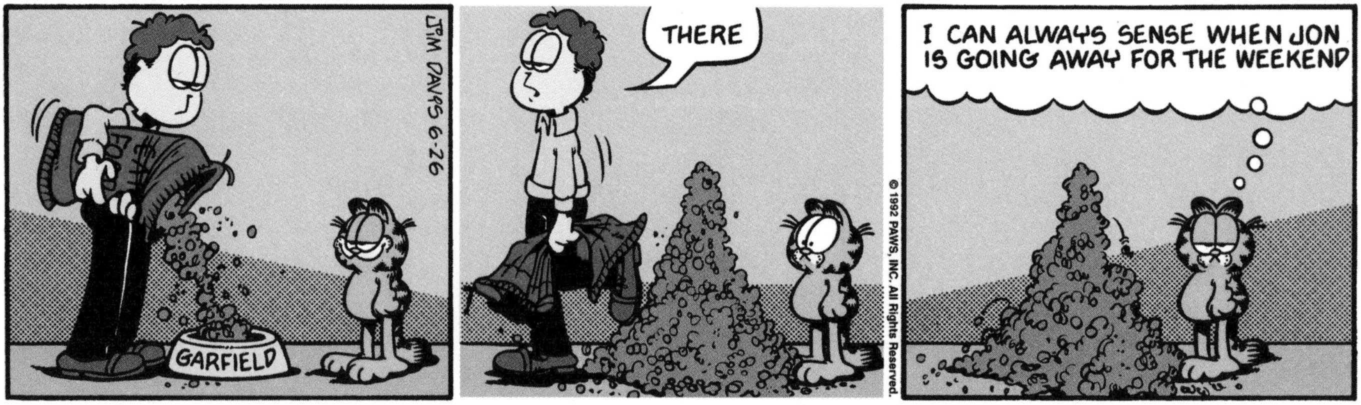
JIM DAVIS 6-26
GARFIELD
THERE
© 1992 PAWS, INC. All Rights Reserved.
I CAN ALWAYS SENSE WHEN JON IS GOING AWAY FOR THE WEEKEND

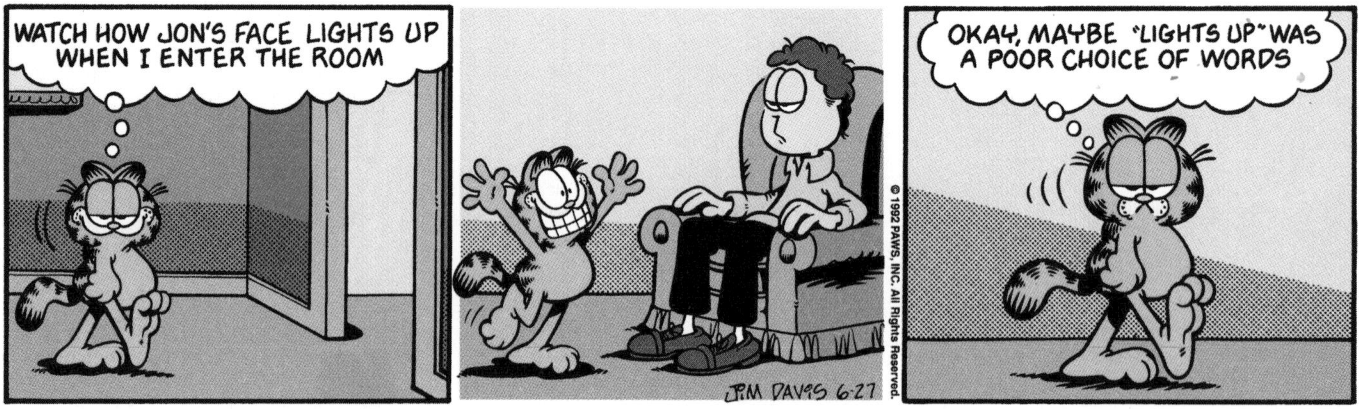
WATCH HOW JON'S FACE LIGHTS UP WHEN I ENTER THE ROOM
JIM DAVIS 6-27
© 1992 PAWS, INC. All Rights Reserved.
OKAY, MAYBE "LIGHTS UP" WAS A POOR CHOICE OF WORDS

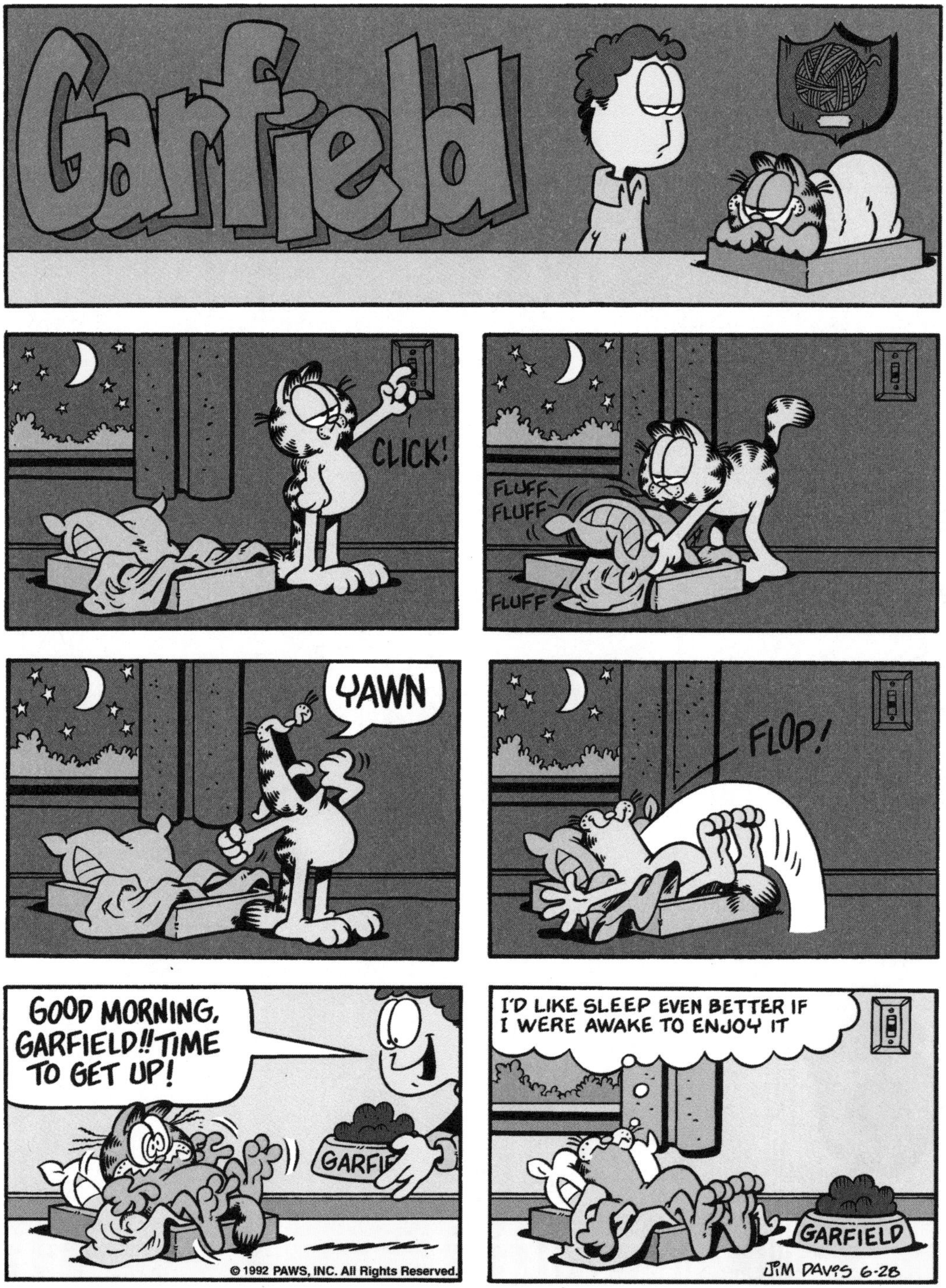
Garfield
CLICK!
FLUFF
FLUFF
FLUFF
YAWN
FLOP!
GOOD MORNING, GARFIELD!! TIME TO GET UP!
GARFIELD
I'D LIKE SLEEP EVEN BETTER IF I WERE AWAKE TO ENJOY IT
GARFIELD
JIM DAVIS 6-28

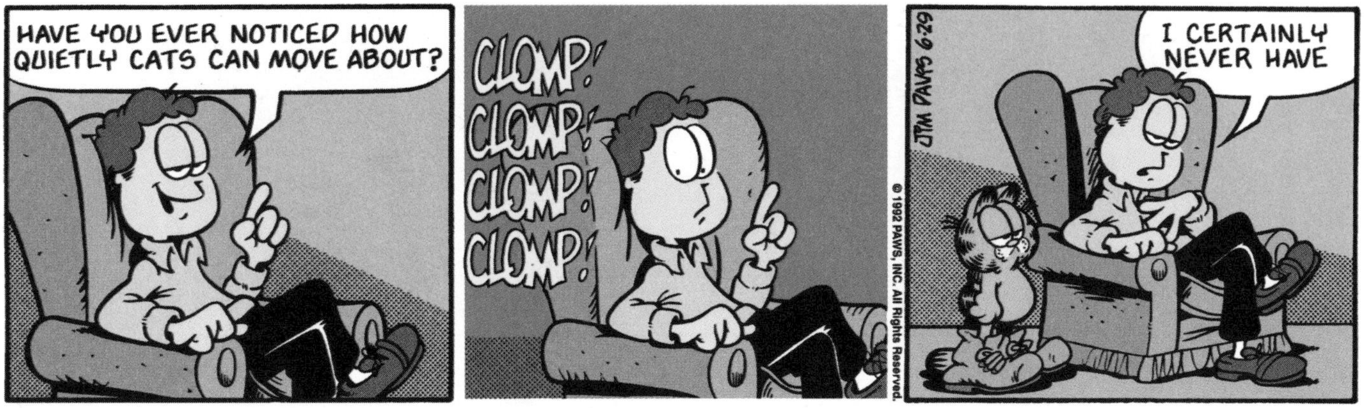
HAVE YOU EVER NOTICED HOW QUIETLY CATS CAN MOVE ABOUT?
CLOMP! CLOMP! CLOMP! CLOMP!
JIM DAVIS 6-29
© 1992 PAWS, INC. All Rights Reserved.
I CERTAINLY NEVER HAVE

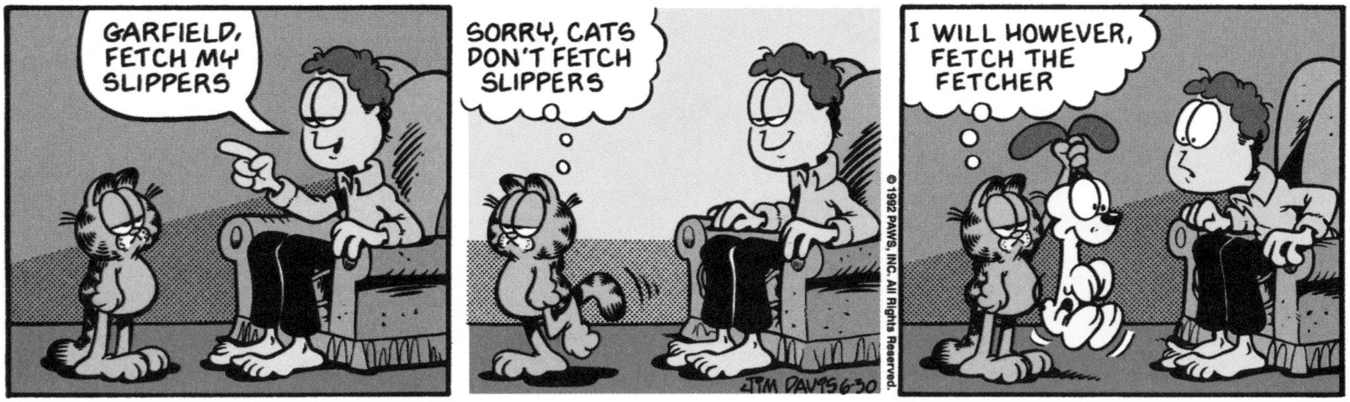
GARFIELD, FETCH MY SLIPPERS
SORRY, CATS DON'T FETCH SLIPPERS
JIM DAVIS 6-30
© 1992 PAWS, INC. All Rights Reserved.
I WILL HOWEVER, FETCH THE FETCHER

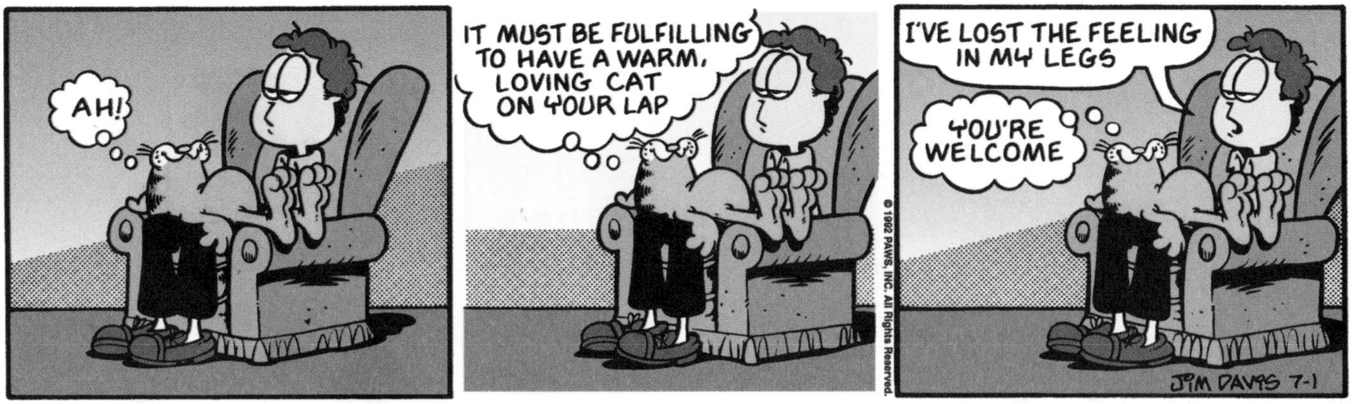
AH!
IT MUST BE FULFILLING TO HAVE A WARM, LOVING CAT ON YOUR LAP
© 1992 PAWS, INC. All Rights Reserved.
I'VE LOST THE FEELING IN MY LEGS
YOU'RE WELCOME
JIM DAVIS 7-1

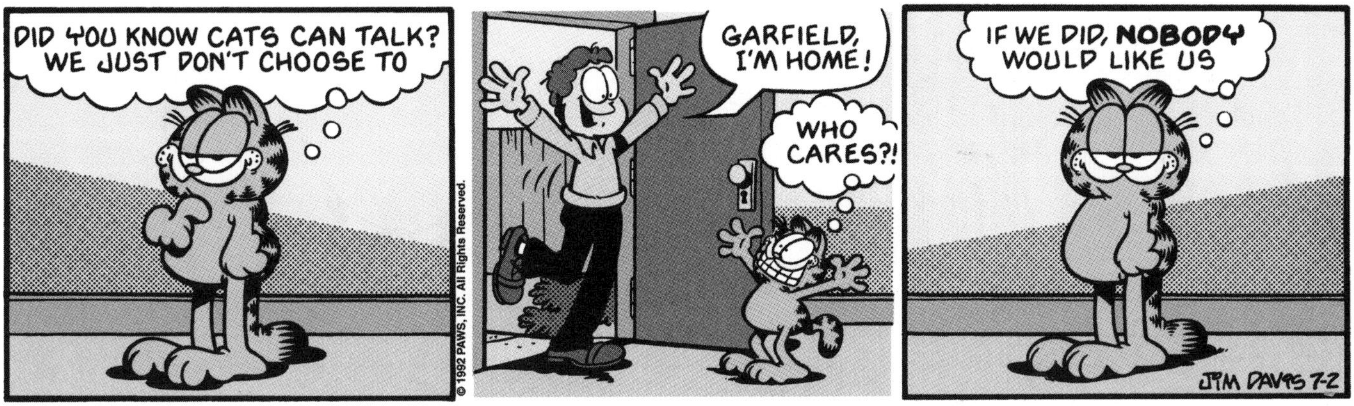
DID YOU KNOW CATS CAN TALK? WE JUST DON'T CHOOSE TO
© 1992 PAWS, INC. All Rights Reserved.
GARFIELD, I'M HOME!
WHO CARES?!
IF WE DID, **NOBODY** WOULD LIKE US
JIM DAVIS 7-2

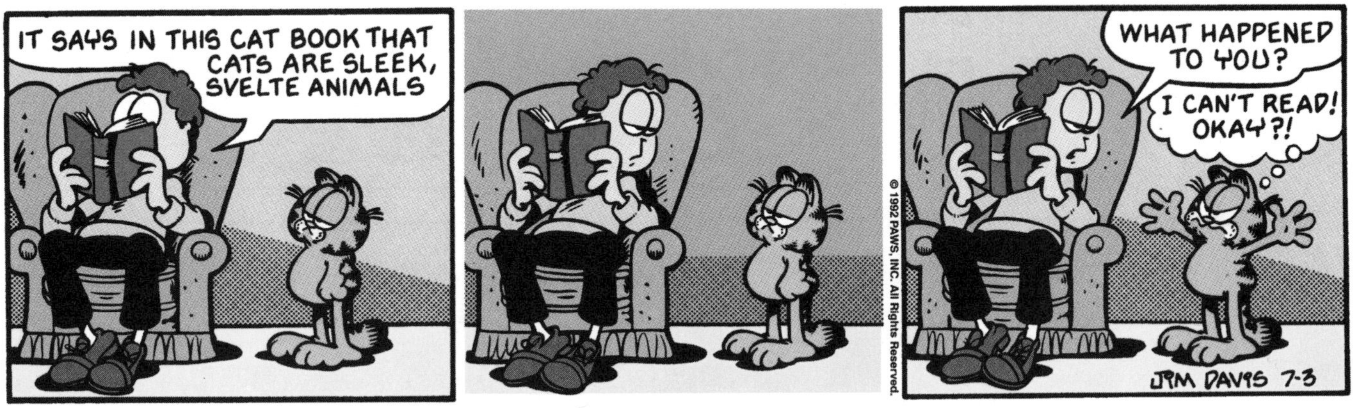
IT SAYS IN THIS CAT BOOK THAT CATS ARE SLEEK, SVELTE ANIMALS
© 1992 PAWS, INC. All Rights Reserved.
WHAT HAPPENED TO YOU?
I CAN'T READ! OKAY?!
JIM DAVIS 7-3

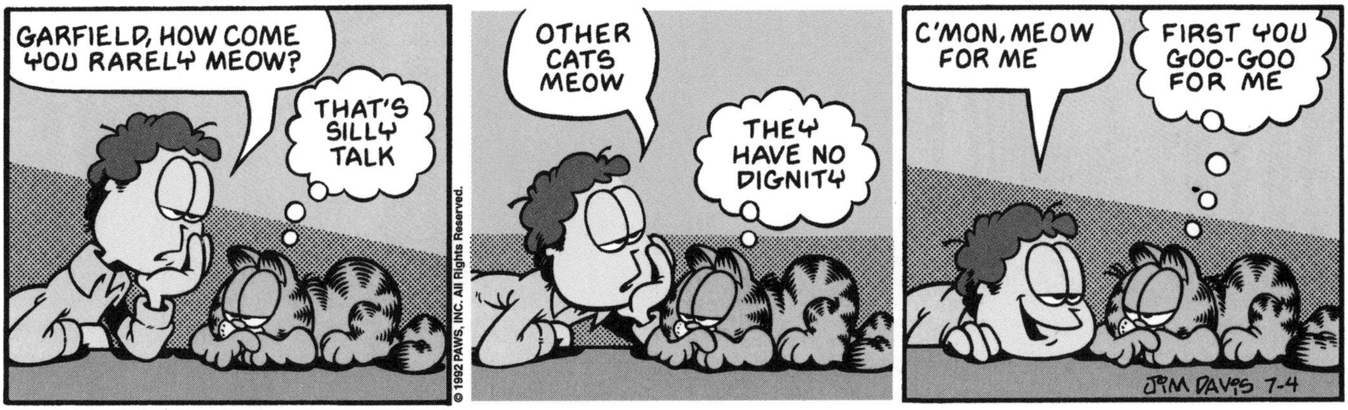
GARFIELD, HOW COME YOU RARELY MEOW?
THAT'S SILLY TALK
© 1992 PAWS, INC. All Rights Reserved.
OTHER CATS MEOW
THEY HAVE NO DIGNITY
C'MON, MEOW FOR ME
FIRST YOU GOO-GOO FOR ME
JIM DAVIS 7-4

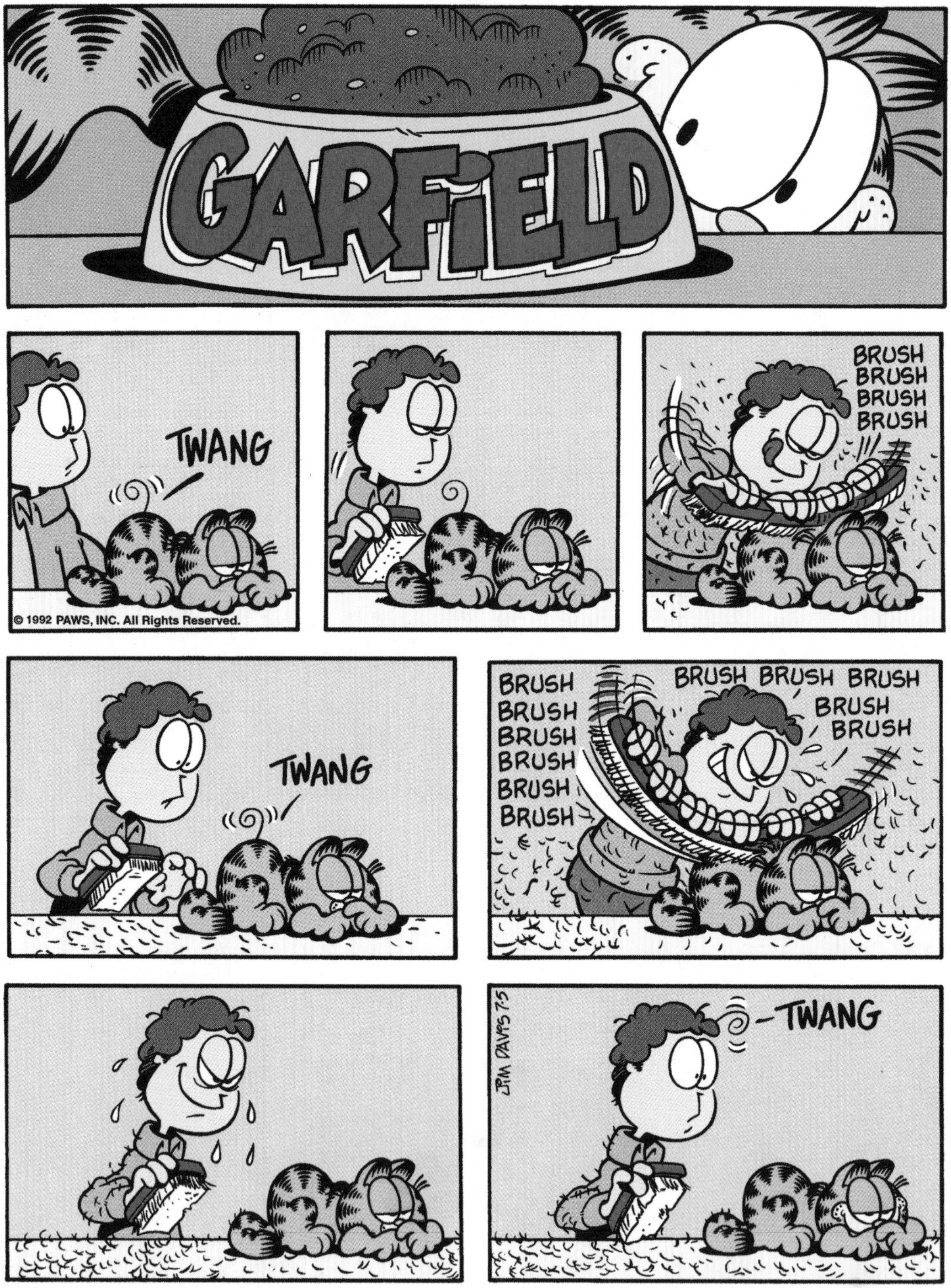
GARFIELD
TWANG
© 1992 PAWS, INC. All Rights Reserved.
BRUSH BRUSH BRUSH BRUSH
TWANG
BRUSH BRUSH BRUSH BRUSH BRUSH BRUSH
BRUSH BRUSH BRUSH
BRUSH BRUSH
JIM DAVIS 7-5
TWANG

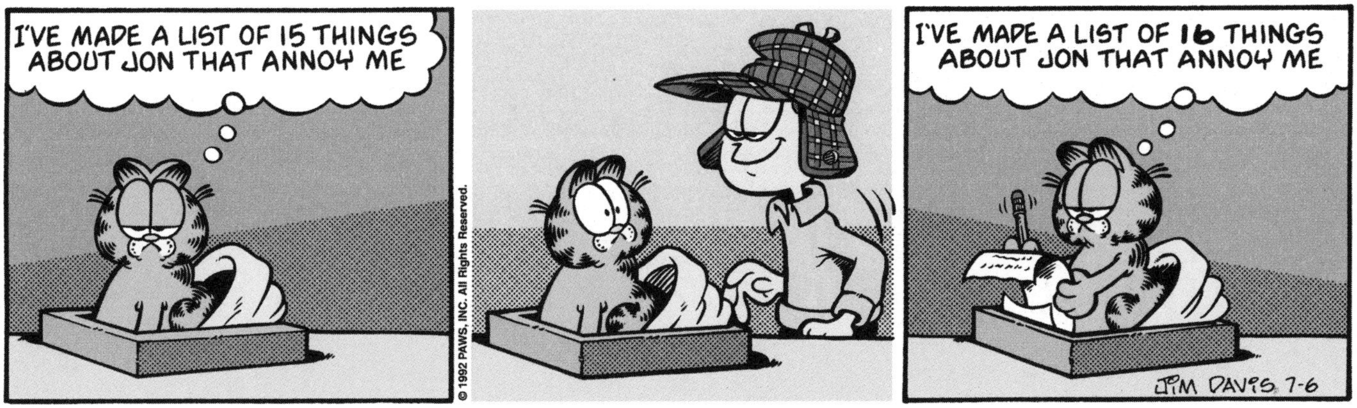
I'VE MADE A LIST OF 15 THINGS ABOUT JON THAT ANNOY ME
© 1992 PAWS, INC. All Rights Reserved.
I'VE MADE A LIST OF 16 THINGS ABOUT JON THAT ANNOY ME
JIM DAVIS 7-6

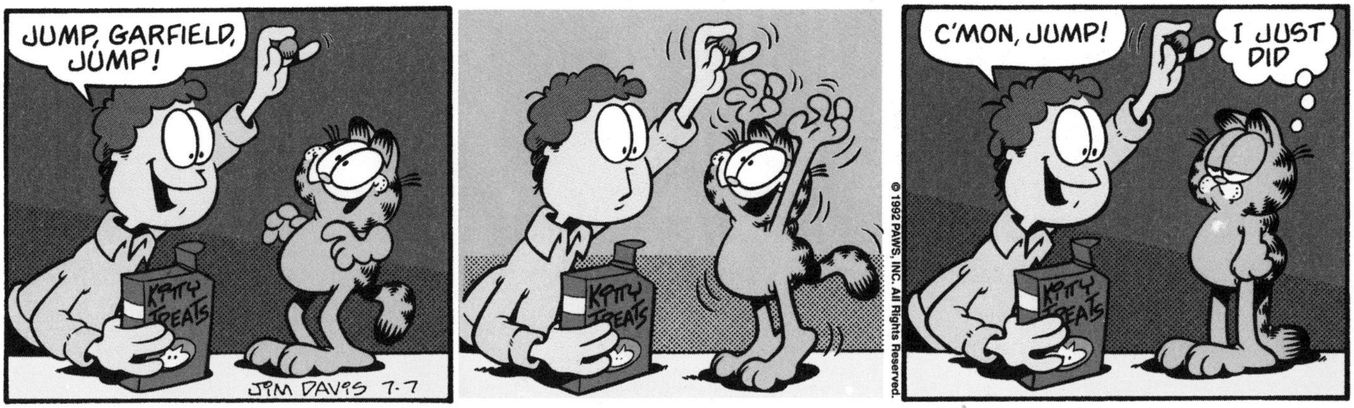
JUMP, GARFIELD, JUMP!
KITTY TREATS
JIM DAVIS 7-7
© 1992 PAWS, INC. All Rights Reserved.
C'MON, JUMP!
I JUST DID

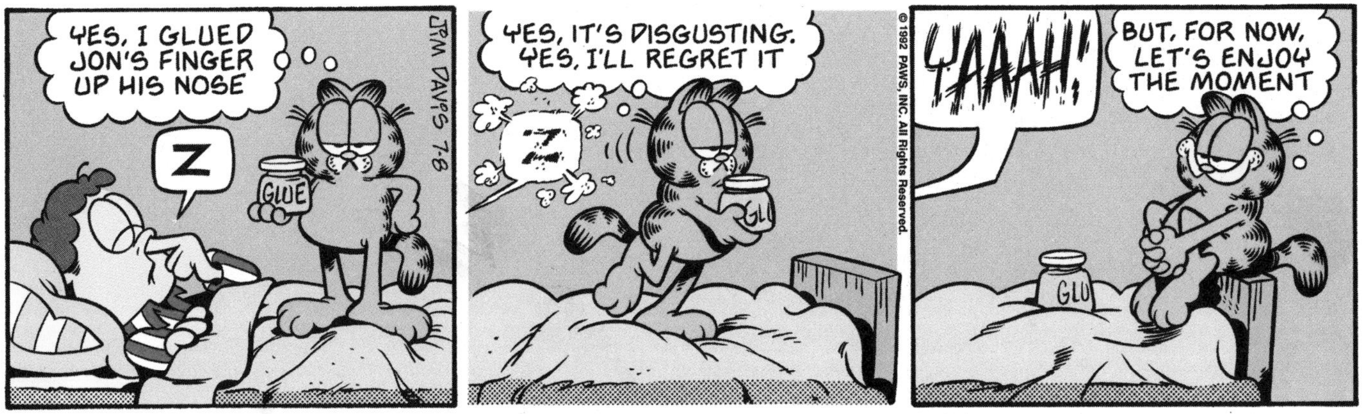
YES, I GLUED JON'S FINGER UP HIS NOSE
Z
GLUE
JIM DAVIS 7-8
YES, IT'S DISGUSTING. YES, I'LL REGRET IT
Z
© 1992 PAWS, INC. All Rights Reserved.
YAAAH!
BUT, FOR NOW, LET'S ENJOY THE MOMENT
GLU

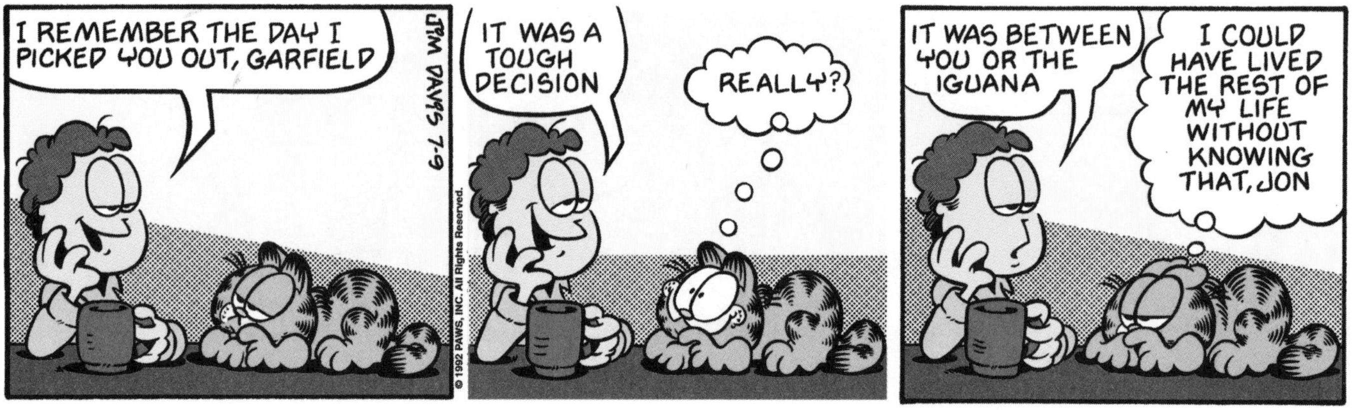
I REMEMBER THE DAY I PICKED YOU OUT, GARFIELD
IT WAS A TOUGH DECISION
REALLY?
IT WAS BETWEEN YOU OR THE IGUANA
I COULD HAVE LIVED THE REST OF MY LIFE WITHOUT KNOWING THAT, JON
JIM DAVIS 7-9
© 1992 PAWS, INC. All Rights Reserved.

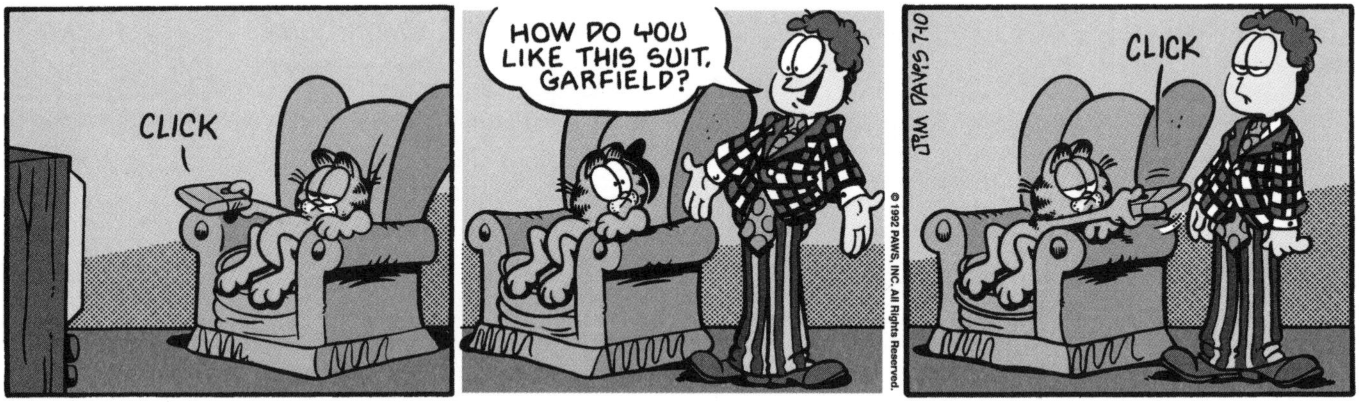
CLICK
HOW DO YOU LIKE THIS SUIT, GARFIELD?
CLICK
JIM DAVIS 7-10
© 1992 PAWS, INC. All Rights Reserved.

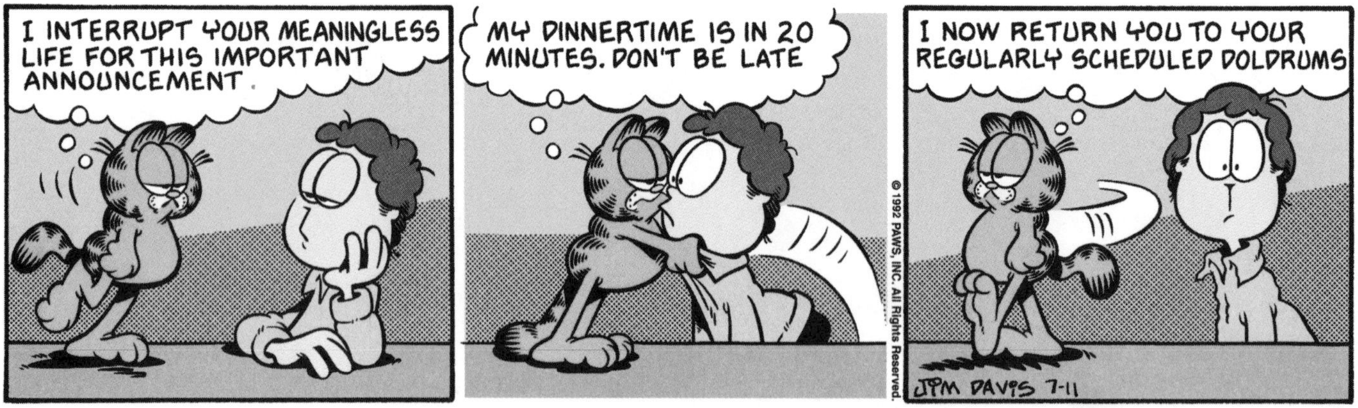
I INTERRUPT YOUR MEANINGLESS LIFE FOR THIS IMPORTANT ANNOUNCEMENT
MY DINNERTIME IS IN 20 MINUTES. DON'T BE LATE
I NOW RETURN YOU TO YOUR REGULARLY SCHEDULED DOLDRUMS
JIM DAVIS 7-11
© 1992 PAWS, INC. All Rights Reserved.

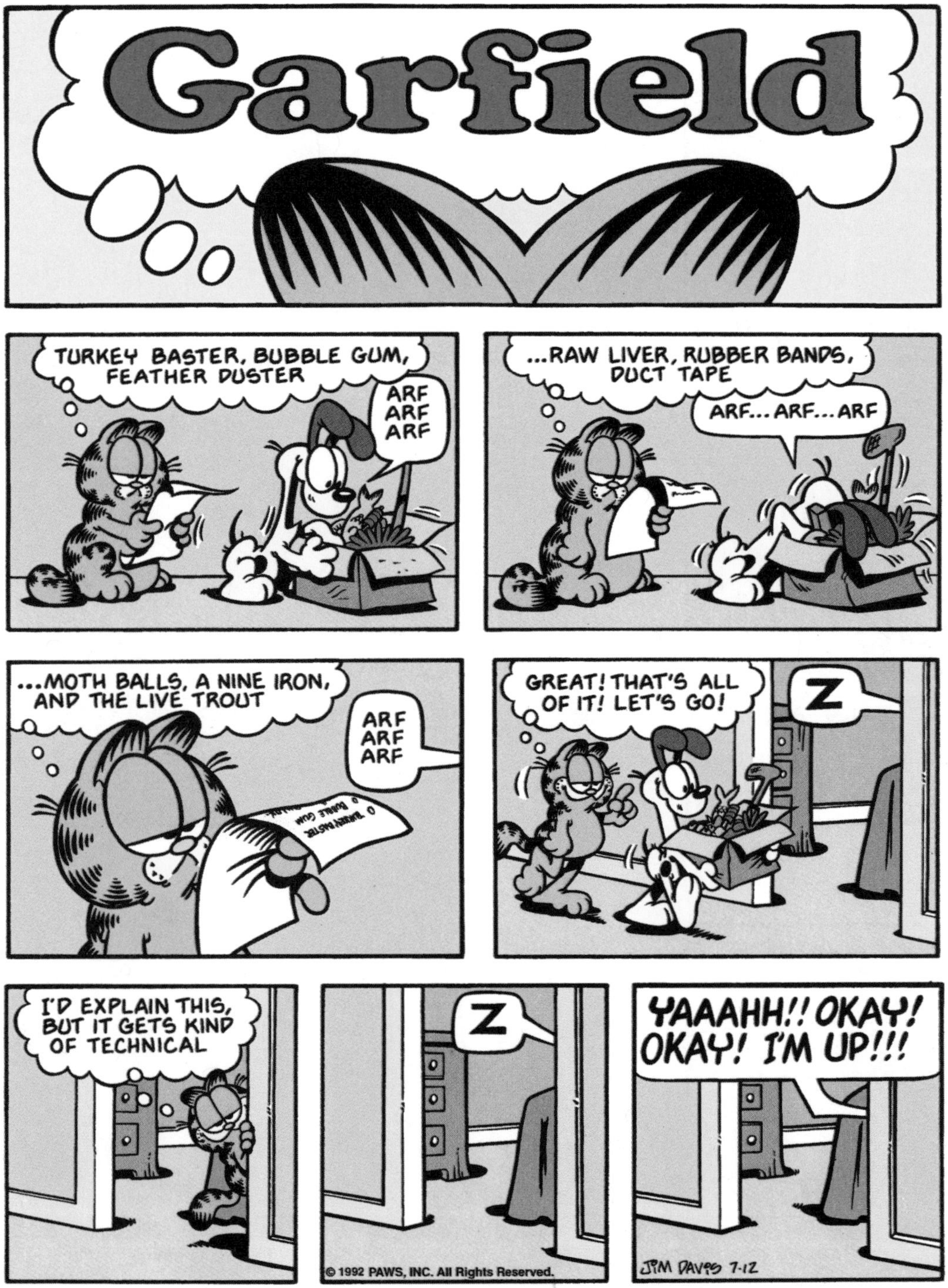
Garfield
TURKEY BASTER, BUBBLE GUM, FEATHER DUSTER
ARF ARF ARF
...RAW LIVER, RUBBER BANDS, DUCT TAPE
ARF... ARF... ARF
...MOTH BALLS, A NINE IRON, AND THE LIVE TROUT
ARF ARF ARF
GREAT! THAT'S ALL OF IT! LET'S GO!
Z
I'D EXPLAIN THIS, BUT IT GETS KIND OF TECHNICAL
Z
YAAAHH!! OKAY! OKAY! I'M UP!!!
© 1992 PAWS, INC. All Rights Reserved.
JIM DAVIS 7-12

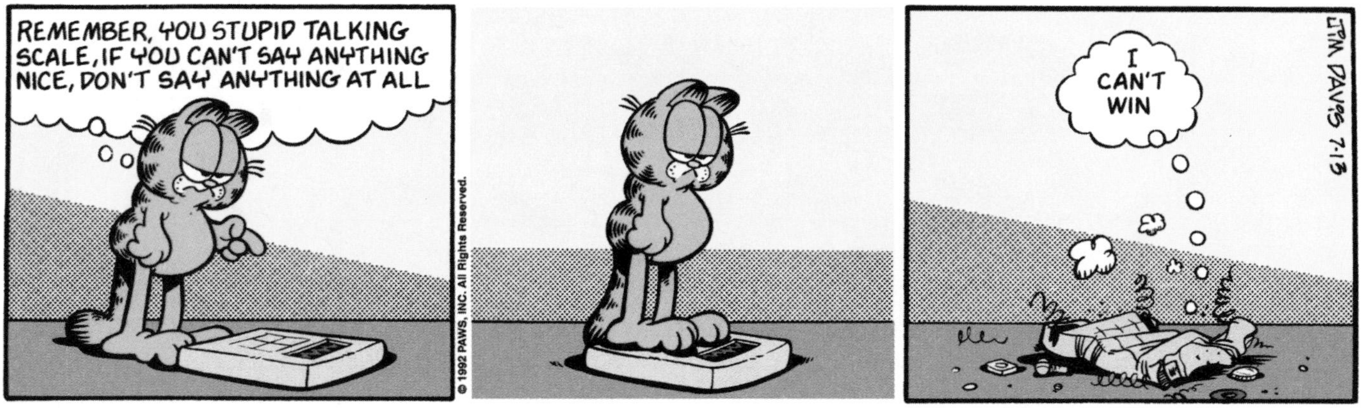
REMEMBER, YOU STUPID TALKING SCALE, IF YOU CAN'T SAY ANYTHING NICE, DON'T SAY ANYTHING AT ALL
© 1992 PAWS, INC. All Rights Reserved.
I CAN'T WIN
JIM DAVIS 7-13

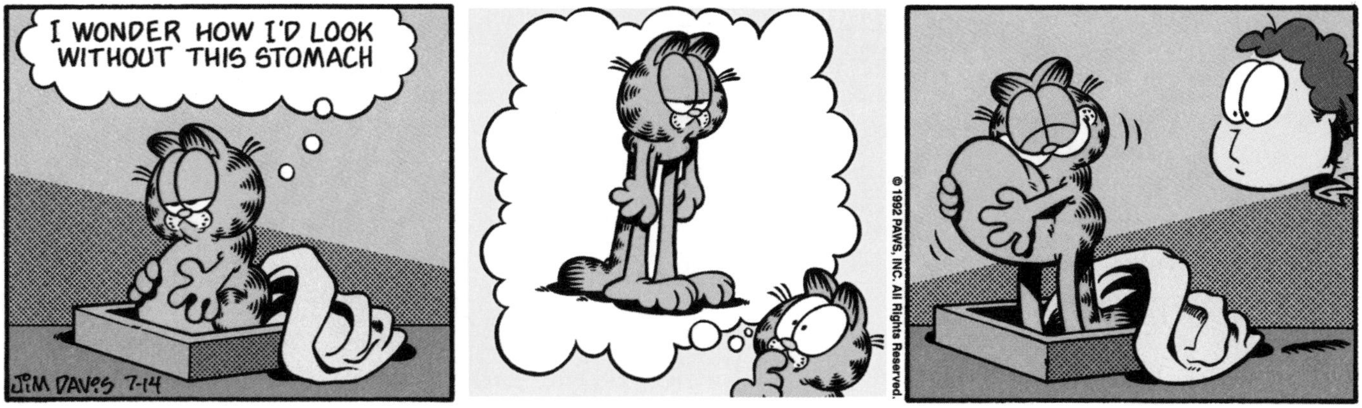
I WONDER HOW I'D LOOK WITHOUT THIS STOMACH
JIM DAVIS 7-14
© 1992 PAWS, INC. All Rights Reserved.

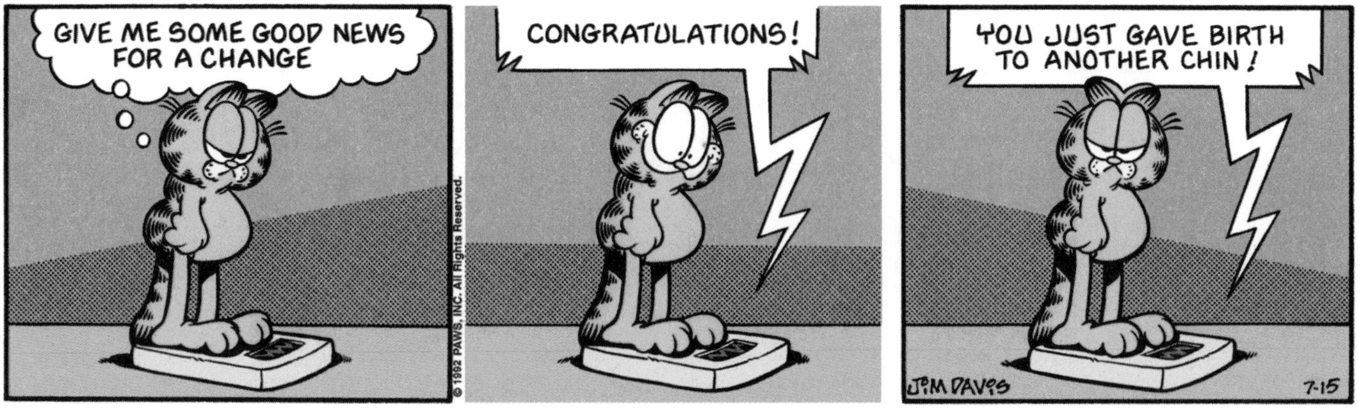
GIVE ME SOME GOOD NEWS FOR A CHANGE
© 1992 PAWS, INC. All Rights Reserved.
CONGRATULATIONS!
YOU JUST GAVE BIRTH TO ANOTHER CHIN!
JIM DAVIS
7-15

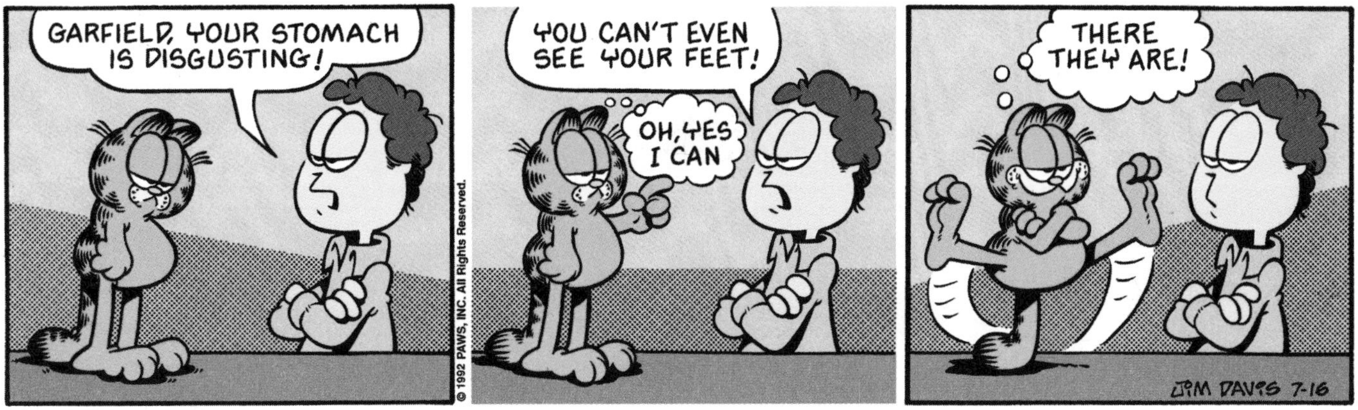
GARFIELD, YOUR STOMACH IS DISGUSTING!
© 1992 PAWS, INC. All Rights Reserved.
YOU CAN'T EVEN SEE YOUR FEET!
OH, YES I CAN
THERE THEY ARE!
JIM DAVIS 7-16

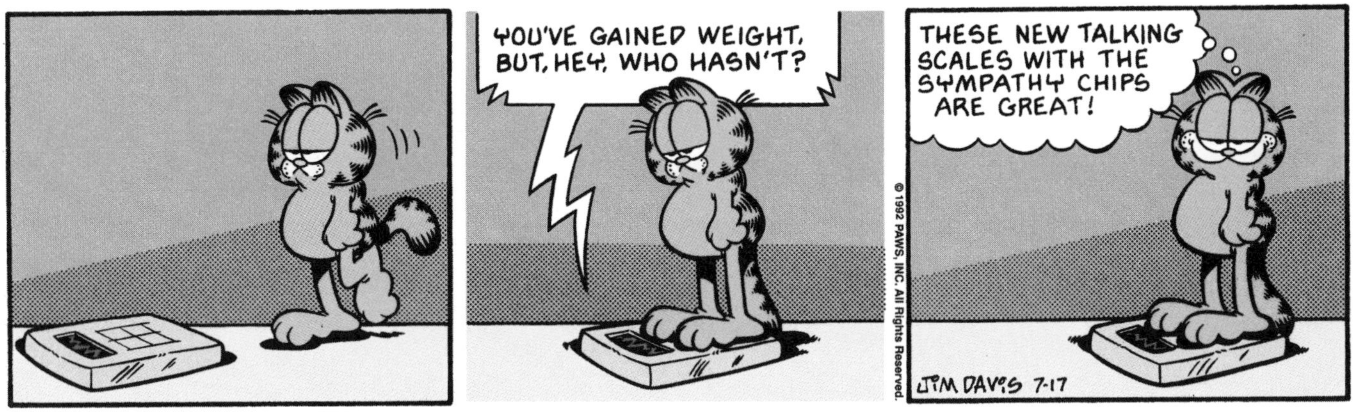
YOU'VE GAINED WEIGHT. BUT, HEY, WHO HASN'T?
© 1992 PAWS, INC. All Rights Reserved.
THESE NEW TALKING SCALES WITH THE SYMPATHY CHIPS ARE GREAT!
JIM DAVIS 7-17

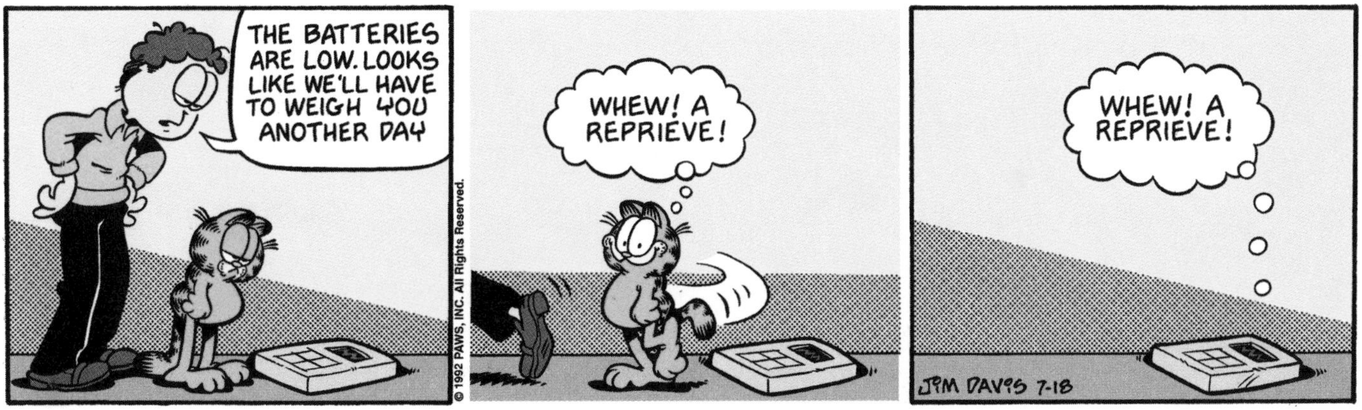
THE BATTERIES ARE LOW. LOOKS LIKE WE'LL HAVE TO WEIGH YOU ANOTHER DAY
© 1992 PAWS, INC. All Rights Reserved.
WHEW! A REPRIEVE!
WHEW! A REPRIEVE!
JIM DAVIS 7-18

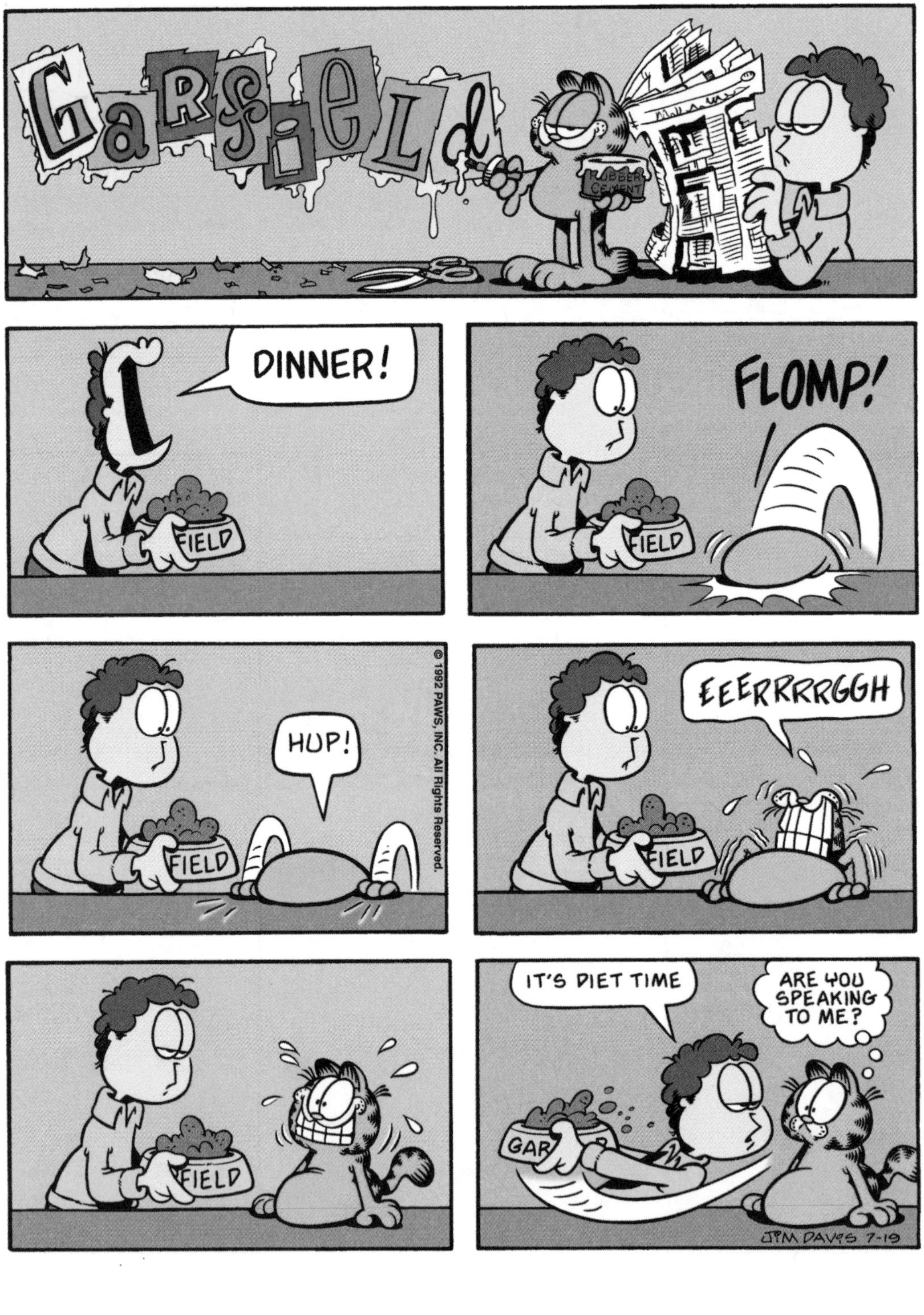
GARFIELD
RUBBER CEMENT
DINNER!
FIELD
FLOMP!
FIELD
HUP!
FIELD
© 1992 PAWS, INC. All Rights Reserved.
EEERRRRGGH
FIELD
FIELD
IT'S DIET TIME
ARE YOU SPEAKING TO ME?
GAR
JIM DAVIS 7-19

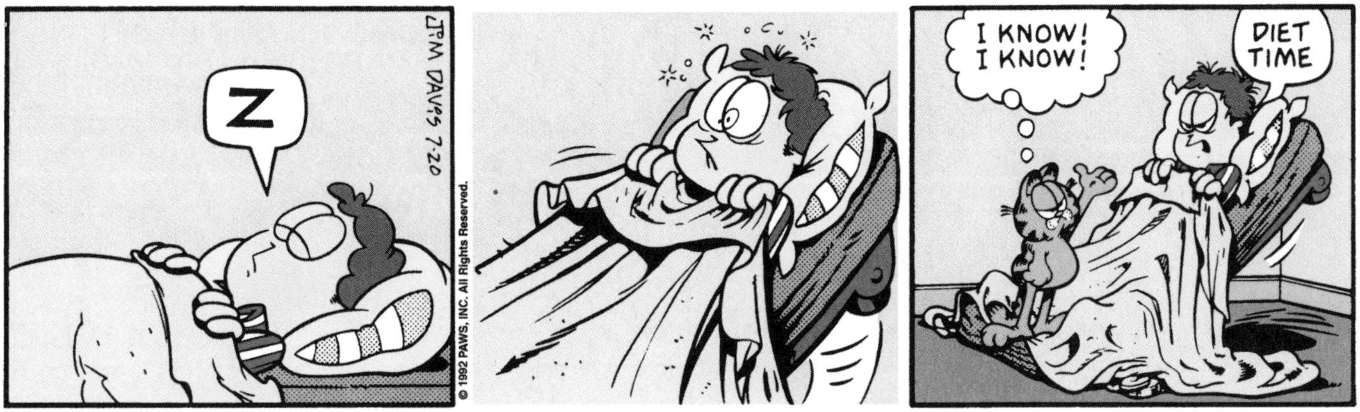
Z
JIM DAVIS 7-20
I KNOW! I KNOW!
DIET TIME

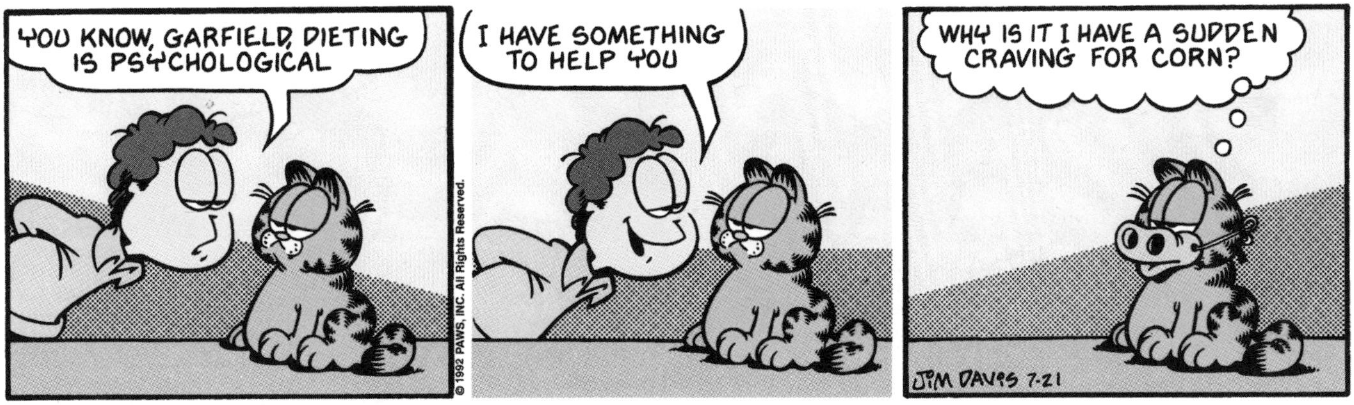
YOU KNOW, GARFIELD, DIETING IS PSYCHOLOGICAL
I HAVE SOMETHING TO HELP YOU
WHY IS IT I HAVE A SUDDEN CRAVING FOR CORN?
JIM DAVIS 7-21

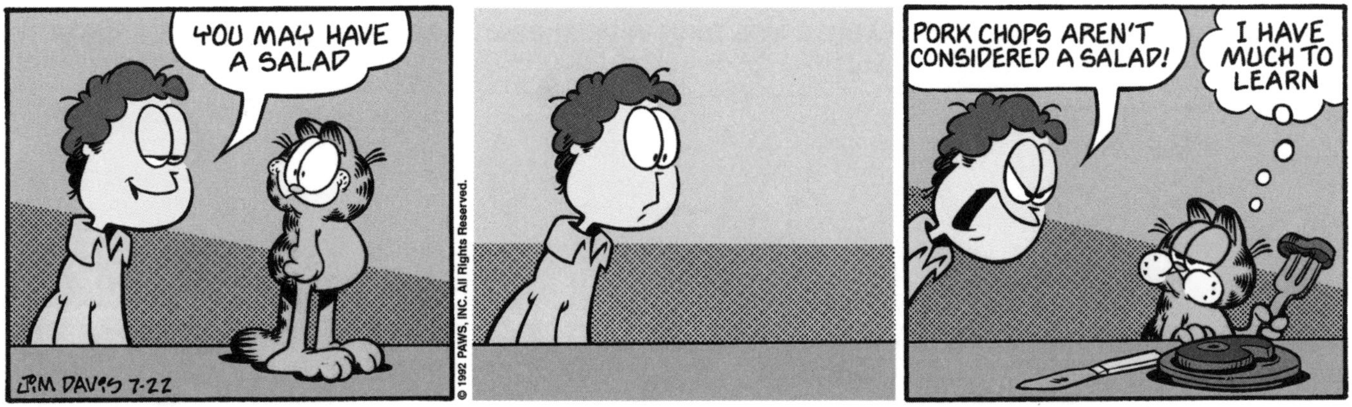
YOU MAY HAVE A SALAD
JIM DAVIS 7-22
PORK CHOPS AREN'T CONSIDERED A SALAD!
I HAVE MUCH TO LEARN

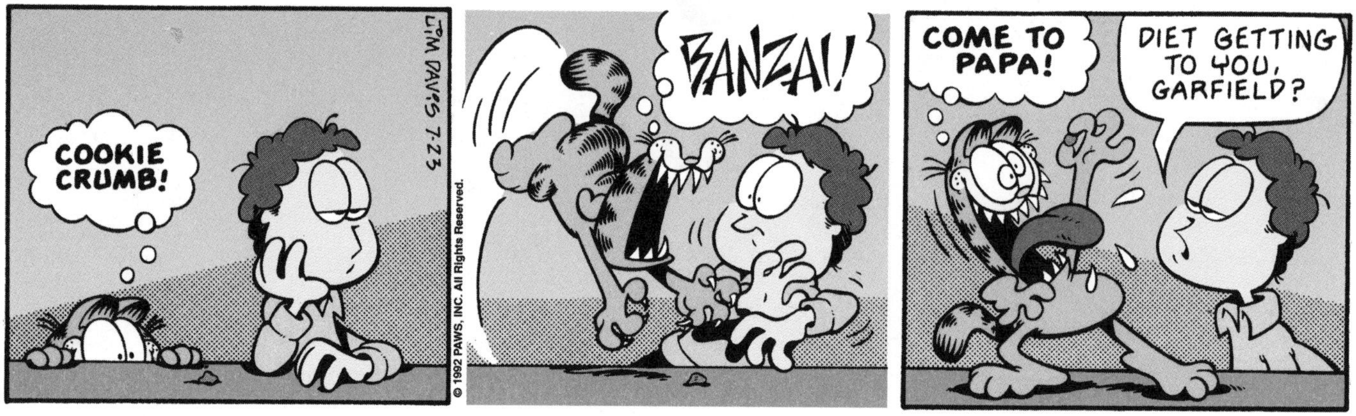
COOKIE CRUMB!
JIM DAVIS 7-23
© 1992 PAWS, INC. All Rights Reserved.
BANZAI!
COME TO PAPA!
DIET GETTING TO YOU, GARFIELD?

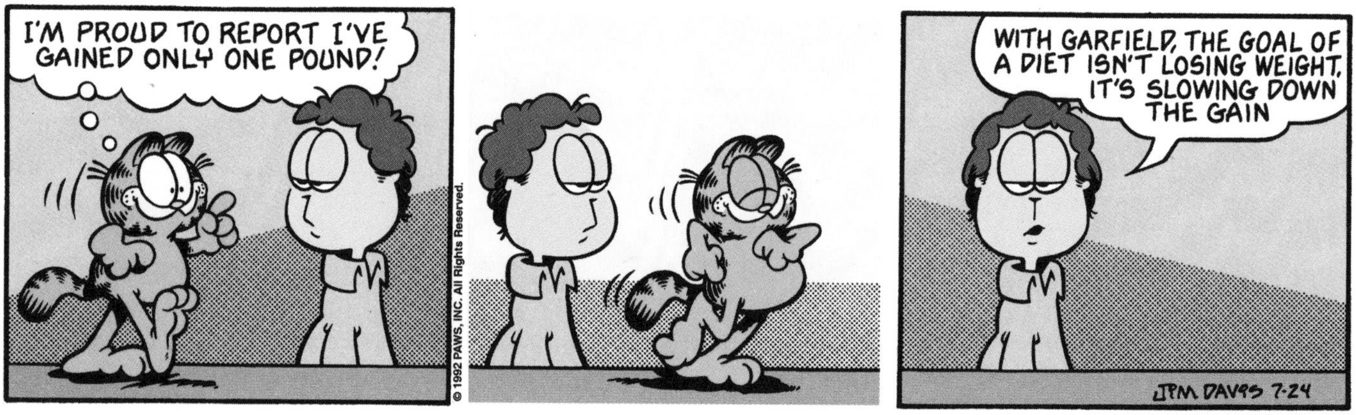
I'M PROUD TO REPORT I'VE GAINED ONLY ONE POUND!
© 1992 PAWS, INC. All Rights Reserved.
WITH GARFIELD, THE GOAL OF A DIET ISN'T LOSING WEIGHT, IT'S SLOWING DOWN THE GAIN
JIM DAVIS 7-24

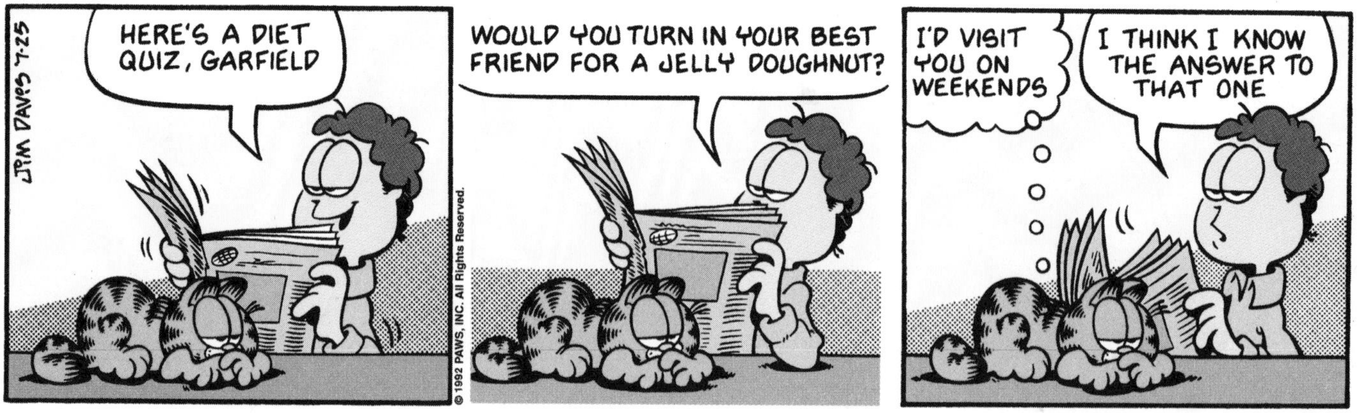
JIM DAVIS 7-25
HERE'S A DIET QUIZ, GARFIELD
© 1992 PAWS, INC. All Rights Reserved.
WOULD YOU TURN IN YOUR BEST FRIEND FOR A JELLY DOUGHNUT?
I'D VISIT YOU ON WEEKENDS
I THINK I KNOW THE ANSWER TO THAT ONE

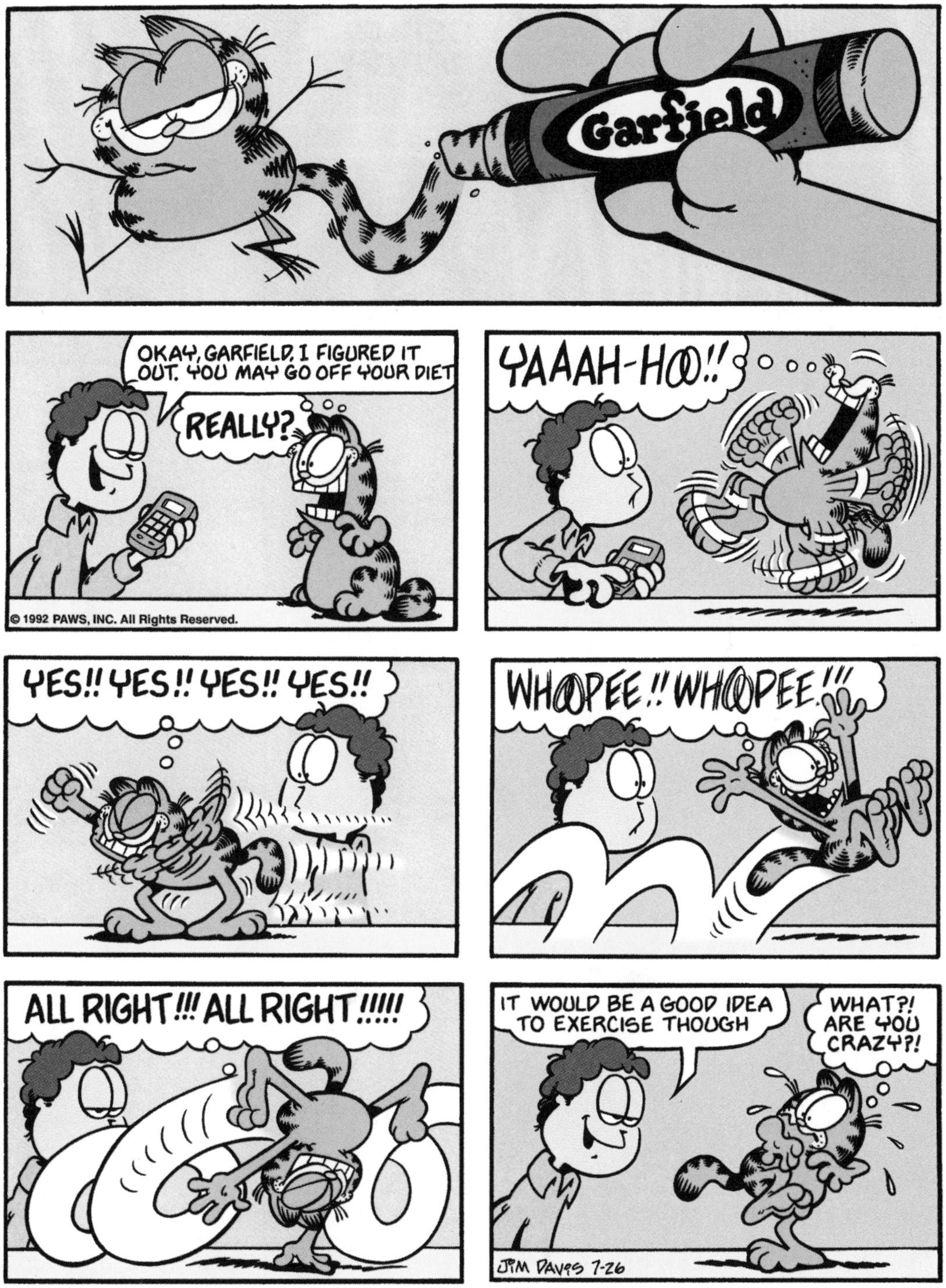
Garfield
OKAY, GARFIELD. I FIGURED IT OUT. YOU MAY GO OFF YOUR DIET
REALLY?
© 1992 PAWS, INC. All Rights Reserved.
YAAAH-HOO!!
YES!! YES!! YES!! YES!!
WHOOPEE!! WHOOPEE!!
ALL RIGHT!!! ALL RIGHT!!!!!
IT WOULD BE A GOOD IDEA TO EXERCISE THOUGH
WHAT?! ARE YOU CRAZY?!
JIM DAVIS 7-26

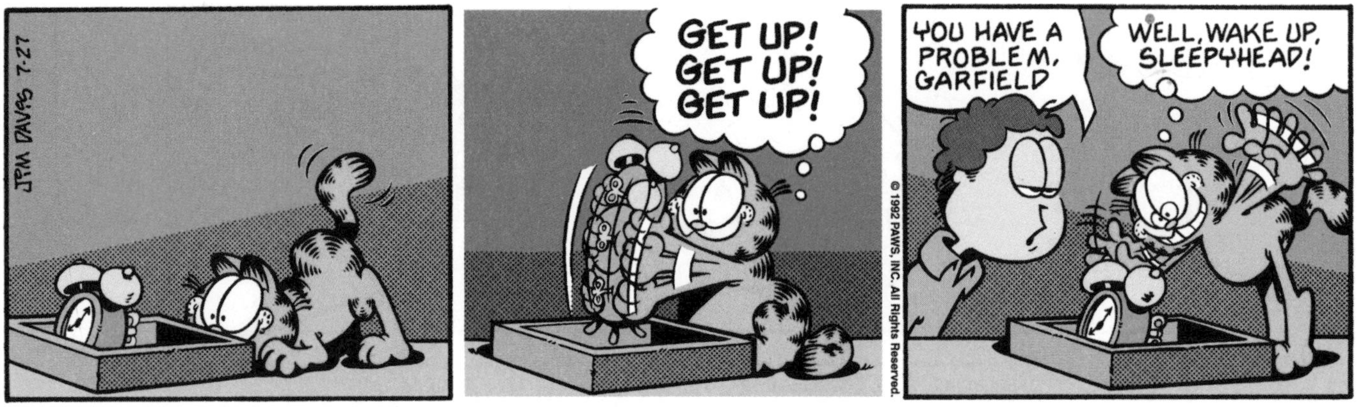
JPM DAVPS 7-27
GET UP! GET UP! GET UP!
© 1992 PAWS, INC. All Rights Reserved.
YOU HAVE A PROBLEM, GARFIELD
WELL, WAKE UP, SLEEPYHEAD!

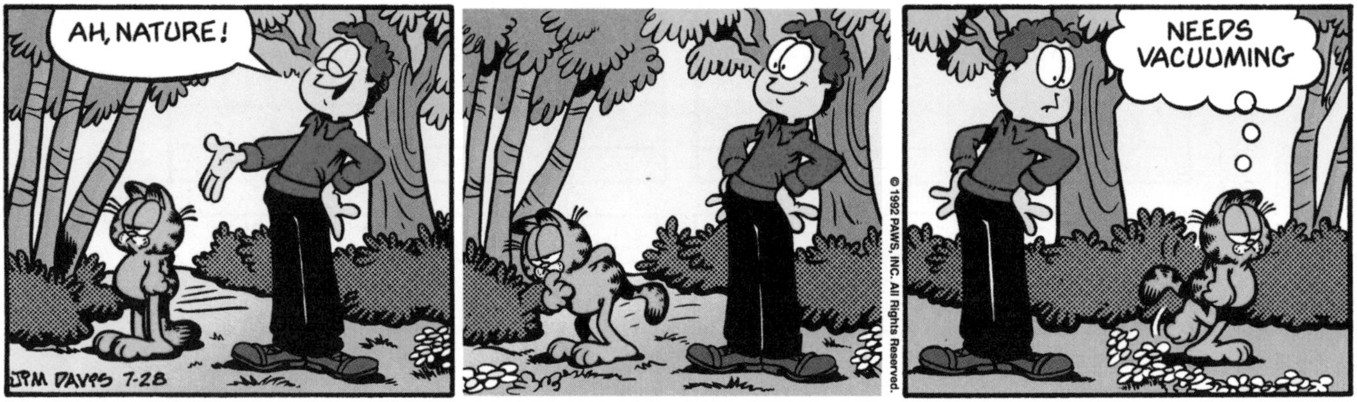
AH, NATURE!
JPM DAVPS 7-28
© 1992 PAWS, INC. All Rights Reserved.
NEEDS VACUUMING

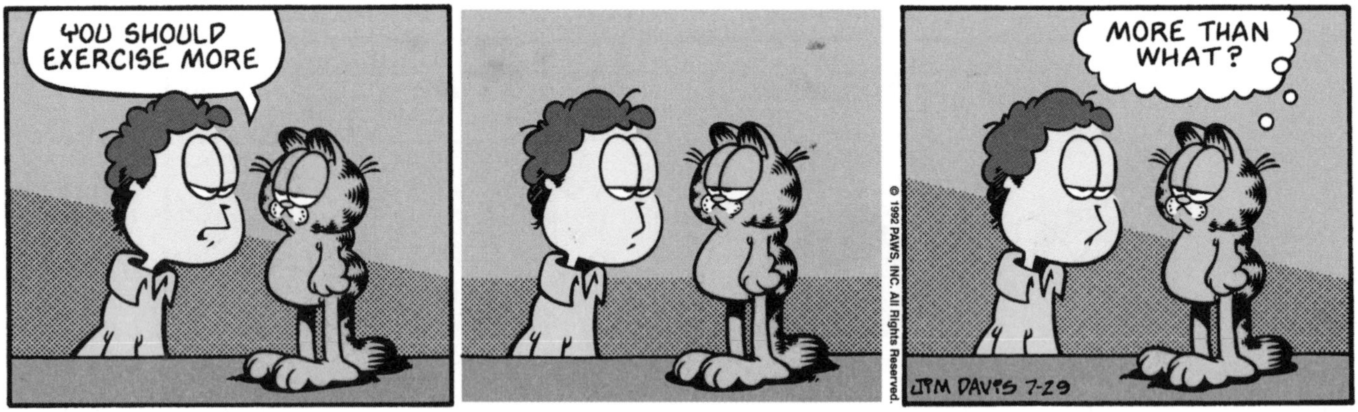
YOU SHOULD EXERCISE MORE
© 1992 PAWS, INC. All Rights Reserved.
MORE THAN WHAT?
JPM DAVPS 7-29

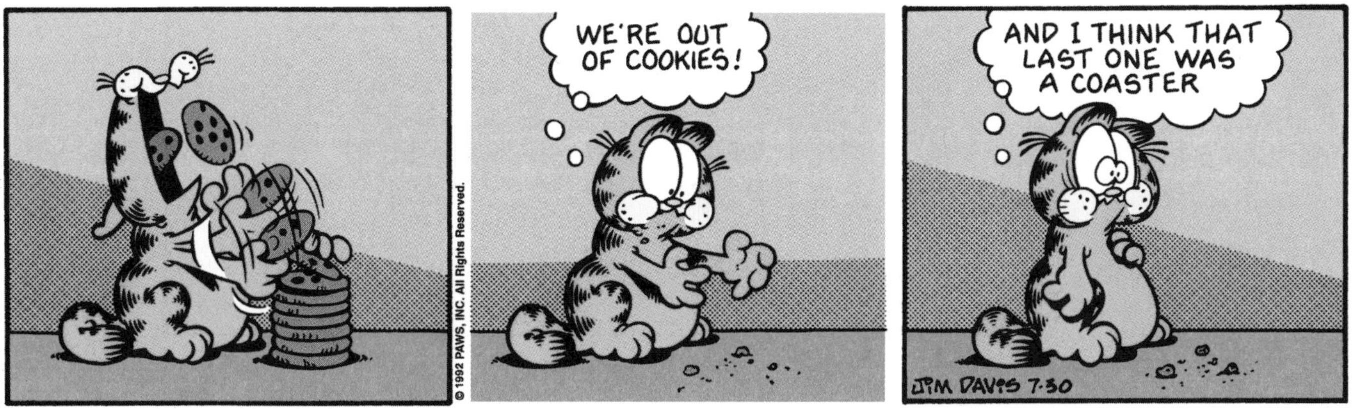
© 1992 PAWS, INC. All Rights Reserved.
WE'RE OUT OF COOKIES!
AND I THINK THAT LAST ONE WAS A COASTER
JIM DAVIS 7-30

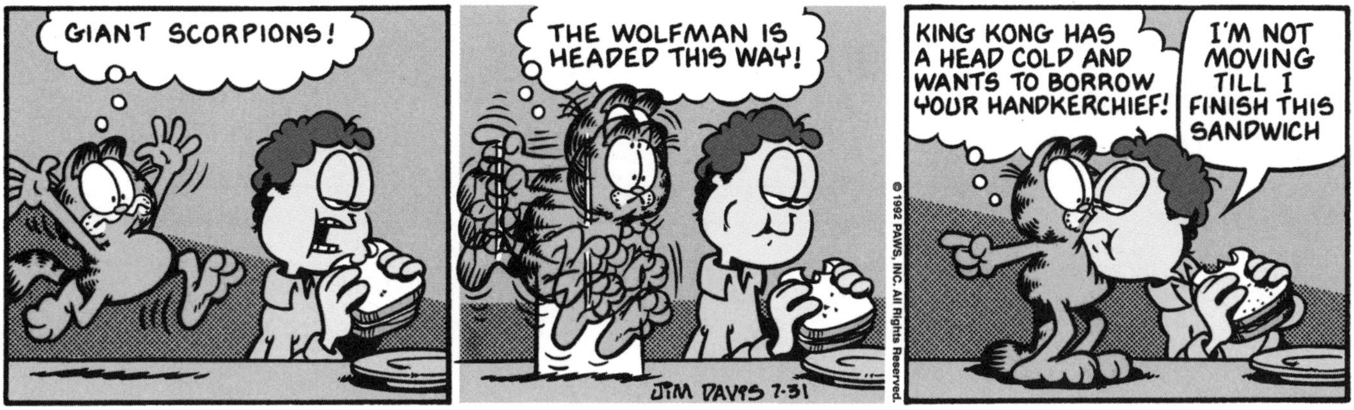
GIANT SCORPIONS!
THE WOLFMAN IS HEADED THIS WAY!
JIM DAVIS 7-31
© 1992 PAWS, INC. All Rights Reserved.
KING KONG HAS A HEAD COLD AND WANTS TO BORROW YOUR HANDKERCHIEF!
I'M NOT MOVING TILL I FINISH THIS SANDWICH

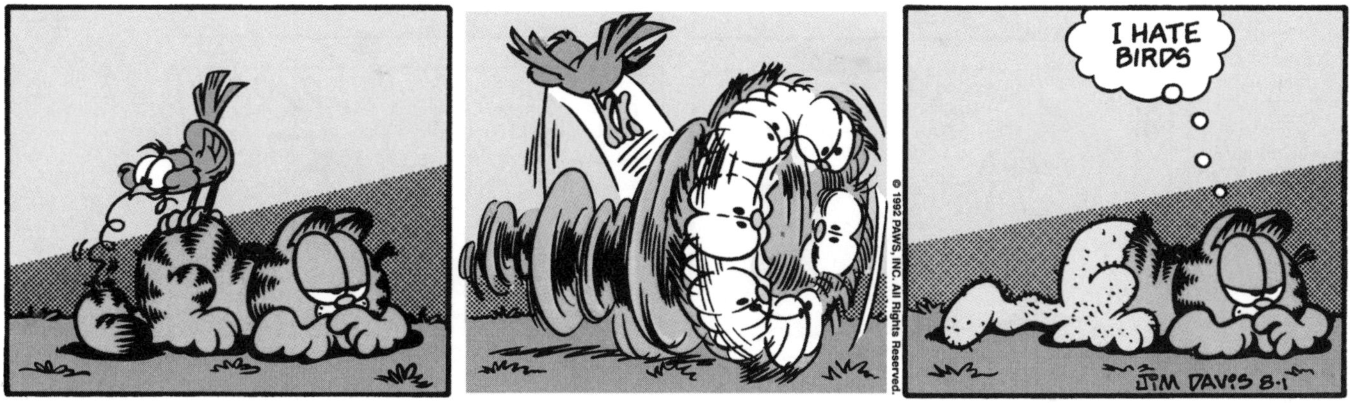
© 1992 PAWS, INC. All Rights Reserved.
I HATE BIRDS
JIM DAVIS 8-1

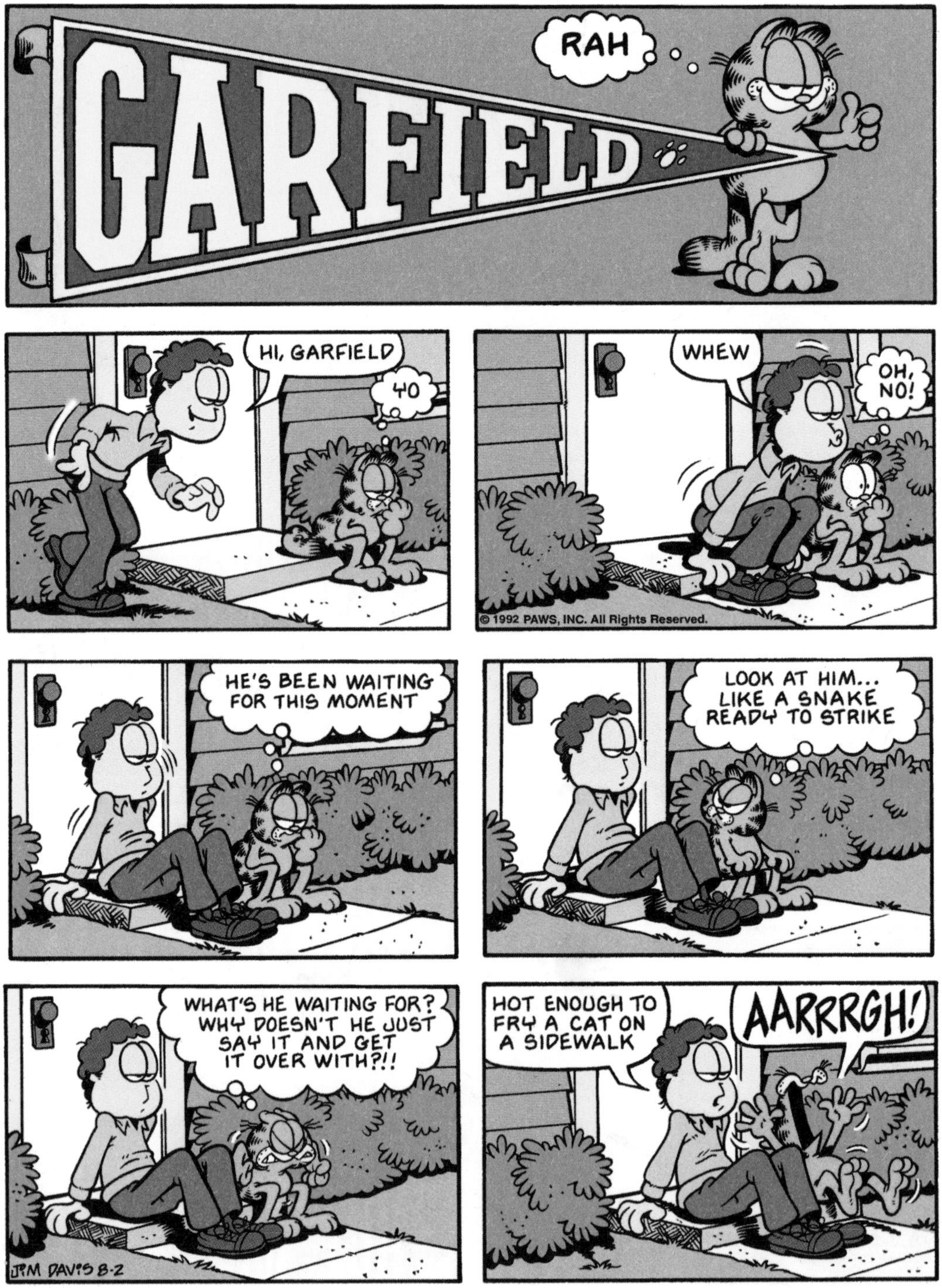
GARFIELD
RAH
HI, GARFIELD
40
WHEW
OH, NO!
© 1992 PAWS, INC. All Rights Reserved.
HE'S BEEN WAITING FOR THIS MOMENT
LOOK AT HIM... LIKE A SNAKE READY TO STRIKE
WHAT'S HE WAITING FOR? WHY DOESN'T HE JUST SAY IT AND GET IT OVER WITH?!!
JIM DAVIS 8-2
HOT ENOUGH TO FRY A CAT ON A SIDEWALK
AARRRGH!

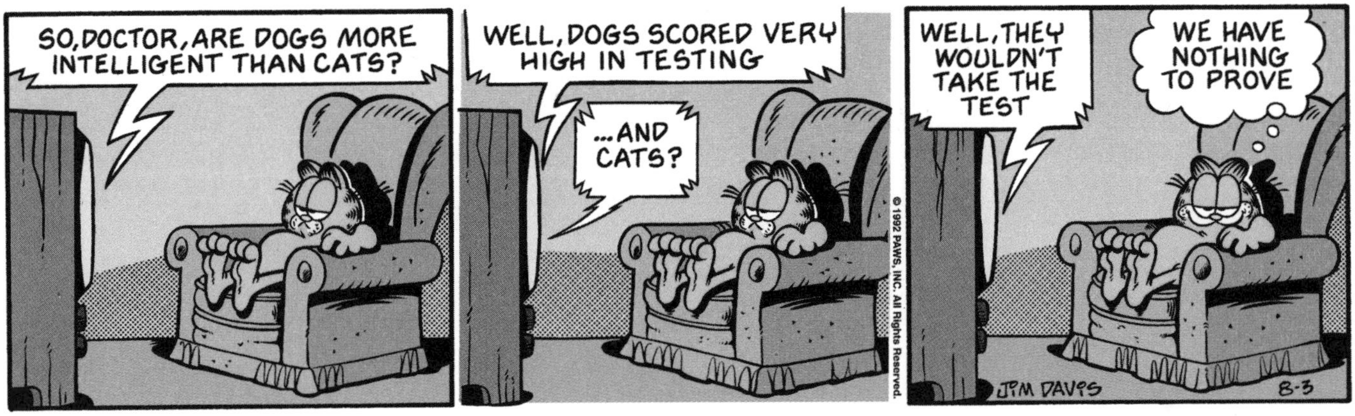
SO, DOCTOR, ARE DOGS MORE INTELLIGENT THAN CATS?
WELL, DOGS SCORED VERY HIGH IN TESTING
...AND CATS?
WELL, THEY WOULDN'T TAKE THE TEST
WE HAVE NOTHING TO PROVE
© 1992 PAWS, INC. All Rights Reserved.
JIM DAVIS 8-3

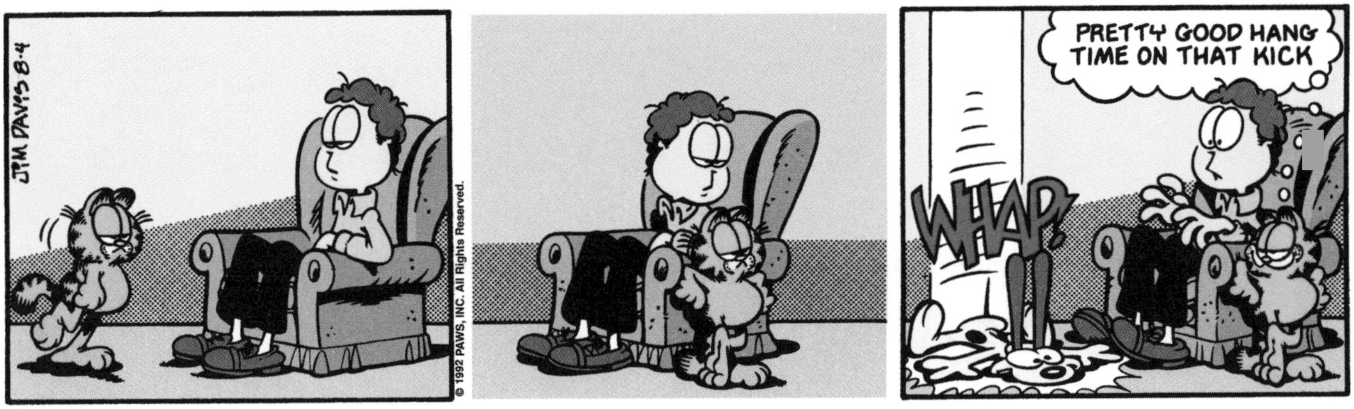
JIM DAVIS 8-4
© 1992 PAWS, INC. All Rights Reserved.
WHAP!
PRETTY GOOD HANG TIME ON THAT KICK

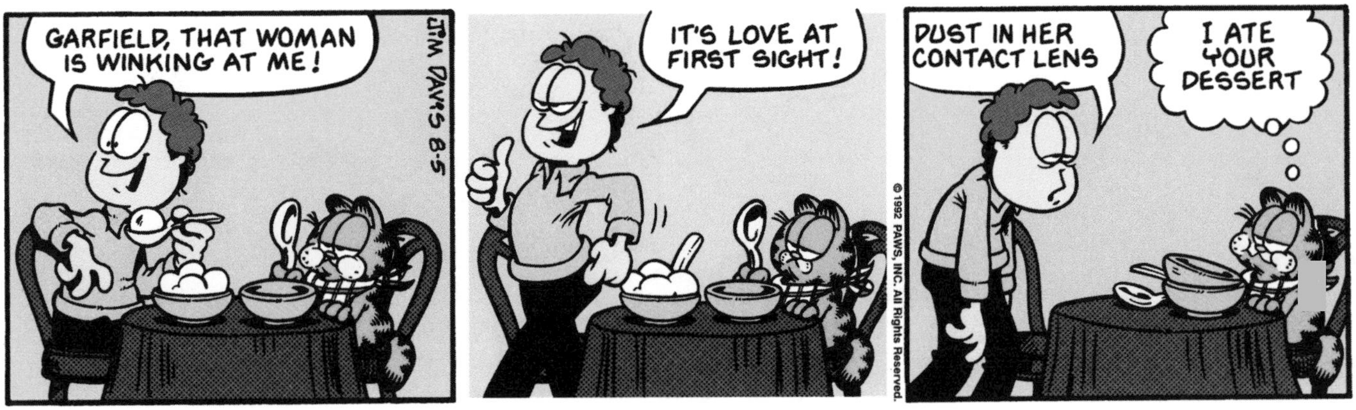
GARFIELD, THAT WOMAN IS WINKING AT ME!
JIM DAVIS 8-5
IT'S LOVE AT FIRST SIGHT!
© 1992 PAWS, INC. All Rights Reserved.
DUST IN HER CONTACT LENS
I ATE YOUR DESSERT

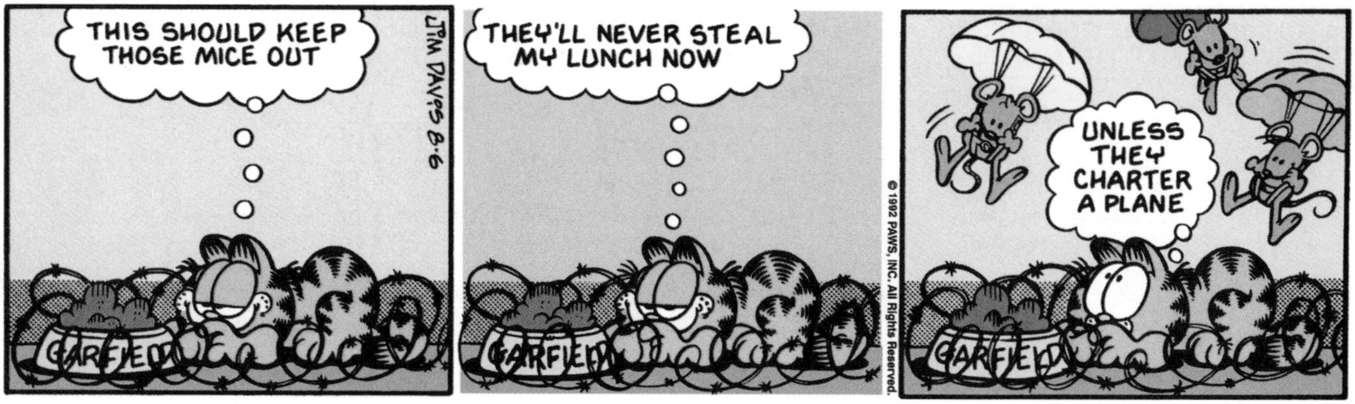
THIS SHOULD KEEP THOSE MICE OUT
JIM DAVIS 8-6
THEY'LL NEVER STEAL MY LUNCH NOW
© 1992 PAWS, INC. All Rights Reserved.
UNLESS THEY CHARTER A PLANE
GARFIELD

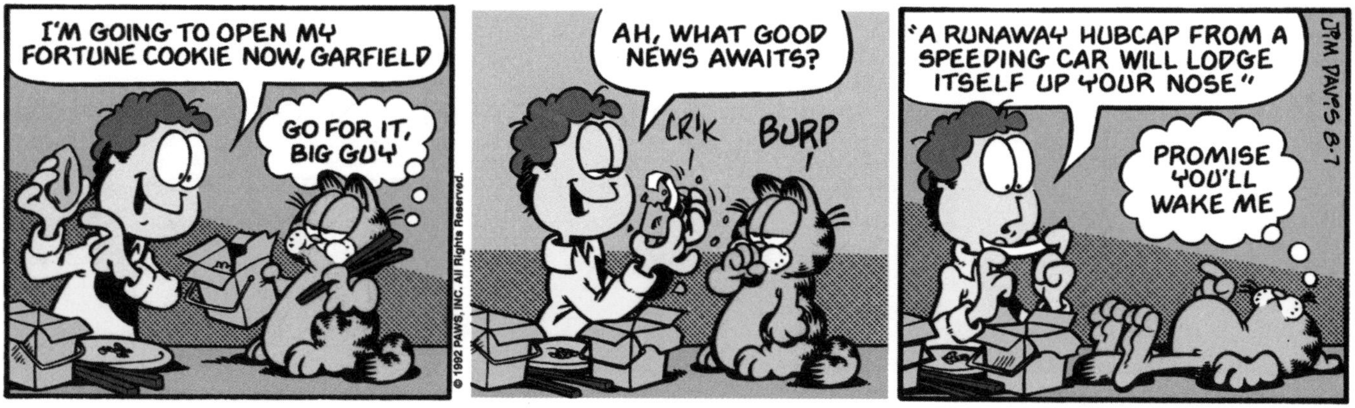
I'M GOING TO OPEN MY FORTUNE COOKIE NOW, GARFIELD
GO FOR IT, BIG GUY
© 1992 PAWS, INC. All Rights Reserved.
AH, WHAT GOOD NEWS AWAITS?
CR'K
BURP
"A RUNAWAY HUBCAP FROM A SPEEDING CAR WILL LODGE ITSELF UP YOUR NOSE"
PROMISE YOU'LL WAKE ME
JIM DAVIS 8-7

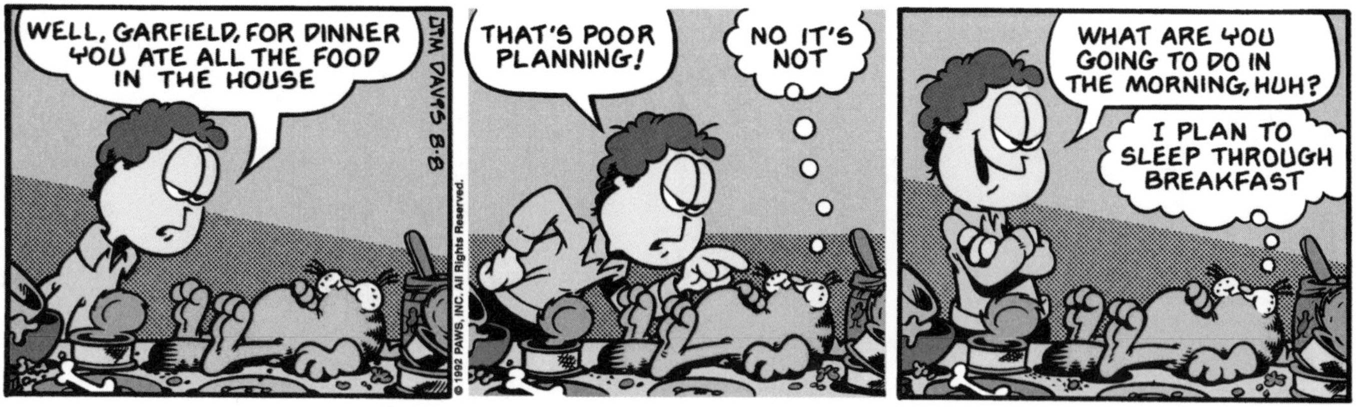
WELL, GARFIELD, FOR DINNER YOU ATE ALL THE FOOD IN THE HOUSE
JIM DAVIS 8-8
© 1992 PAWS, INC. All Rights Reserved.
THAT'S POOR PLANNING!
NO IT'S NOT
WHAT ARE YOU GOING TO DO IN THE MORNING, HUH?
I PLAN TO SLEEP THROUGH BREAKFAST

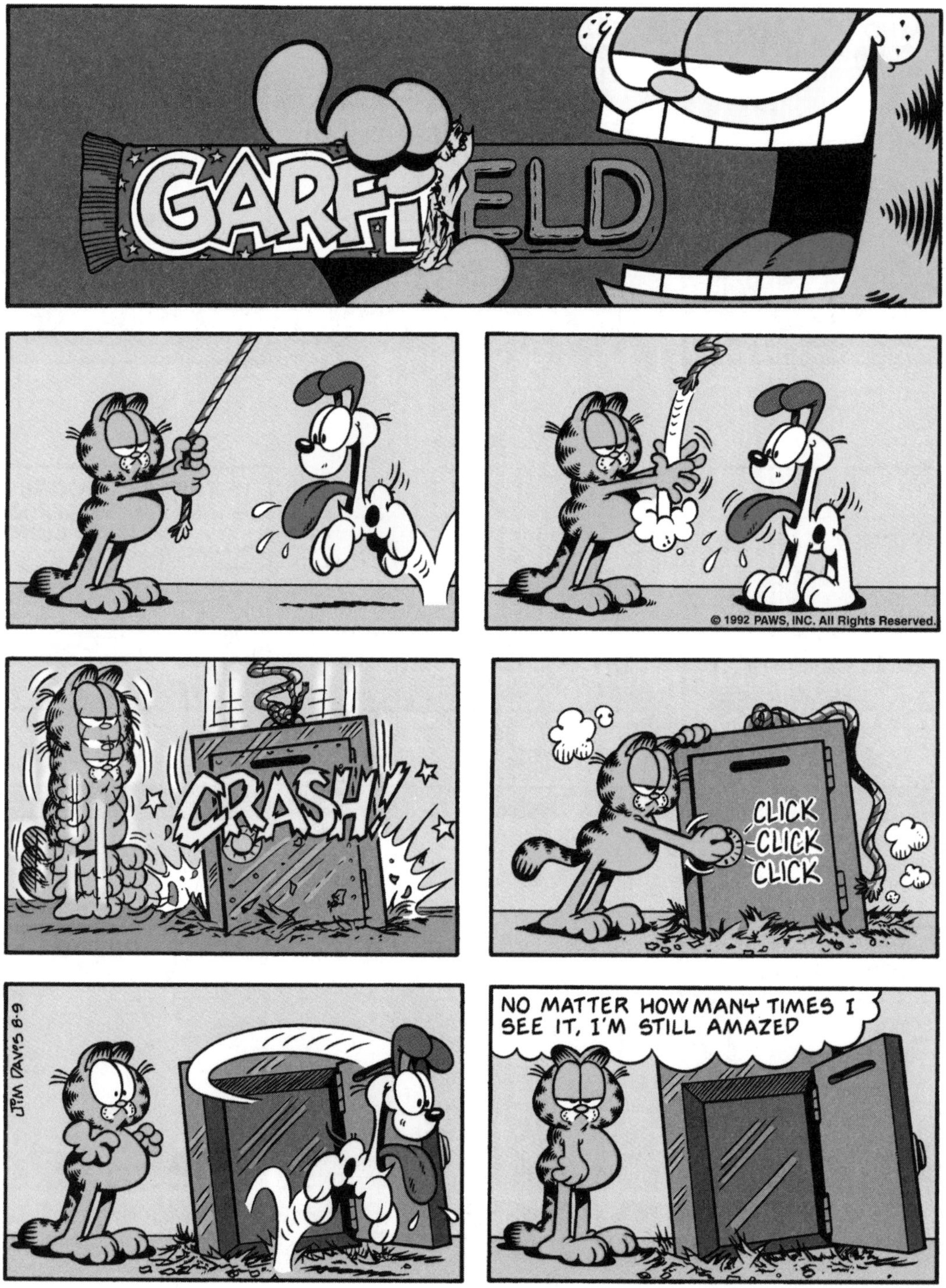
GARFIELD
© 1992 PAWS, INC. All Rights Reserved.
CRASH!
CLICK
CLICK
CLICK
JIM DAVIS 8-9
NO MATTER HOW MANY TIMES I SEE IT, I'M STILL AMAZED

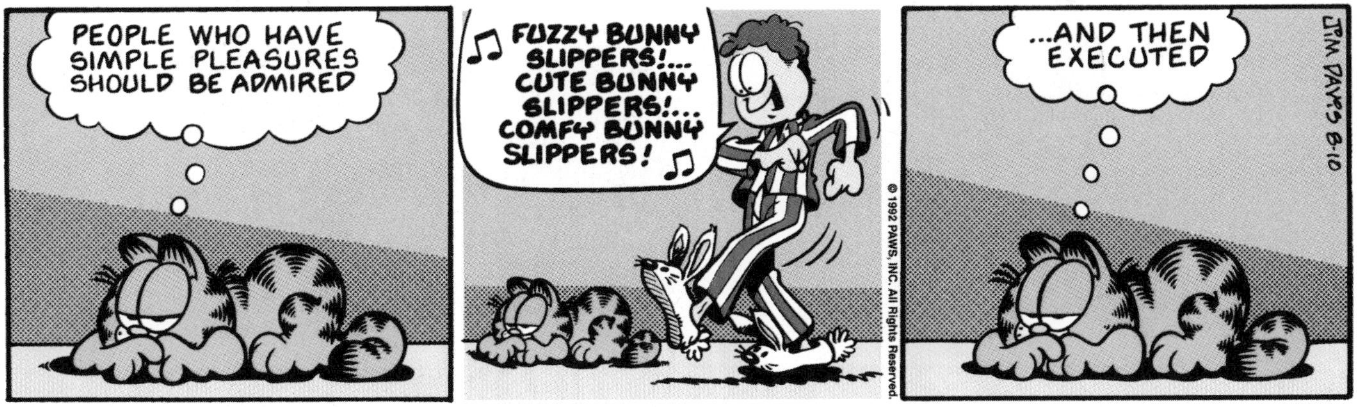
PEOPLE WHO HAVE SIMPLE PLEASURES SHOULD BE ADMIRED
FUZZY BUNNY SLIPPERS!... CUTE BUNNY SLIPPERS!... COMFY BUNNY SLIPPERS!
© 1992 PAWS, INC. All Rights Reserved.
...AND THEN EXECUTED
JIM DAVIS 8-10

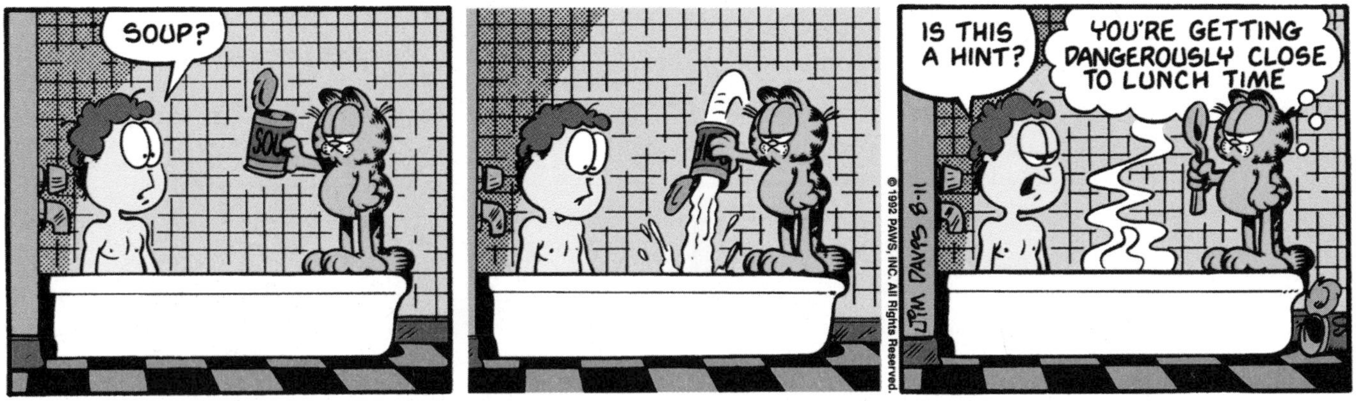
SOUP?
© 1992 PAWS, INC. All Rights Reserved.
JIM DAVIS 8-11
IS THIS A HINT?
YOU'RE GETTING DANGEROUSLY CLOSE TO LUNCH TIME

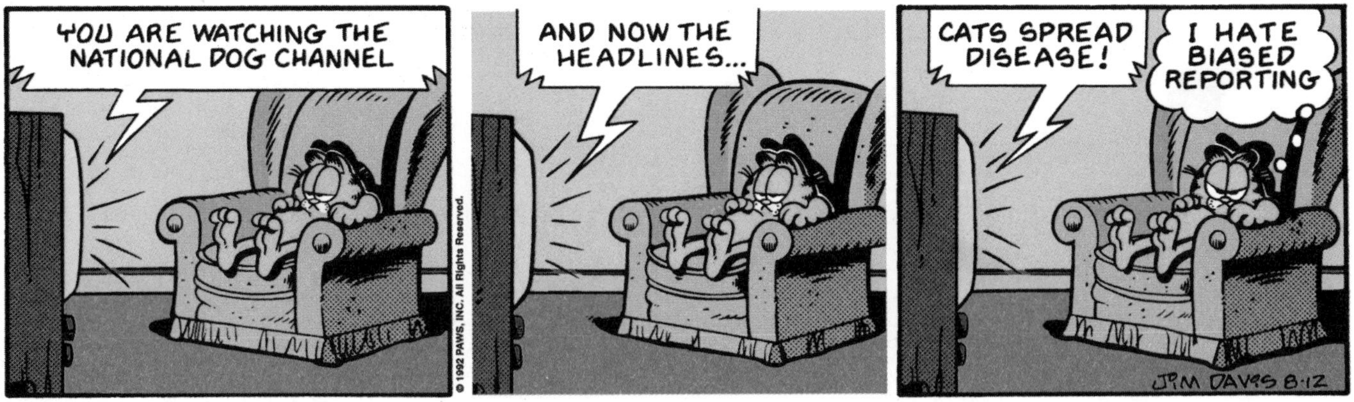
YOU ARE WATCHING THE NATIONAL DOG CHANNEL
© 1992 PAWS, INC. All Rights Reserved.
AND NOW THE HEADLINES...
CATS SPREAD DISEASE!
I HATE BIASED REPORTING
JIM DAVIS 8-12

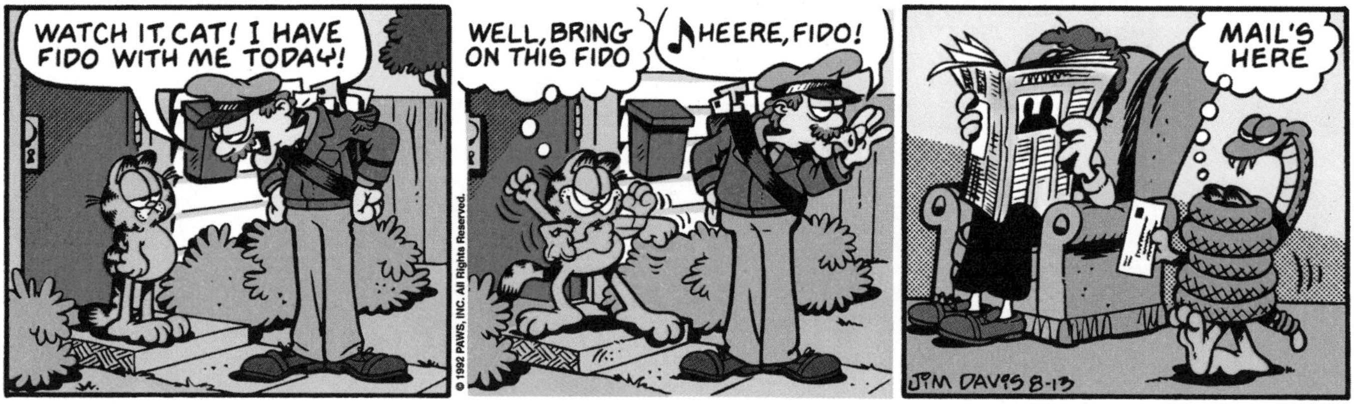
WATCH IT, CAT! I HAVE FIDO WITH ME TODAY!
WELL, BRING ON THIS FIDO
♪HEERE, FIDO!
© 1992 PAWS, INC. All Rights Reserved.
MAIL'S HERE
JIM DAVIS 8-13

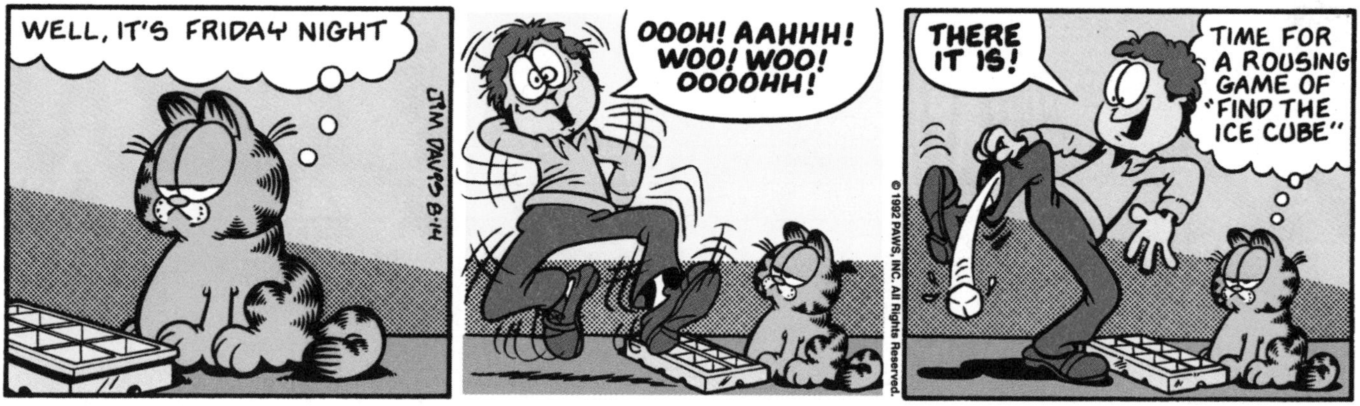
WELL, IT'S FRIDAY NIGHT
JIM DAVIS 8-14
OOOH! AAHHH! WOO! WOO! OOOOHH!
© 1992 PAWS, INC. All Rights Reserved.
THERE IT IS!
TIME FOR A ROUSING GAME OF "FIND THE ICE CUBE"

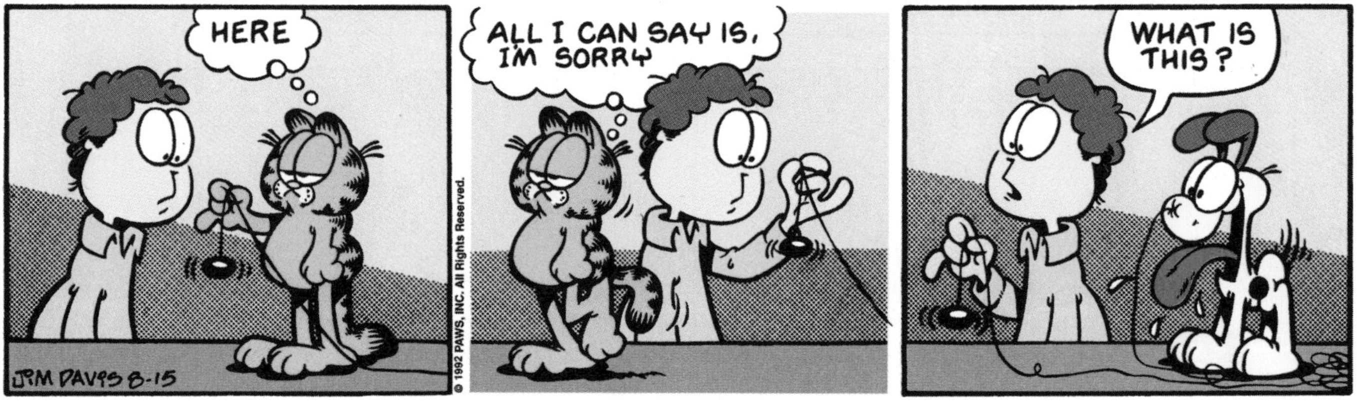
HERE
JIM DAVIS 8-15
© 1992 PAWS, INC. All Rights Reserved.
ALL I CAN SAY IS, I'M SORRY
WHAT IS THIS?

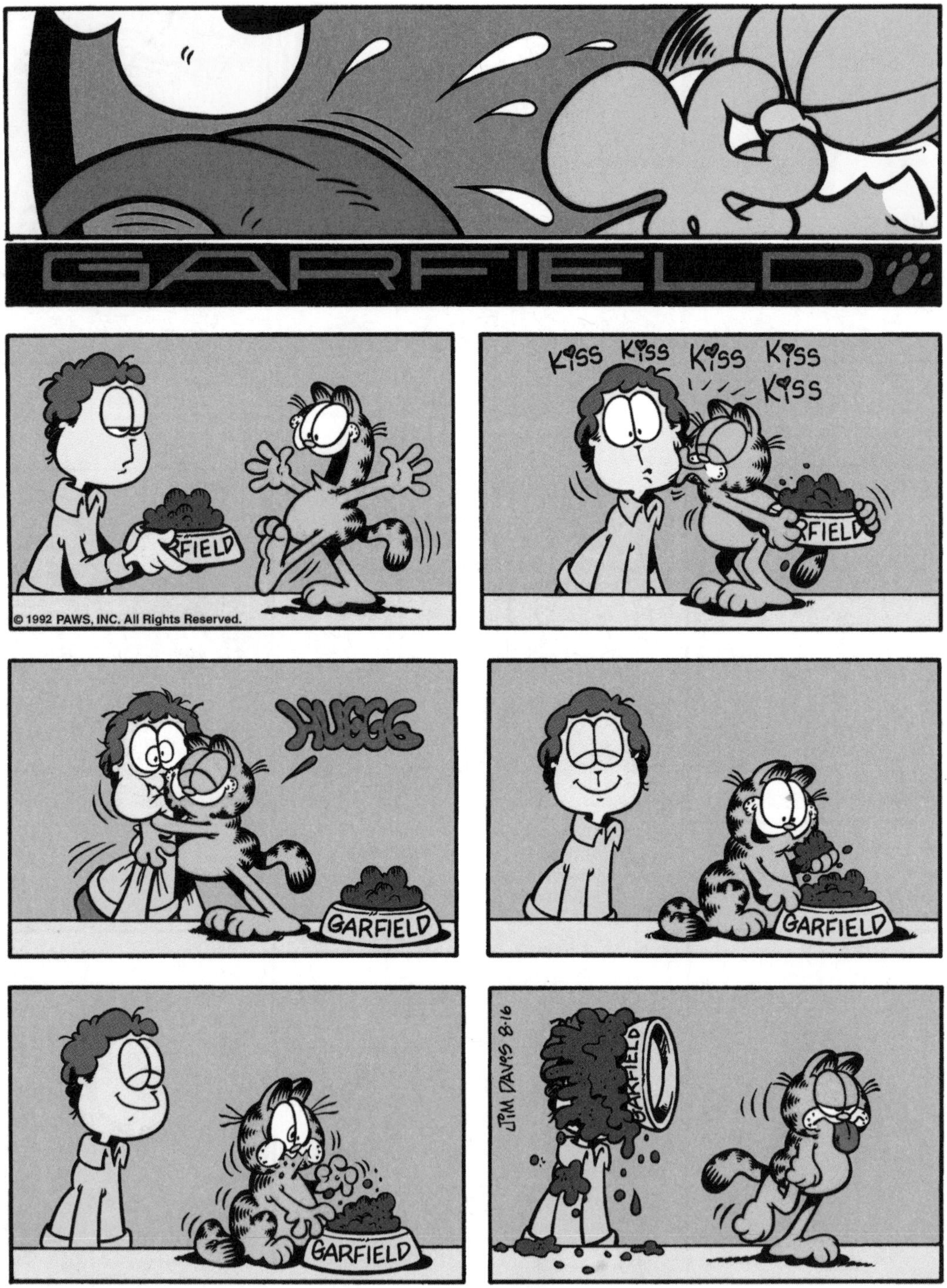
GARFIELD
© 1992 PAWS, INC. All Rights Reserved.
FIELD
KISS KISS KISS KISS
KISS
FIELD
HUGGG
GARFIELD
GARFIELD
GARFIELD
JIM DAVIS 8·16
GARFIELD

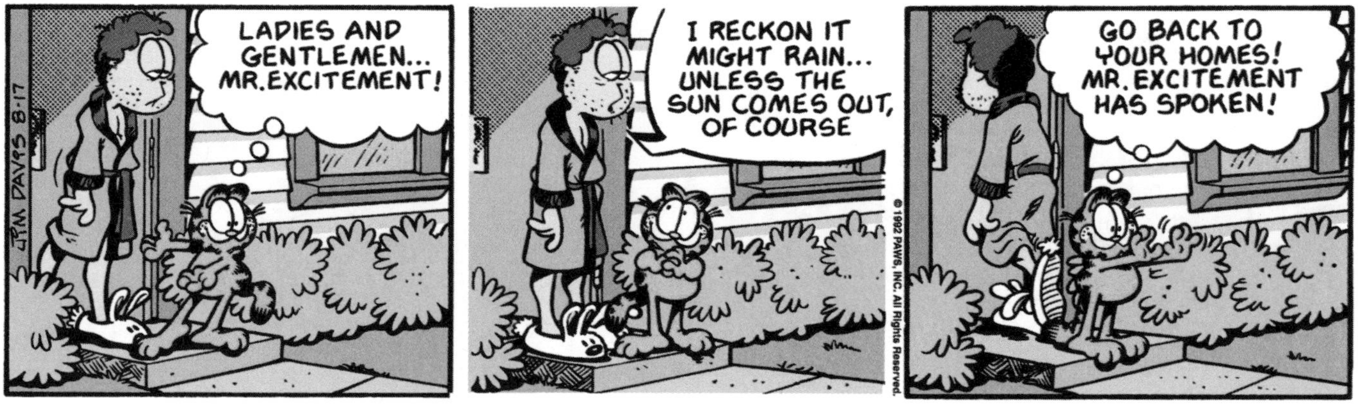
JIM DAVIS 8-17
LADIES AND GENTLEMEN... MR. EXCITEMENT!
I RECKON IT MIGHT RAIN... UNLESS THE SUN COMES OUT, OF COURSE
© 1992 PAWS, INC. All Rights Reserved.
GO BACK TO YOUR HOMES! MR. EXCITEMENT HAS SPOKEN!

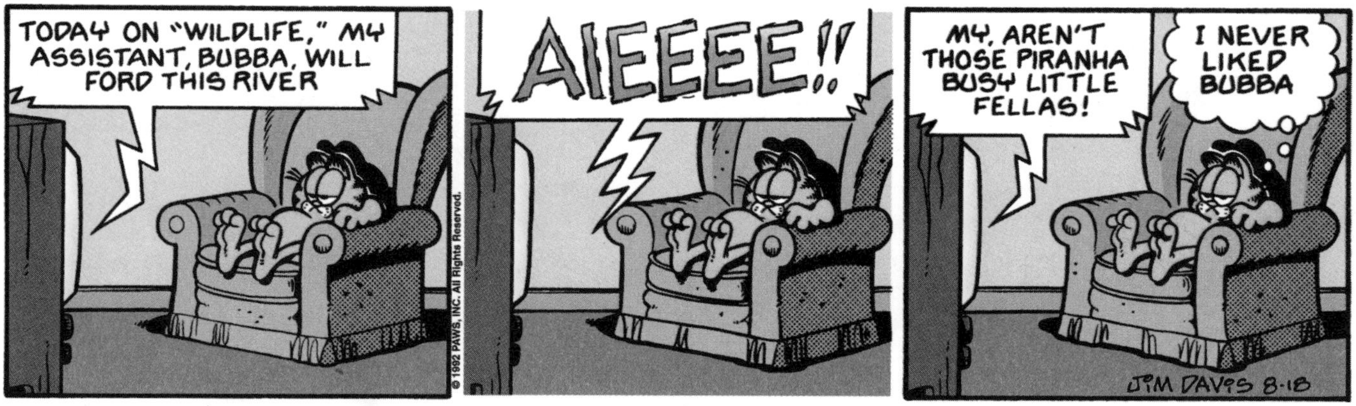
TODAY ON "WILDLIFE," MY ASSISTANT, BUBBA, WILL FORD THIS RIVER
© 1992 PAWS, INC. All Rights Reserved.
AIEEEEE!!
MY, AREN'T THOSE PIRANHA BUSY LITTLE FELLAS!
I NEVER LIKED BUBBA
JIM DAVIS 8-18

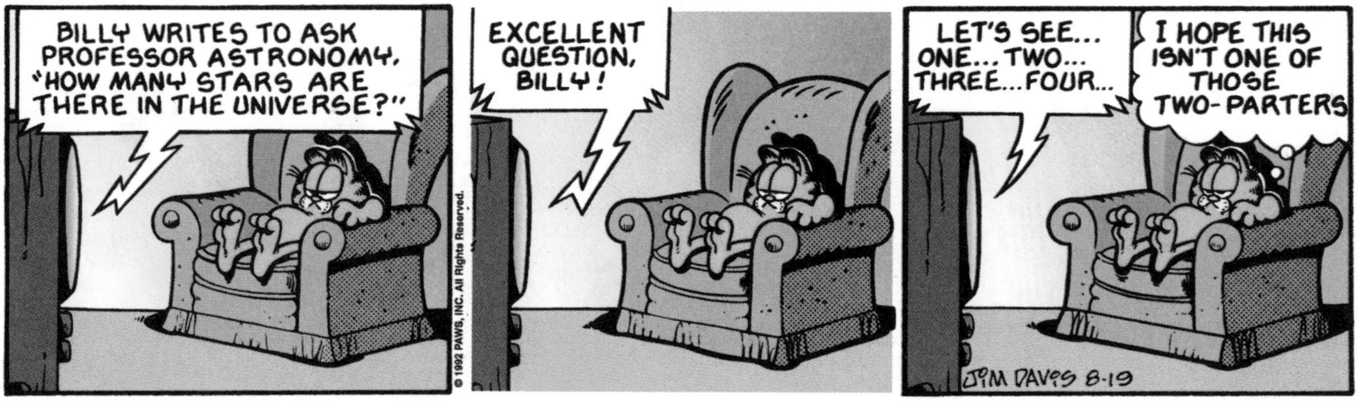
BILLY WRITES TO ASK PROFESSOR ASTRONOMY, "HOW MANY STARS ARE THERE IN THE UNIVERSE?"
© 1992 PAWS, INC. All Rights Reserved.
EXCELLENT QUESTION, BILLY!
LET'S SEE... ONE... TWO... THREE... FOUR...
I HOPE THIS ISN'T ONE OF THOSE TWO-PARTERS
JIM DAVIS 8-19

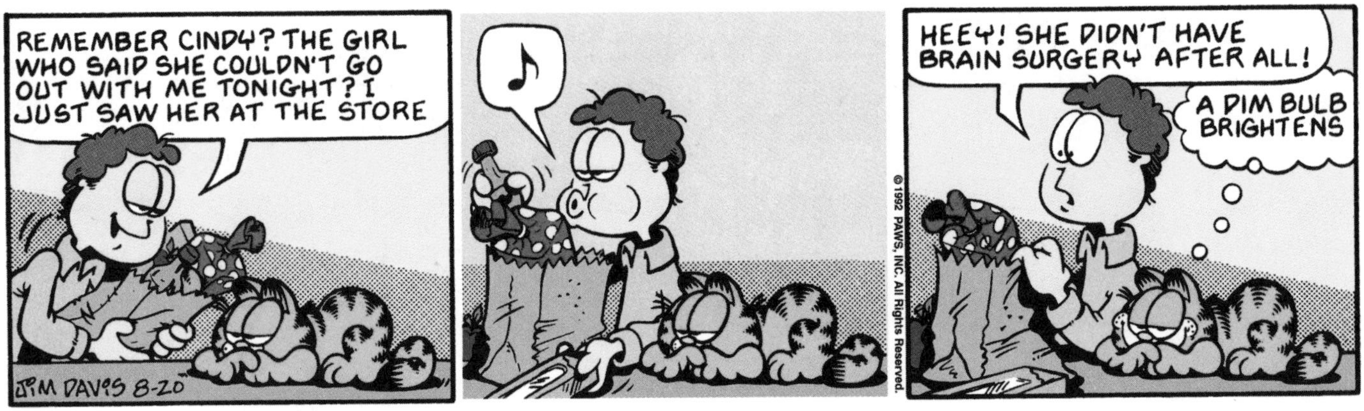
REMEMBER CINDY? THE GIRL WHO SAID SHE COULDN'T GO OUT WITH ME TONIGHT? I JUST SAW HER AT THE STORE
♪
HEEY! SHE DIDN'T HAVE BRAIN SURGERY AFTER ALL!
A DIM BULB BRIGHTENS
JIM DAVIS 8-20
© 1992 PAWS, INC. All Rights Reserved.

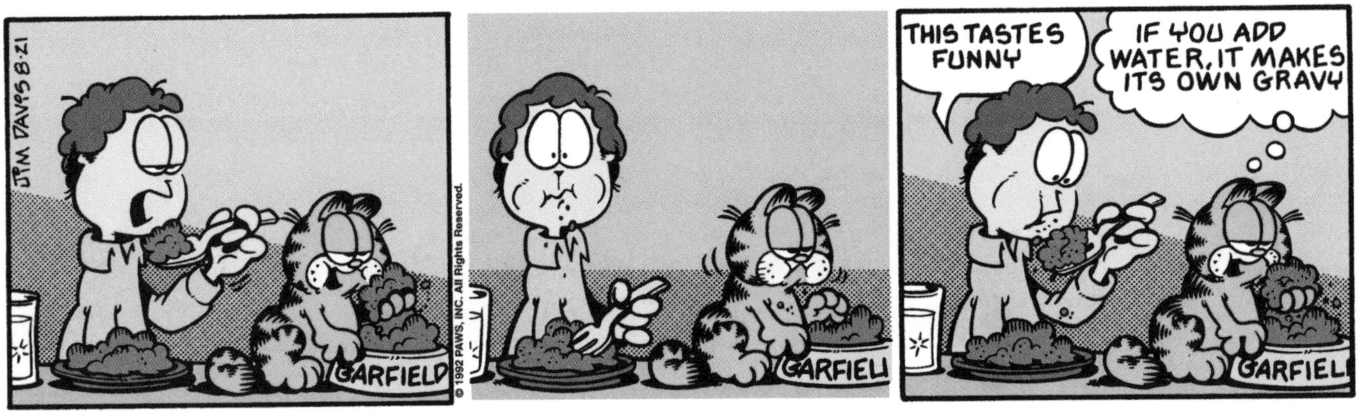
JIM DAVIS 8-21
GARFIELD
© 1992 PAWS, INC. All Rights Reserved.
THIS TASTES FUNNY
IF YOU ADD WATER, IT MAKES ITS OWN GRAVY

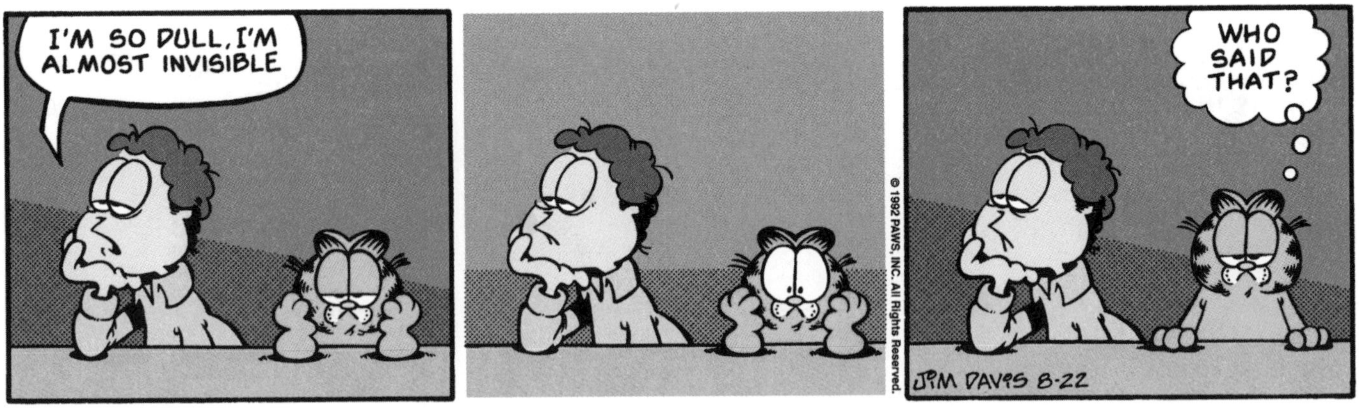
I'M SO DULL, I'M ALMOST INVISIBLE
© 1992 PAWS, INC. All Rights Reserved.
WHO SAID THAT?
JIM DAVIS 8-22

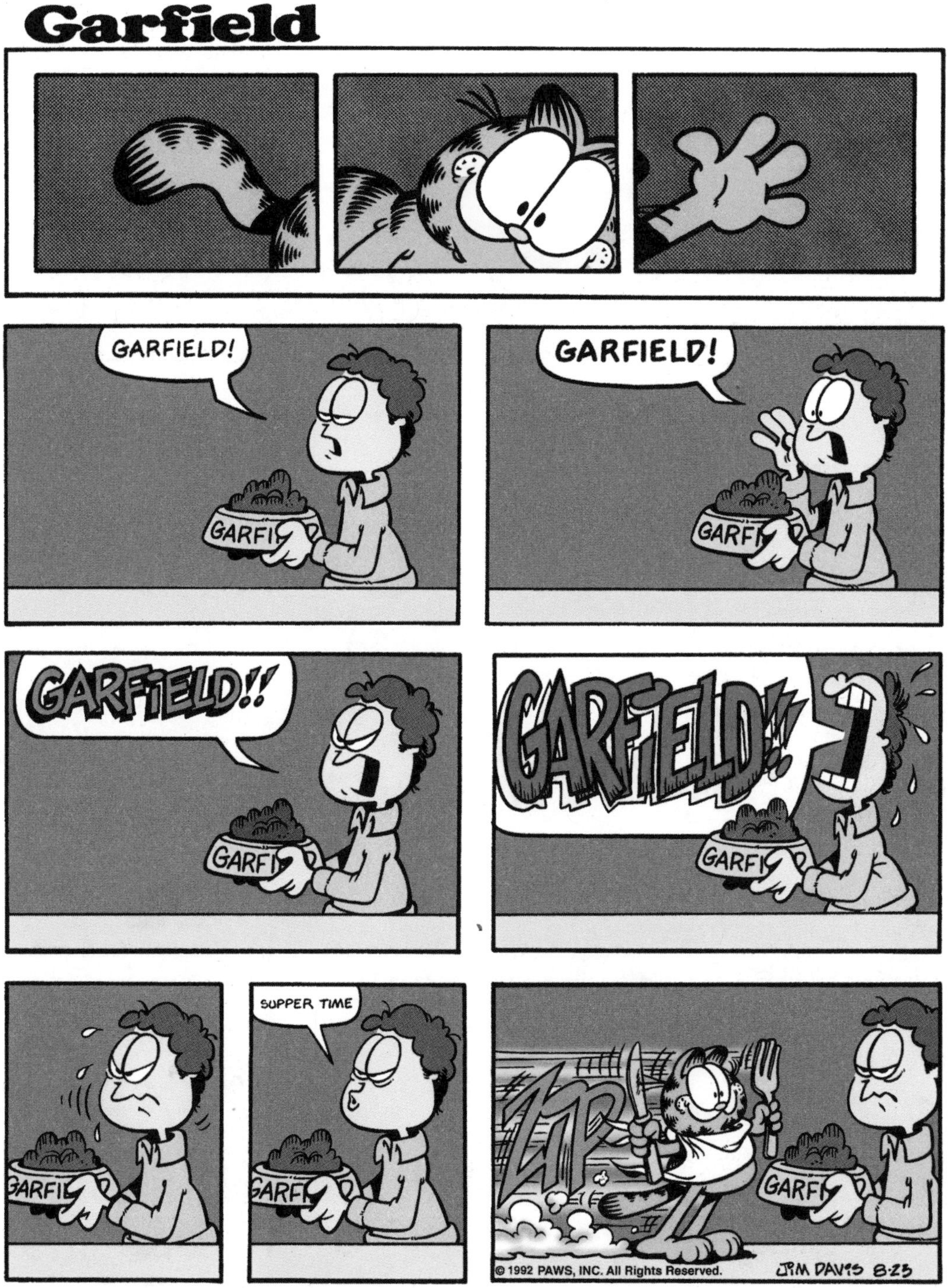
Garfield
GARFIELD!
GARFIELD!
GARFIELD!!
GARFIELD!!
SUPPER TIME
ZIP
GARFI
© 1992 PAWS, INC. All Rights Reserved.
JIM DAVIS 8-23

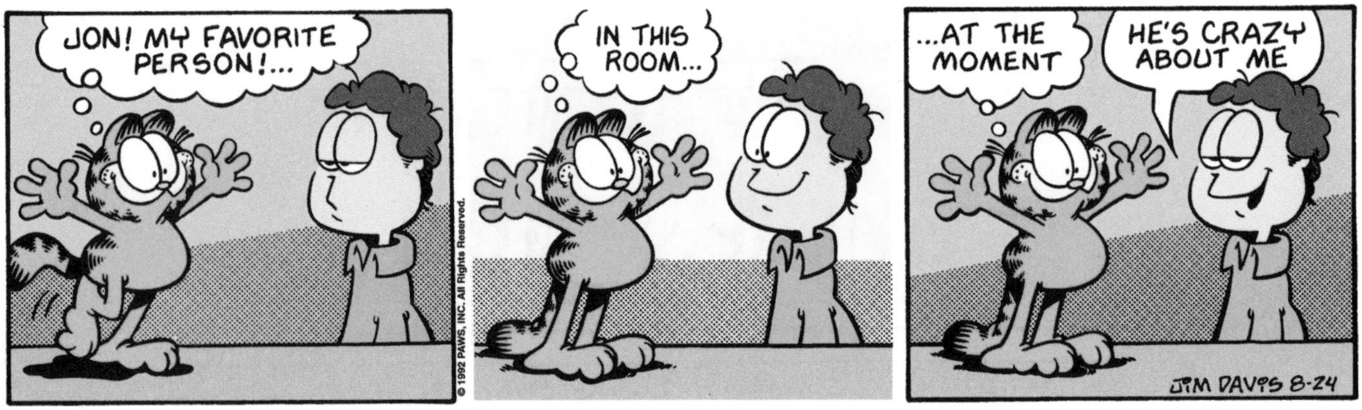
JON! MY FAVORITE PERSON!...
IN THIS ROOM...
...AT THE MOMENT
HE'S CRAZY ABOUT ME
© 1992 PAWS, INC. All Rights Reserved.
JIM DAVIS 8-24

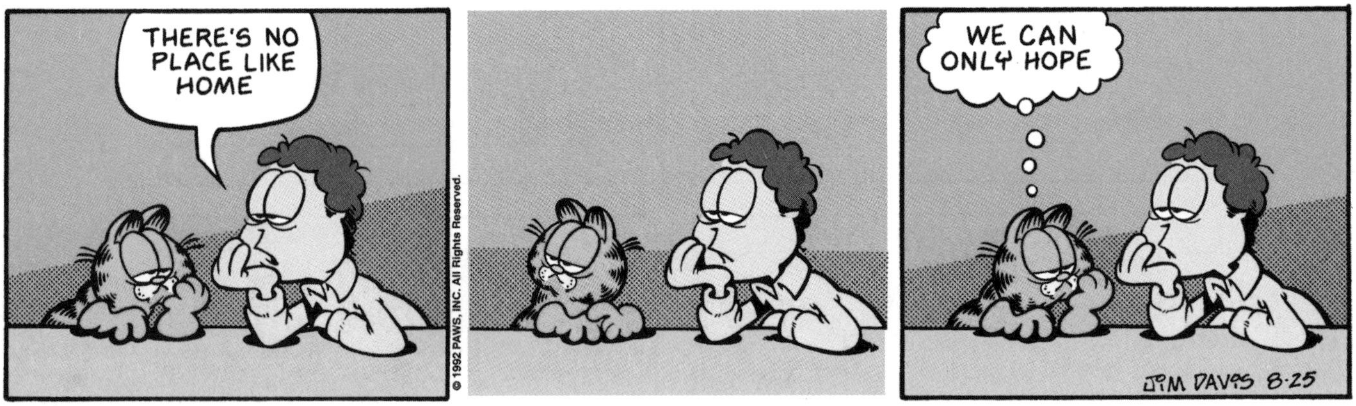
THERE'S NO PLACE LIKE HOME
WE CAN ONLY HOPE
© 1992 PAWS, INC. All Rights Reserved.
JIM DAVIS 8-25

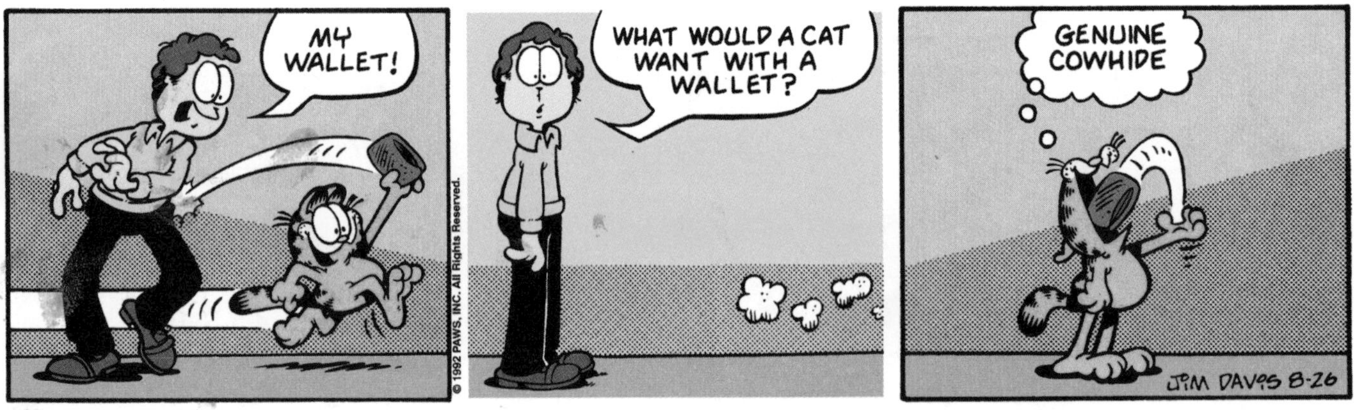
MY WALLET!
WHAT WOULD A CAT WANT WITH A WALLET?
GENUINE COWHIDE
© 1992 PAWS, INC. All Rights Reserved.
JIM DAVIS 8-26

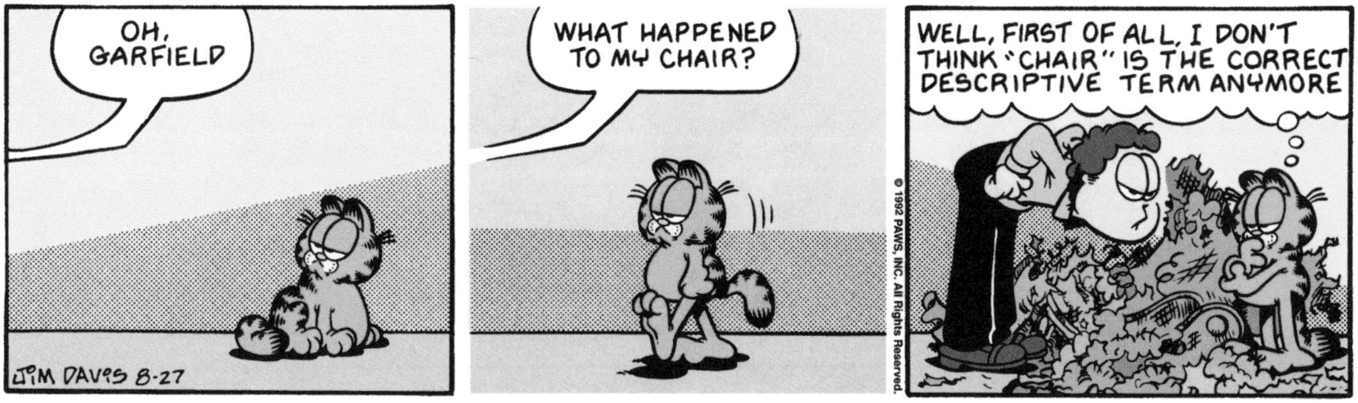
OH, GARFIELD
WHAT HAPPENED TO MY CHAIR?
WELL, FIRST OF ALL, I DON'T THINK "CHAIR" IS THE CORRECT DESCRIPTIVE TERM ANYMORE
JIM DAVIS 8-27
© 1992 PAWS, INC. All Rights Reserved.

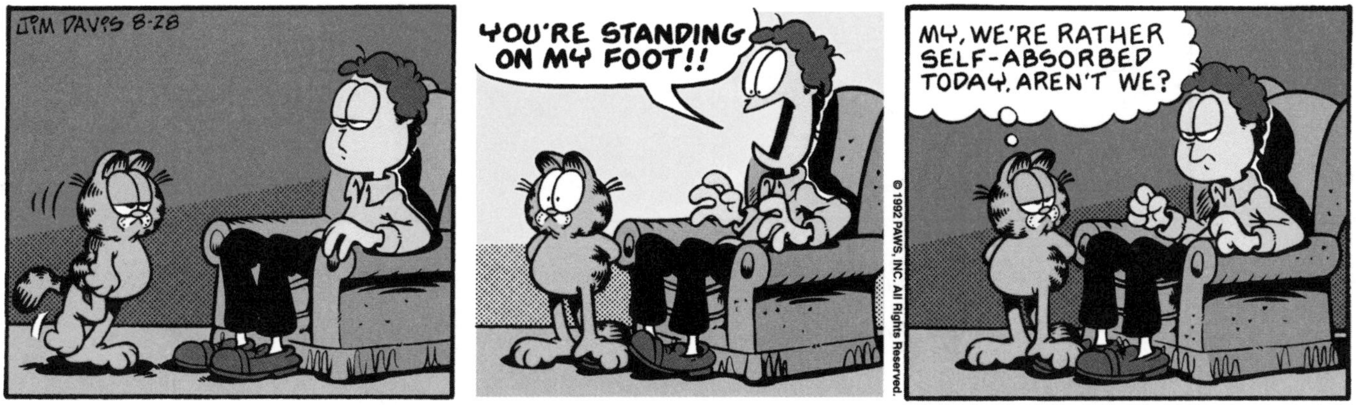
JIM DAVIS 8-28
YOU'RE STANDING ON MY FOOT!!
MY, WE'RE RATHER SELF-ABSORBED TODAY, AREN'T WE?
© 1992 PAWS, INC. All Rights Reserved.

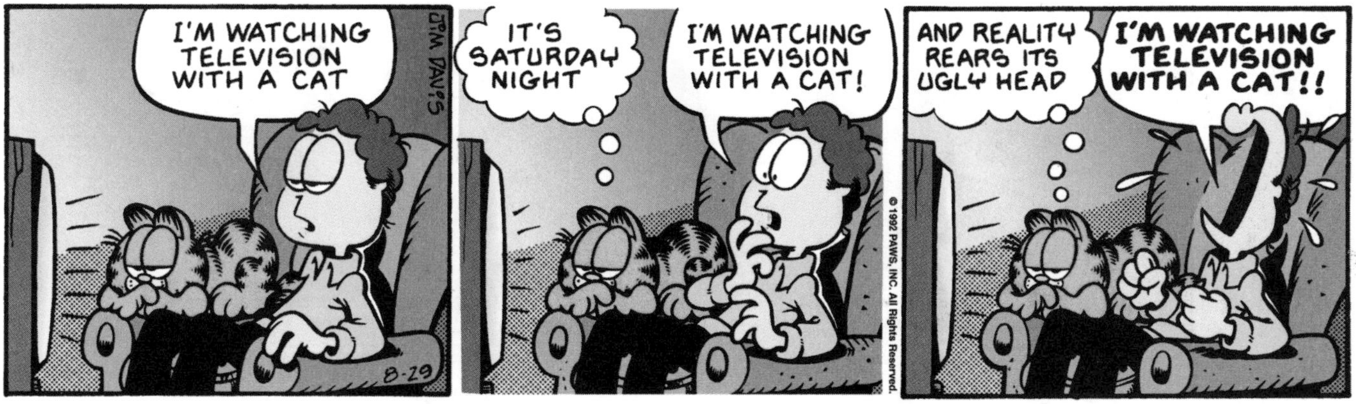
I'M WATCHING TELEVISION WITH A CAT
JIM DAVIS
8-29
IT'S SATURDAY NIGHT
I'M WATCHING TELEVISION WITH A CAT!
AND REALITY REARS ITS UGLY HEAD
I'M WATCHING TELEVISION WITH A CAT!!
© 1992 PAWS, INC. All Rights Reserved.

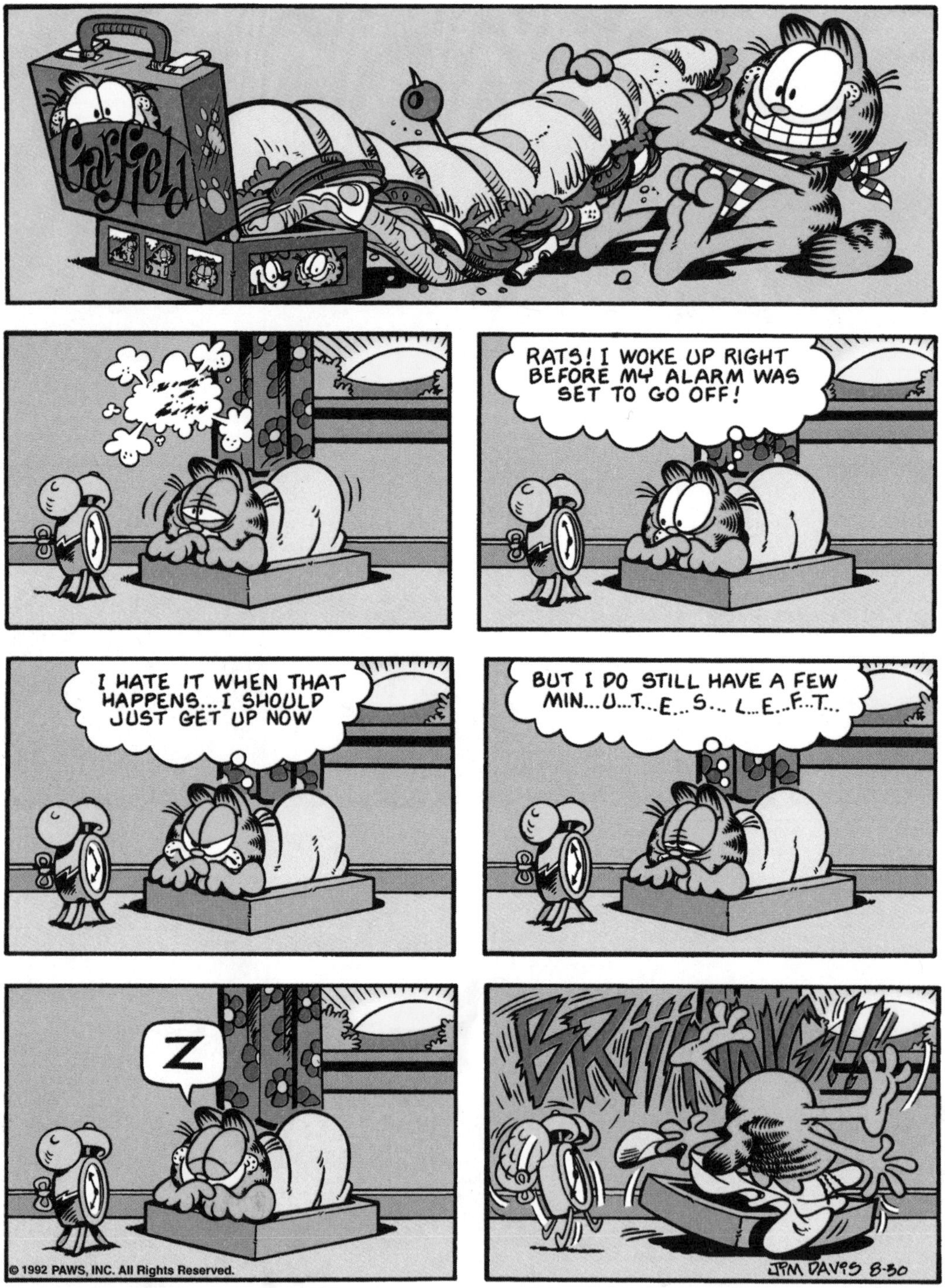
RATS! I WOKE UP RIGHT BEFORE MY ALARM WAS SET TO GO OFF!
I HATE IT WHEN THAT HAPPENS... I SHOULD JUST GET UP NOW
BUT I DO STILL HAVE A FEW MIN...U...T...E...S... L...E...F...T...
Z
JIM DAVIS 8-30

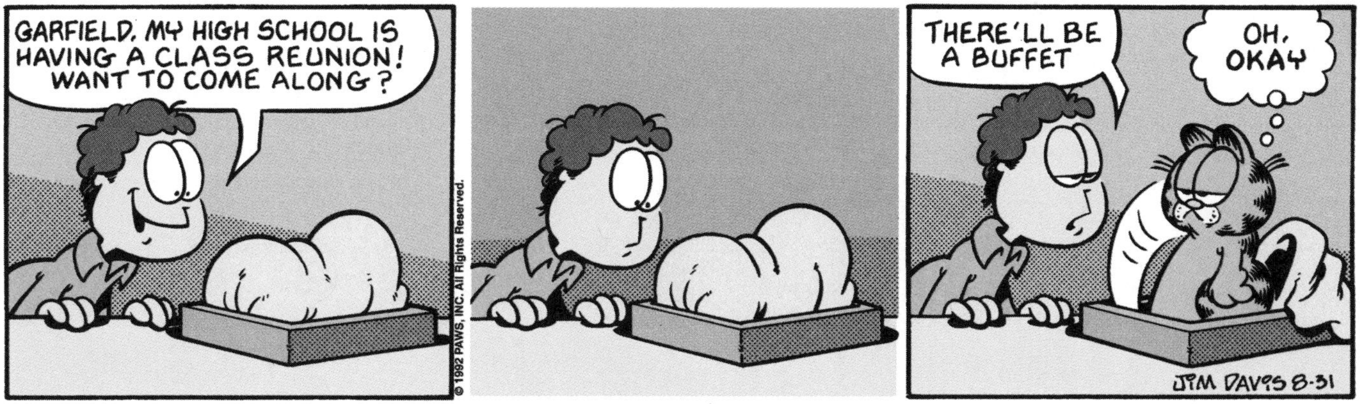
GARFIELD, MY HIGH SCHOOL IS HAVING A CLASS REUNION! WANT TO COME ALONG?
© 1992 PAWS, INC. All Rights Reserved.
THERE'LL BE A BUFFET
OH, OKAY
JIM DAVIS 8-31

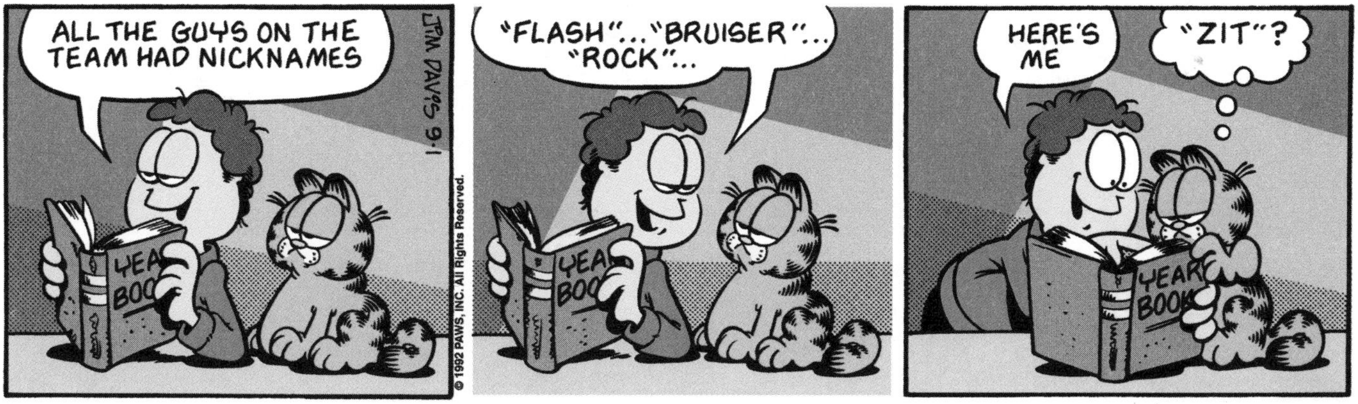
ALL THE GUYS ON THE TEAM HAD NICKNAMES
JIM DAVIS 9-1
© 1992 PAWS, INC. All Rights Reserved.
"FLASH"..."BRUISER"... "ROCK"...
HERE'S ME
"ZIT"?

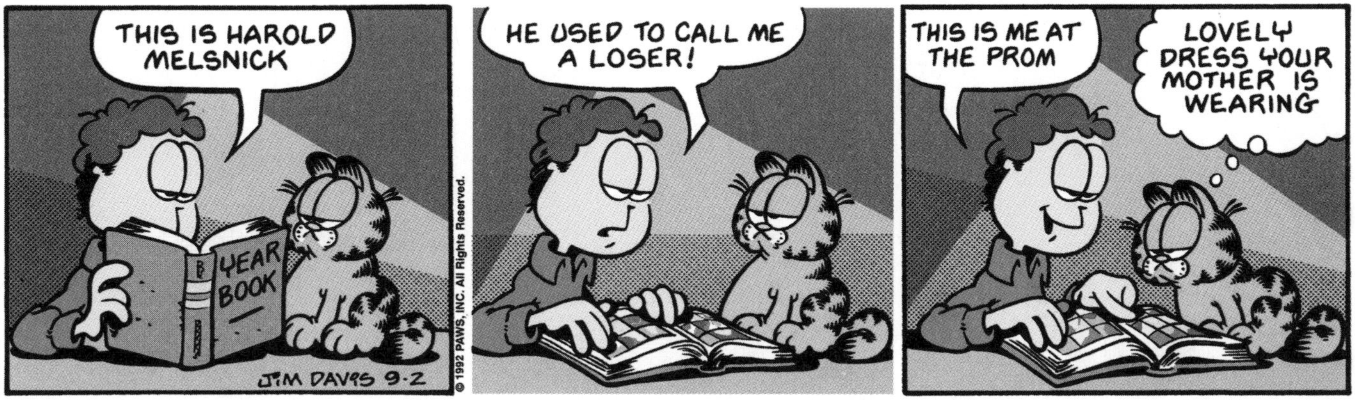
THIS IS HAROLD MELSNICK
JIM DAVIS 9-2
© 1992 PAWS, INC. All Rights Reserved.
HE USED TO CALL ME A LOSER!
THIS IS ME AT THE PROM
LOVELY DRESS YOUR MOTHER IS WEARING

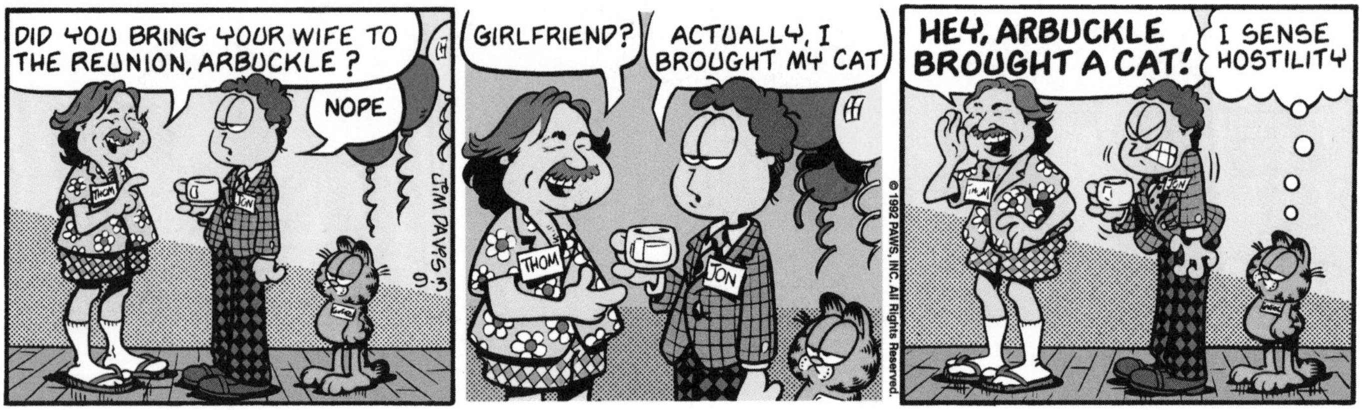
DID YOU BRING YOUR WIFE TO THE REUNION, ARBUCKLE?
NOPE
GIRLFRIEND?
ACTUALLY, I BROUGHT MY CAT
HEY, ARBUCKLE BROUGHT A CAT!
I SENSE HOSTILITY
THOM
JON
JIM DAVIS 9-3
© 1992 PAWS, INC. All Rights Reserved.

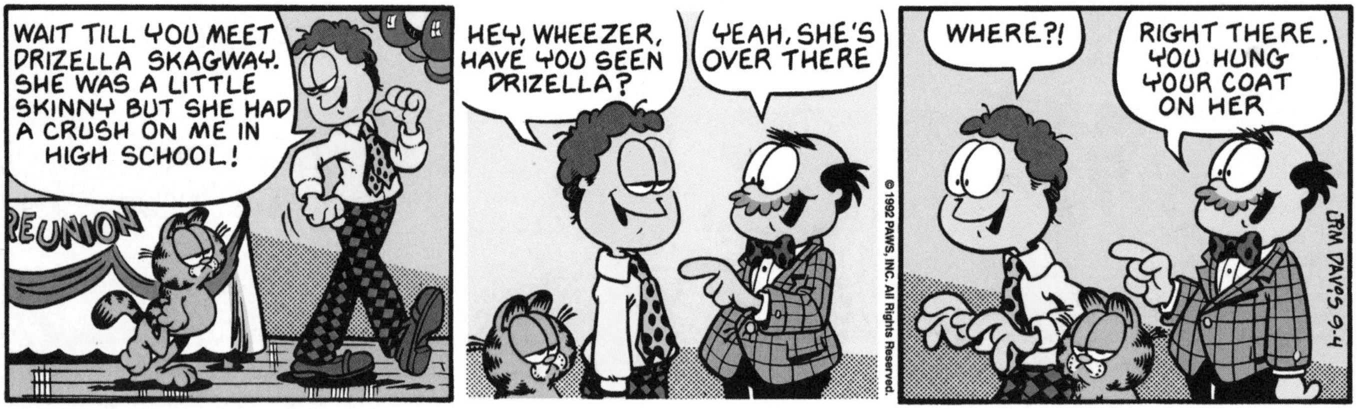
WAIT TILL YOU MEET DRIZELLA SKAGWAY. SHE WAS A LITTLE SKINNY BUT SHE HAD A CRUSH ON ME IN HIGH SCHOOL!
REUNION
HEY, WHEEZER, HAVE YOU SEEN DRIZELLA?
YEAH, SHE'S OVER THERE
WHERE?!
RIGHT THERE. YOU HUNG YOUR COAT ON HER
JIM DAVIS 9-4
© 1992 PAWS, INC. All Rights Reserved.

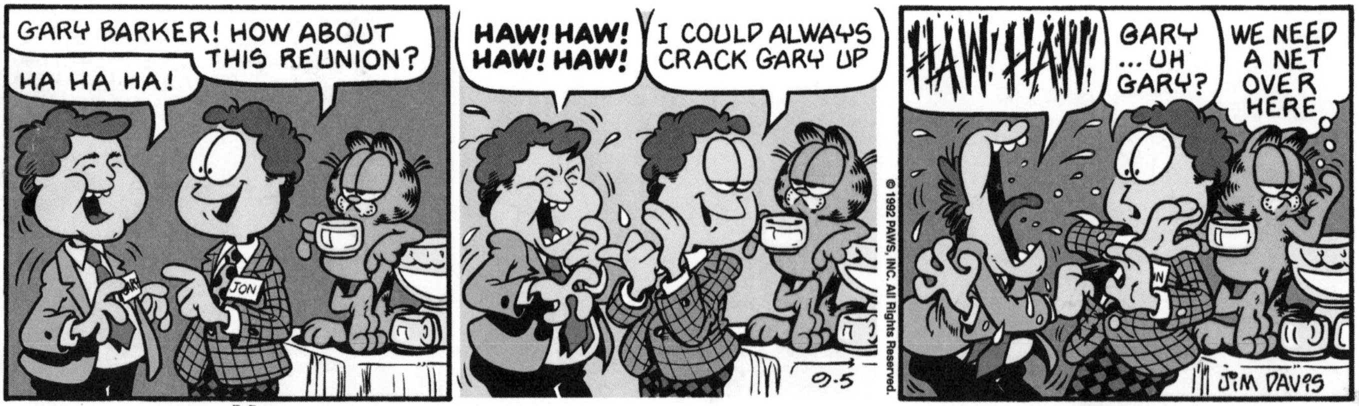
GARY BARKER! HOW ABOUT THIS REUNION?
HA HA HA!
JON
HAW! HAW! HAW! HAW!
I COULD ALWAYS CRACK GARY UP
9-5
HAW! HAW!
GARY ... UH GARY?
WE NEED A NET OVER HERE
JIM DAVIS
© 1992 PAWS, INC. All Rights Reserved.

TOP TEN COMIC STRIPS JIM DAVIS TRIED BEFORE GARFIELD

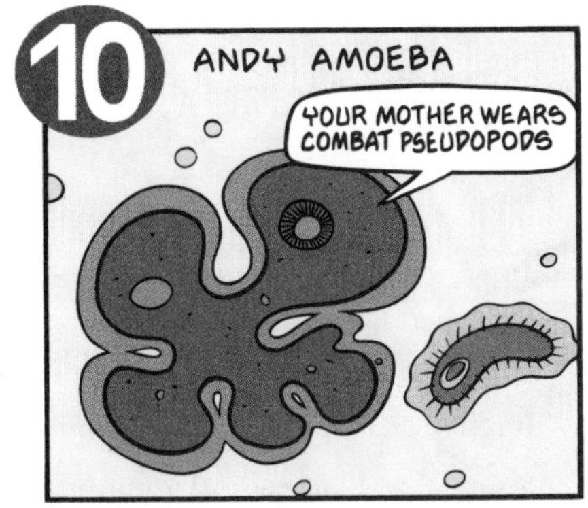
10
ANDY AMOEBA
YOUR MOTHER WEARS COMBAT PSEUDOPODS

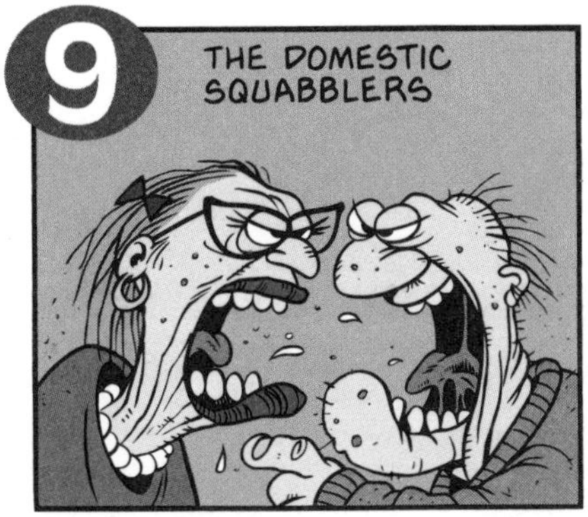
9
THE DOMESTIC SQUABBLERS

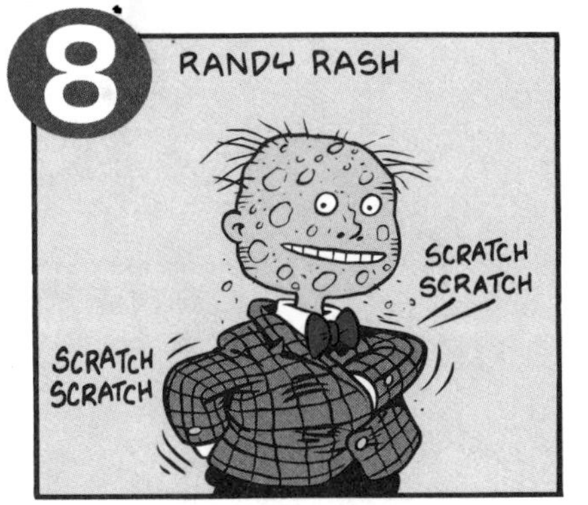
8
RANDY RASH
SCRATCH SCRATCH
SCRATCH SCRATCH

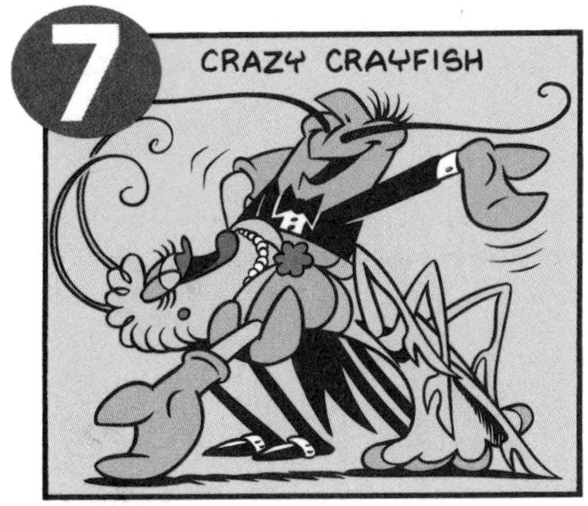
7
CRAZY CRAYFISH

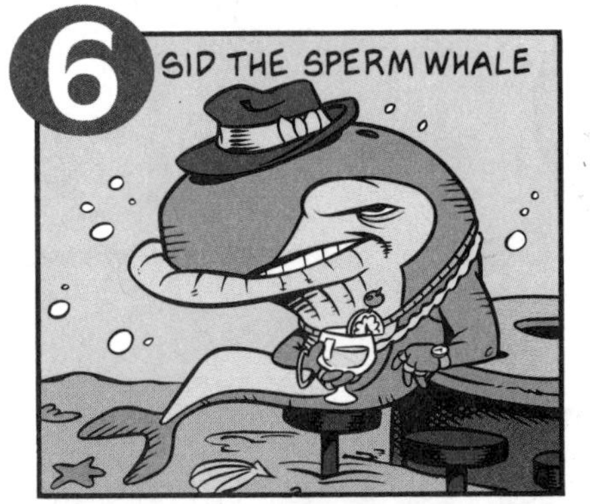
6
SID THE SPERM WHALE

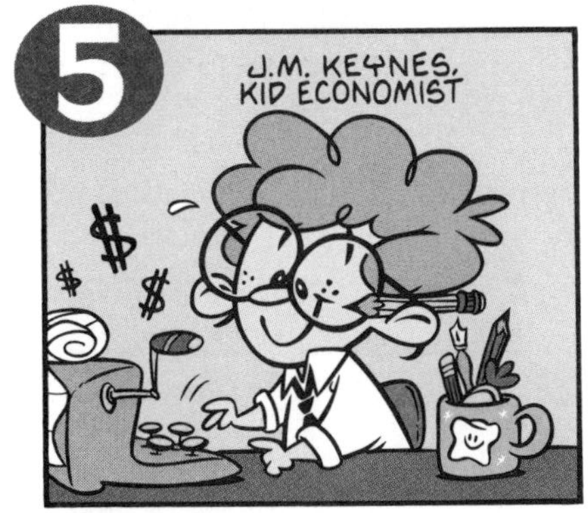
5
J.M. KEYNES, KID ECONOMIST
$
$
$

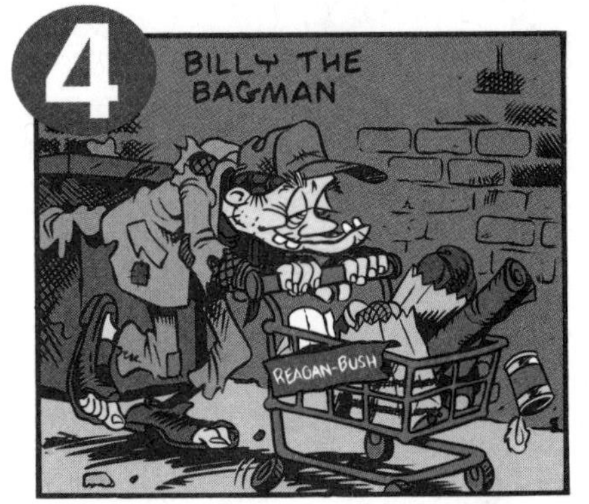
4
BILLY THE BAGMAN
REAGAN-BUSH

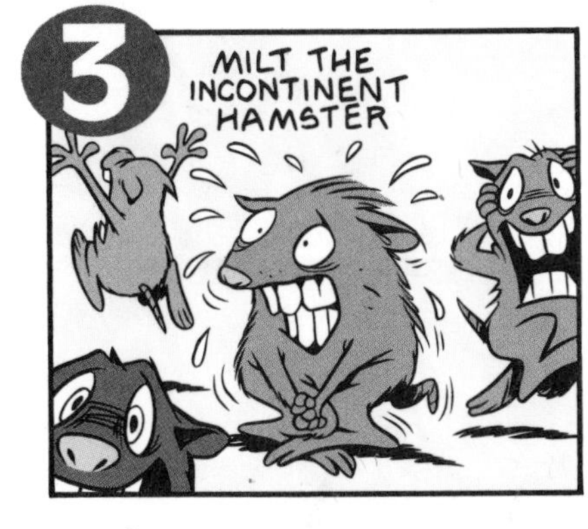
3
MILT THE INCONTINENT HAMSTER

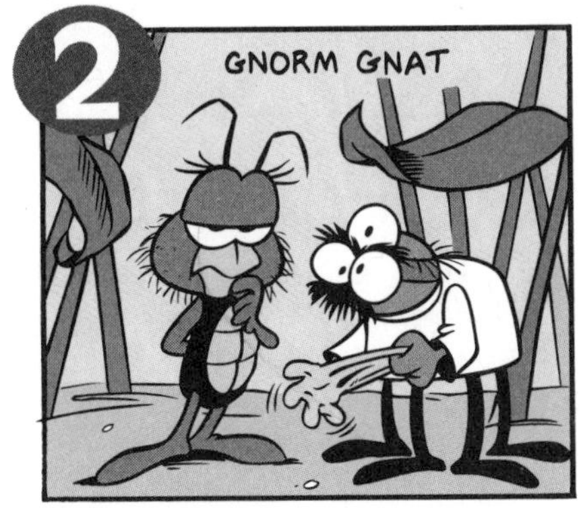
2
GNORM GNAT

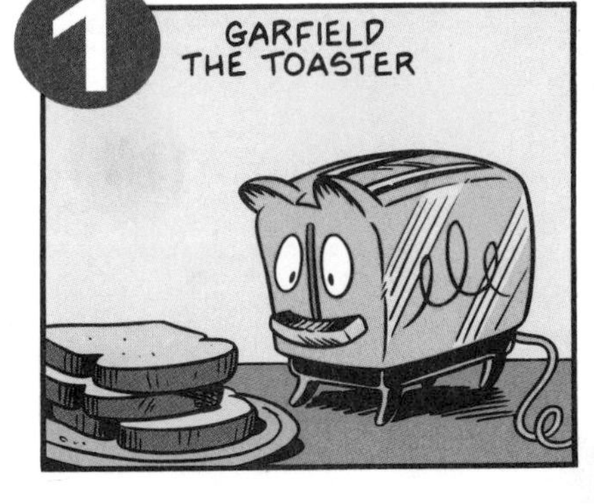
1
GARFIELD THE TOASTER

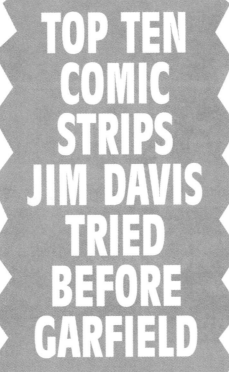

Watch. Read. Shop. Play.

DON'T FORGET THE SNACKS!

garfield.com

✳ *The Garfield Show*
An all-new animated TV show on Cartoon Network!
Watch FREE episodes online!

✳ The Comic Strip
Search & read thousands of GARFIELD® comic strips!

✳ Garfield on Facebook & Twitter
Read daily posts from Garfield. Share photos
and connect with other Garfield fans!

✳ Shop all the Garfield stores!
Original art & comic strips, books, apparel, personalized products, & mo

✳ Play FREE Garfield games!
Plus, buy Garfield apps & games for your iPhone or iPod touch.